THE ARMENIAN GENOCIDE
IN PERSPECTIVE

THE ARMENIAN GENOCIDE IN PERSPECTIVE

Edited by
Richard G. Hovannisian

Introduction by Terrence Des Pres

Preface by Israel W. Charny

Transaction Books
New Brunswick (U.S.A.) and Oxford (U.K.)

Library of Congress Catalog Number: 85-29038
ISBN: 0-88738-096-4 (cloth), 0-88738-636-9 (paper)
Printed in the United States of America

Library of Congress Cataloging in Publication Data
Main entry under title:
The Armenian genocide in perspective.
   1. Armenian massacres, 1915–1923—Turkey—Addresses,
essays, lectures. 2. Armenia—History—1901–   —
Addresses, essays, lectures. I. Hovannisian, Richard G.
DS195.5.A739 1986   956.6′201   85-29038
ISBN 0-88738-096-4 (pbk.)

Contents

Foreword

Richard G. Hovannisian

During the deportations and massacres of the Armenian population in the Ottoman Empire in 1915, hundreds of descriptive articles and books were written about the genocide by eyewitnesses, diplomats, correspondents, and humanitarians of many nationalities. Scholarly study of the subject, however, is only just beginning. This may be explained in part by the fact that for years the exiled survivor generation concentrated its energies on adapting to new environments, rescuing and caring for family members who somehow had remained alive, and organizing schools and churches to perpetuate, as well as possible, a national cultural heritage in diverse and often alien surroundings. Moreover, the failure of the Allied Powers after World War I to fulfill their pledges to repatriate the survivors and to create a separate Armenian state, and the subsequent international abandonment of the Armenian Question in 1923, deprived the Armenians of the status and resources that could have encouraged and facilitated scholarly investigation of the genocide. But perhaps the main reason for the general disregard for scientific study was the feeling that there was neither need for, nor purpose in, dwelling upon that which the entire world accepted as common knowledge, that is, the systematic dislocation and annihilation of the Armenian population by a dictatorial regime bent on creating a radically different political order with a radically different ethnoreligious composition. With the humiliating but accurate phrase "starving Armenian" broadcast the world over, the survivors would have found it unimaginable that within a generation there might be those who would either deny or else try to minimize the scope of their victimization by casting it into the context of the general horror and havoc of war. Ironically, however, that is exactly what happened. And with great new international crises gripping the world in the 1930s and 1940s, the Armenian experience in World War I became the "forgotten genocide."

1

It was not until the fiftieth anniversary of the genocide in 1965 that the children and grandchildren of the survivors were able to penetrate the wall of silence around them just a little and to voice their pleas for international recognition and rectification of an outstanding crime against humanity. Many younger Armenians, affected by the transgenerational trauma of genocide, became involved in political and demonstrative activities. The Turkish government, on the other hand, came to regard the modest revival of interest in the Armenian case as a serious menace. Since the 1960s it has engaged in an intense campaign of denial and refutation, using to advantage its geopolitical position, its international diplomatic, military, and economic associations, and its organized machinery of state. The determination of that government to prevent the Armenian Question from ever again becoming a subject for international consideration has led it into extreme positions, not excluding threat and intimidation. Indeed, most of the papers in this volume, presented during the International Conference on the Holocaust and Genocide in Tel Aviv in 1982, were delivered under the heavy shadow of intimidation. Yet in spite of the pressure to exclude discussion of the Armenian genocide or else cancel the conference, people of good conscience prevailed, refusing to put political considerations above moral and humanitarian imperatives. It was because of such people that the Tel Aviv conference became reality.

Since the preparation of the papers in this volume, the campaign of denial has been unrelenting. Public relations firms have been engaged to refine the tactics and strategy. School boards and public officials have been visited by delegations with publications and materials aimed at placing in question the truth and scope of the Armenian genocide. Repeated attempts have been made to preclude discussion of the genocide in textbooks and in public forums. The advocates of denial hold forth the defense interests of the United States and of NATO, play upon the fear of international terrorism, appeal to a sense of fair play, and demand with allusions to legal action equal time to present their views. In 1985, on the seventieth anniversary of the genocide, the Turkish government exerted such extraordinary pressure as to prompt the Department of State, the Department of Defense, and the White House to lobby against passage of a congressional joint resolution designating April 24 as a day of remembrance of man's inhumanity to man with particular reference to the Armenian tragedy. National defense requirements were invoked by many who participated in the effort to obscure the historical record, evidence of which abounds in the National Archives, almost within sight of both the Capitol and the White House. Sadly, some academics, too, have lent their support to this campaign, raising the specter of possible things to come once the Holocaust generation has passed from the scene. Fortunately, however, there are still many conscientious people who will not submit to the coercion nor acquiesce in the perversion of national interests to thwart the quest for truth and justice. These have been the bold and the brave, those who have withstood the pressure, who have gone forward with forums and programs on the Armenian genocide, and who remain committed to remembering the past for the sake of the present and the future.

This volume includes the papers presented at the Tel Aviv conference, together with contributions by Leo Kuper, Robert Melson, and Donald and Lorna Miller. The informative conference papers of Professors Vahakn Dadrian, Alen Salerian, and Avedis Sanjian do not appear in this volume but may be published elsewhere. The variety in discipline and specialization of the authors is clearly reflected in the content, focus, interpretation, and style of the individual articles. Collectively, however, the anthology may be viewed as an attempt to address a few of the complex issues relating to the Armenian genocide and its manifold consequences. It may provide answers to some questions regarding the Armenian past and, it is hoped, will be of use to those dedicated to the prevention and punishment of the crime of genocide.

Preface
One Is Either for Human Life or Not

Israel W. Charny

I am honored and pleased to have been invited to write the preface to this important volume, and gratified that much of the work it contains was first developed for and presented at the International Conference on the Holocaust and Genocide, held in Tel Aviv in 1982. Although in a basic philosophical sense the task is endless, I am sure that the excellent papers presented here constitute a major contribution or our knowledge of the Armenian genocide. The Armenian genocide was a cataclysmic event to the Armenian people—indeed to all people—and to the very process we call civilization. To study the Armenian genocide is to do honor to the Armenian people and their history, and it is also to affirm a commitment to protect and fight for the rights of all peoples.

I write this piece shortly after returning to Jerusalem from Boston, where I participated in a noteworthy conference on the theme, "Seventy Years after the Genocide: Lessons from the Armenian Experience." I am impressed by the increasing range and depth of scholarship on the Armenian genocide. I also sense an upsurge of pride in one's Armenian heritage, a greater resoluteness in articulating the story of the injustice done to the Armenians. In addition, it is very heartening that an increasing number of Armenian scholars and leaders are ready to join scholars and leaders of other ethnic, national, and religious communities in studying the history of different genocides in a broad human rights perspective, and out of a shared concern for the future fate of all peoples.

I would like to think that the milestone conference in 1982 and the continuing work of our Institute of the International Conference on the Holocaust and Genocide have something to do with these developments. If I have understood my Armenian colleagues correctly, the conference was the first time in several decades that the Armenian case was presented

5

in an international forum of scholars. I remember vividly the deep concern and sometimes outright anxiety of Armenian participants when the conference organizers took a stand against the Turkish government's heavy pressures to have the Armenian topic removed from the conference and against the Israeli government, which, to the unending shame of many of us, succumbed to Turkish demands and attempted to close down the conference. It was a powerful lesson that Armenians and Jews—and all other peoples—must stand together in a common battle against those responsible for past events of genocide, and against all those who seek to deny the truth of such past events.

I often wonder what it meant to Armenians to see some of us Jews, and our beloved Jewish state, bow to realpolitik and agree to suppress Armenian history. Even in 1985, upon returning to Israel from Boston, I found that the government had attempted to pressure the mayor of Jerusalem, Teddy Kollek, not to participate in a meeting at the Hebrew University on Mt. Scopus in commemoration of the Armenian genocide. Happily, I have also been encouraged by a strong editorial in the *Jerusalem Post* (April 25, 1985) insisting that "no political considerations can supersede the imperative against joining the forgetters and distorters of the genocide of another people." This is the Israel I believe in, and the voice of human integrity that I am always thrilled to hear.

Nonetheless, it is a fact that among the people who experienced the Holocaust there are individuals who are willing to collaborate with the killer-apologists of another people because it serves their immediate sense of self-interest. This sobering restatement of truth about human nature and the potential evil that exists in people is not unrelated to the very dynamics from which sprang both the Armenian genocide and the Holocaust. Sadly, a readiness to court violence and to revel in power is present in all peoples. Thus, in the burst of a new Armenian pride these last years, there has also emerged a terrorist movement that has claimed the lives of Turkish diplomats, their families, and other innocent people. Although many of us can readily understand the deep rage felt by the Armenians against the Turkish government, which is currently engaged in massive campaigns to obliterate the history of the Armenian genocide, the killing of innocent people cannot be the way for those of us who believe that the essential evil in all genocide is the preempting of another human being's inherent right to life.

Similarly, the Jewish national experience in its reconstituted homeland instructs us again in the truth about human nature. Even a victimized people, with their deep sensitivity to suffering, must guard against the hubris of power, the corruption of pragmatism, and the lure of militarism. One can but hope that the ethical traditions of Judaism and the basic democratic structure of the State of Israel, along with the never-to-be-forgotten legacy of the Holocaust, will prevail in reestablishing the Israeli commitment to "purity of arms," that is, a commitment to power only for self-defense, and never for inflicting or cooperating in a reckless destruction of another people. We who have been victims have a profound responsibility to guard against wanton violence even in our struggles against our oppressors. Each and every human being, at any given time in human history, has a connection with all the genocides that have taken place in the past, and with the potential for genocide against any people whatsoever in the future. *One is either for human life or not. There is no such thing as indifference on this issue.*

The new forms of mass murder available today on our planet threaten the continuation of human existence. It is the responsibility of us all to be aware of the dangers of nuclear holocausts, multiple genocides, or omnicide that can obliterate millions of human beings belonging to many different groups.

We should not forget Pastor Niemoeller's brilliant epigraph to the Holocaust:

> *First they came for the Jews*
> *And I did not speak out—*
> *Because I was not a Jew.*
>
> *Then they came for the communists*
> *And I did not speak out—*
> *Because I was not a communist.*
>
> *Then they came for the trade*
> *Unionists and I did not speak out—*
> *Because I was not a trade unionist.*
>
> *Then they came for me—*
> *And there was no one left*
> *To speak out for me.*

Introduction
Remembering Armenia

Terrence Des Pres

May 5, 1985: The President of the United States travels to Bitburg to honor German troops who died in World War II, among them forty-nine members of the Nazi SS. Despite great protest against an event that honors Hitler's killer elite, Ronald Reagan goes on record as saying that between the murderers and the victims there is no distinction; that the crimes of the past are better forgotten; and that this vastly powerful signal to the world—the champion of holocaustal weapons absolving the agents of the Holocaust—is "morally right."

The contempt for history is plain to see. So is the pain caused to survivors, those of the death camps as well as those who endured or fought to stop the Nazi onslaught. Even worse is the news that "SS Veterans Feel 'Rehabilitated' by Reagan Visit" (*New York Times,* May 3, 1985). Worse yet, there is the damage such an action inflicts upon ethical consciousness, on our capacity to distinguish, and believe in, the difference between good and evil. Conscience, as Schopenhauer put it, arises from humankind's knowledge concerning what it has done. The message of the Bitburg visit is that conscience does not count.

After the fury has subsided and the long view again becomes possible, the U.S. homage to fascism will take *its* place in history, and we shall look back upon it as an emblematic gesture, a potent sign of the times. For Ronald Reagan is nothing if not timely, the perfectly representative man for an age increasingly committed to military solutions, to brute force and carnage. Now vicitimization is taken for granted. Now nations are written off, whole peoples dismissed as "acceptable loss." The line between war and genocide blurs, and we may expect to see increasing hostility toward those of us who would salvage distinctions. Such political hostility is, in fact, the challenge that this volume of essays rises to meet.

9

The issue is nothing less than power versus truth, and we have the Bitburg incident as evidence that politics disdains the historical record. In the Orwellian world of modern governments, the past is rewritten or excised as shifting policy dictates.

One wishes the Bitburg blunder were the isolated event that, magnified by press coverage, it might at first have seemed to be. But in the West, no less than in the East, history submits to politics. The will to truth is cowed by pressure of numerous kinds, reasons of state on the one hand, economic necessities on the other, and, not least, the pure careerism of intellectuals who put their expertise in the service of power as a matter of course. When governments and professional elites find reward in the sophistries of might makes right, truth is bound to suffer. Some of the damage can be gauged by observing that nowadays the delivery of fact comes in two formats: "official" and "alleged." There are, furthermore, "two sides to every issue," which leaves the outcome to cosmetics and the technologies of persuasion. We live in an age of intense propaganda, and the demand for "acceptable" versions of events would seem to suggest that old-fashioned bringers of bad news—witnesses, scholars, serious journalists—may henceforth expect hard going.

Milan Kundera, the exiled Czech novelist, has written that "the struggle of man against power is the struggle of memory against forgetting." This single remark, in my view, sums up the human predicament today and puts the burden of responsibility exactly where it falls—on writers, and now more than ever, on scholars. Kundera is obsessed by the spectacle of Soviet tanks rolling into Prague. Such a concrete historical image, in turn, becomes the emblem of culture besieged; and any people or nation, we need to keep in mind, is only as strong as its culture's integrity. National catastrophes can be survived if (and perhaps only if) those to whom disaster happens can recover themselves through knowing the truth of their suffering. Great powers, on the other hand, would vanquish not only the peoples they subjugate but also the cultural mechanisms that would sustain vital memory of historical crimes.

Franz Werfel defended memory when he wrote *The Forty Days of Musa Dagh,* and I find it significant that Werfel spent the first third of his life in Prague, the second third in Vienna, and the last as a permanent exile initially in France and finally in the United States, a species of diaspora that Kundera calls the "typically Central European biography." After 1915, how many thousands of Armenians wandered in exactly the same way? By now the biography of exile has become standard, a universal type, and not for individuals only. Kundera's sympathies, like those of Franz Werfel, are for peoples threatened by obliteration. When modern states make way for geopolitical power plays, they are not above removing everything—nations, cultures, homelands—in their path. Great powers regularly demolish other peoples' claims to dignity and place, and sometimes, as we know, the outcome is genocide. In a very real sense, therefore, Kundera is right: against historical crimes we fight as best we can, and a cardinal part of this engagement is "the struggle of memory against forgetting."

I say "we," and have in mind a definite group, those among us disciplined in the recovery of facts and the validation of lost worlds. I am addressing the community of scholars, thinkers, and writers whose profession is the work of remembering. Even more specifically, I am concerned with men and women for whom the labor of truth takes them into areas of conflict where the older ideals of humane enlightenment—the values of detachment, suspended judgment, and the long view—no longer suffice or cannot be counted on.

The problem today is that scholarship has had thrust upon it the *necessity* of partisan practice, and about this I would like to be very exact. When power of any sort, be it political, professional, or institutional, takes a hostile stance toward certain directions of study and the results of such study, then scholars can no longer pretend to escape political consequence. Antigone might wish only to give her brother decent burial, but Creon has ruled otherwise and, like it or not, she is forced to perform her private duties within a context defined by the king. This is what I mean by "political intrusion," by now a nearly universal affliction in private as in public lives, for men and women dedicated to knowledge no less than for men and women committed to action. The curse is general, and scholars are neither immune nor exempt.

We have come, I think, to a parting of roads. As scholars beset by political pressures, we can beg off, plead innocence, and allow established policy to go on directing our interests. Or we can find a niche within the power structure and speak with that authority. Or—the militant course in a militant time—we can counter these temptations by deliberately setting our work against any approach to, or from, worldly agencies of power, with a special distrust for ideological blandishments, whether from left or right or from the deceptive middle. The unpalatable fact, in this age of disinformation, is that political order requires the subservience of knowledge. How to respond is everyone's problem. For scholars repelled by politics, one solution is to take up an oppositional or antithetical style of inquiry. What this means in practice is to proceed with healthy disrespect for things official. As a spokesman for the U.S. Department of State quipped, "Don't believe anything until it's officially denied." The willing suspension of belief has always been a part of academic method, but never more so than now.

The political control of knowledge goes deeper than censorship and is more subtle than outright propaganda. It includes the conditions under which research will be funded and given a forum, and also the designation of legitimacy to be conferred or withheld in specific fields of inquiry. Jobs, tenure, professional advancement, all can come to depend on taking the approved line. Adjacent to these disturbing developments in the academy, the high-pressure phenomenon of the "institute" and "think tank" proliferates, with, in most cases, government backing of one sort or another. What all this scrambling means, finally, is that the struggle of memory against forgetting must compete with official versions and special interests, with public and private demands for serviceable knowledge, with the kinds of on-line information geared to expedient needs. Amid this din the scholar's independent voice is hard to hear, unless, of course, it too is "backed."

We who pride ourselves on learning must now decide if research is to become the service industry that governments require. We are accustomed to denigrating Marxist distortions, and we point with scorn to situations in which Soviet scholars produce results useful to the state. Such cases are highly visible, and the means of coercion, which include exile and imprisonment, make the Soviet example impressive. But coercion may take other forms as well—appointments and grants, for example— which remind us that the economic factor is always active; or the bias of one's profession, which opens its best avenues of advancement to those whose methods have been duly authorized; or finally, the influence of nationality, by which I mean the need to display in one's work a patriotic spirit, especially in times of political distress. At its worst, pressure of this kind becomes McCarthyist; at its best the subtle nudge of commonweal.

The political manipulation of truth is ruinous to any free society, to the scholarly community especially, for if we cannot trust our standards and each other, our enterprise is groundless. Perhaps, however, my description of this threat has been more extreme than the situation warrants. We can readily agree that things go badly behind the Iron Curtain, and the example of Nazi Germany is ever before us. But surely in our academies, among our intellectuals, the life of the mind bends to no one. Academic discourse, at least among the nations of the Free World, proceeds without interference or intimidation, or so we presume and sometimes boast. But if "academic freedom" were still intact the essays in this volume would not have been written, or rather, they would not be possessed by the urgency that defines their occasion.

Professors Hovannisian, Kuper, and Melson set forth the basic history of the Armenian genocide at the hands of the Turks in 1915–16. Professors

Hamalian and Oshagan trace the imprint of these events upon literary imagination, and Professors Boyajian and Grigorian point up the hypermnesia—the violence of memory—found in survivors and their children, whose ability to deal with historical trauma is vastly complicated by the denial of the events that haunt them. These and other essays offer us a triple perspective. First of all, they increase our understanding of the nature of genocide by examining the Armenian case. Secondly, they stand as a challenge—the challenge of scholarship—to the deliberate policy of denial on the part of the Turkish government, and the policy of support for this denial on the part of the United States government. And lastly, they emerge as a primary instance of scholarship interfered with and intimidated by the state.

As Israel Charny documents, when in 1982 the International Conference on the Holocaust and Genocide was getting under way in Tel Aviv, officials of the Israeli government importuned individual scholars to stay away. This extraordinary action was in response to messages from representatives of Turkey who had approached the Israeli Foreign Ministry with remarks about the well-being of Turkish Jews, remarks that might have been vague and indirect but that caused officials in Israel to attempt to abort the conference. "There was a sense," Charny records, "that actual Jewish lives were at stake." Suddenly, leaders of Jewish communities in the United States and elsewhere were insisting that the conference might better be cancelled. The spiritual leader of the conference, Elie Wiesel, decided (after a visit from Turkish representatives and messages from the Israeli governmernt) not to attend, citing danger to Jews in the Near East. According to the *New York Times* (June 3, 1982), which interviewed Wiesel in Paris, "the Turks let it be known there would be serious difficulties if Armenians took part in the conference." The conference took place as planned, which speaks well for intellectual courage, but the point to keep in mind is that political interests were mobilized against an *academic* conference. It was a gathering of *scholars,* nothing less and nothing more, learned men and women convening to pursue understanding.

It was once fashionable to expend one's pity upon the "starving Armenians," a sort of tea-time sympathy requiring no action but at least recognizing Turkey's attempt, during the war, to exterminate its Armenian population. It is now fashionable to be shocked at Armenian terrorists and to sympathize with "the Turkish side of the story." This sort of windblown compassion is not autonomous; it is the social expression of changes in political outlook. During World War I, when Turkey was allied with Germany, the governments of Great Britain and the United States vigorously condemned the genocide then in progress. By 1923, however, when Turkey achieved its status as a modern nation-state, political allegiance began to shift. As a traditional enemy of Russia, Turkey was worth wooing; and as the Cold War warmed up, the geopolitical importance of Turkey—its strategic position on the border of the Soviet Union, its willingness to transform Mount Ararat into an outpost for Western surveillance—worked to inhibit criticisms of official Turkish policy, in the past as well as in the present. As Jeane Kirkpatrick made clear in her defense of authoritarian governments, political regimes "friendly" to the United States are automatically acceptable, no matter what evils—torture, military rule, contempt for human rights—might need whitewashing. And so it has come about that, at a time when Turkey refuses to admit that a genocide occurred, our State Department backs off from its own records and designates the Armenian genocide as merely "alleged."

My point is that as politics goes, so goes a goodly part of what passes for educated understanding. Far from being something as simple as hypocrisy, the current predicament of scholarship reveals a terribly complicated *modus operandi*. One of the best commentators on the relation of power to knowledge has been Michel Foucault. The bearing of politics upon learning becomes, in his later work, a function of the services knowledge and power perform for each other. Some reciprocal trade-off, in Foucault's view, is always in the works. He argues that more than we have cared to admit, scholarly discourse has depended upon the institutions that permit, control, and legitimate its practice, institutions that are locked into the larger grid of power relations on a spectrum running from the lowliest academic squabble to oil wars and the nuclear terrorism of the superpowers.

The term *discourse* has pretty much replaced the word *truth,* an indication all its own of the way our professional modes of thinking and speaking are controlled by shifts in institutional authorization. Strange to think that the people least likely to use the word *truth* are the sophisticated scholars who staff our universities. There are reasons for this reluctance, no doubt, in particular the victory of rhetoric in matters of public consciousness. Today we possess at most a nostalgia for truth, evident in the persistence of the word, which suggests that *truth* in its nonironic usage might still be, in residue, a term of empowerment. What cannot be doubted are the problems that arise from the deep entanglement of knowledge in the agenda of power, kinds of subversion and complicity that Foucault illuminates in an essay entitled "Truth and Power." In particular, Foucault reminds us that "truth is a thing of this world," not a Platonic entity above and beyond history but very much a bargaining chip in humankind's struggle with power. "Each society," Foucault tells us, "has its regime of truth," and he goes on, "that is, the types of discourse which it accepts and makes function as true; the mechanisms and instances which enable one to distinguish true and false statements, the means by which each is sanctioned; the techniques and procedures accorded value in the acquisition of truth; the status of those who are charged with saying what counts as truth."

That there are "regimes of truth" cannot be doubted. Until some fairly recent date (perhaps midway through the eighteenth century), educated elites openly served their political masters. The Enlightenment, to which Kant assigned the formula "dare to know," then announced the era of independent knowledge. But after only two centuries of intellectual autonomy, of critical thinking vis-à-vis the ruling powers (the heyday of liberalism), the repoliticization of knowledge seems to be gaining momentum. We cannot, perhaps, escape this predicament, but neither are we, by necessity, its absolute victims. If knowledge caters to power, the case is also, as Foucault insists, that power depends on knowledge, a small wedge of hope, perhaps, but one we cannot surrender. Scholarship is under attack because, quite simply, knowledge counts. To judge from increasing attempts to suborn the academy, we might even conclude that knowledge counts a very great deal.

With what general courage the academic community comports itself remains to be seen. In an immediate way, however, our scholarly conduct is put to the test by this question: Will the Armenian genocide of 1915 in Turkey be recognized, or will it go down, with much else, into Orwell's memory hole? It is perhaps evident that the issue here is not only the attempt on the part of the Turkish government to rewrite history and blot out the past. It is the relation of power to knowledge, and how, in real and concrete ways, governments are attempting to deprive academic scholarship of its autonomy and make of it a service industry. The issue, then, is whether or not we wish to be menials, for at the very least, scholars who spend their resources defending the honor of nation-states serve something other than truth.

The case of terrorism, in its present Armenian enactment, is of special interest because on the face of it, such violence ought to invalidate Armenian claims to a hearing. Who will listen to the voice of the victims when, as attacks upon Turkish embassies make clear, the present victims are innocent Turkish officials? And who would have supposed, even a few years ago, that the world-bane of terrorism could have a bearing upon the outcome of scholarly research? In this respect the last essay in this volume, by Professor and Mrs. Miller, seems especially revealing as a study in responses to the trauma of genocide when that trauma includes defeat, dispersal, and the obliteration of national identity.

We might consider that international terrorism (as opposed to state terrorism or the strategic use of violence by indigenous groups in postcolonial conflict) began after World War II with dispossessed German and Japanese groups suffering the deracination of national defeat. Next came the violence of the Palestine Liberation Organization, another group without a country. By now, of course, the kind of terrorism that crosses borders has become universal. But if we take the experience of nations seriously, and therefore consider events such as genocide and defeat in war as sources of psychic upheaval, then we must go on to the case of terrorism, which puts violence at the disposal of international quarrels, and decide to what degree this kind of action arises from loss of nationhood. The burst of Jewish terrorism, directly after World War II, soon ended because a homeland was established. But what of those for whom a homeland was lost?

It should go without saying (but nowadays nothing goes without saying) that the effort to understand terrorism is not a justification. Nothing excuses violence, although we see immediately that the PLO established itself and now operates as a legitimate power precisely through its use of violent measures, and we see also that world opinion would never have taken up the Armenian question ("Who today remembers the annihilation of the Armenians?") had the issue not been forced upon us by Armenian attacks against Turkish diplomats. To the extent that terrorism succeeds, we do live in the shame of a world where might makes right. The most recent example of terrorism making good is the case of the "Contras" or, as they have now earned the right to be called, the "Freedom Fighters" in Nicaragua, a group that began as a small band of terrorists backed by the CIA but that now enjoys Washington's recognition as a political party with rightful claims to "government" in that sad country. The utility of terror, in such instances, is perfectly evident.

Armenian terrorism cannot *go* anywhere, of course; the Armenian part of Turkey is simply gone. But the situation is perhaps hopeful in another, more spiritual way. As the Millers' paper suggests, what drives Armenian extremists to violence is less the hope of a homeland than the deeper need for recompense, which would mean, in this case, to have Turkey and the rest of the world recognize the enormity of Armenian suffering. I mean to suggest a real connection between current acts of terror and Turkish denial. Terrorist violence, in the present situation, is an especially ugly response to the aftermath of genocide when the terrible emotions generated by that legacy find no adequate outlet—emotions like grief, despair, and neurotic repression, but also rage and the pressure of rage to find expression in revenge. An examination of the body of oral testimony confirms that these are common feelings among survivors of the Armenian tragedy, and, as we have learned from study of the children of Holocaust survivors, there is a strong tendency for the present generation to live out the emotional needs of their parents and grandparents. One of the principal discoveries to come out of follow-up studies of the Jewish and Armenian catastrophies is that the impact of historical trauma does not lessen but rather *grows* with time, both in the memory of aging survivors and in the passions of subsequent generations, if, that is, no way to reconciliation presents itself.

Many Armenian survivors and their children are resigned to the geopolitical realities that make recovery of their homeland impossible. What they are not reconciled to, and what increasingly they cannot abide, is the denial of their own historical suffering. That the world refuses to credit the central event of their fate is painful in the extreme and, for some, a cause of violent rage. More than ego, more than politics, what is at stake is the soul of an ancient nation. When one considers the widespread deployment of terrorist tactics by governments of every stripe (the CIA's manual on assassination, for example), it is hardly difficult to make sense of the Armenian case, in which the driving forces are historical tragedy, permanent loss, and the pain of memory mocked by denial.

Because genocide is a crime against humanity, victims naturally appeal to "the world" for redress; and it is not so much the world's indifference as its current collusion with the perpetrators of the crime that turns the victims' appeal into violent expression. Terror is awful in any case, and also self-defeating. The use of violence to voice Armenian claims tends to fuel the righteousness of denial. There is no clear gain, but rather a deepening of desperate confusion. Rage then feeds upon itself, and with it the possibility of yet more terrorist attacks. We must surely wonder how the Armenian agony, caught up in a circle so vicious, might come at last to expiation.

Just here the role of scholars counts more than we might have supposed. I do not refer to those among us busy revising the historical record, but rather to the kind of men and women who, against some very ugly pressures, went ahead with the Tel Aviv conference. In the struggle of memory against forgetting, the situation comes down to this: as things now stand, terrorist actions stain the truth that scholars labor to make clear. But if the truth were made clear, the terrorism would stop. What is now wanted is victory over denial and, in consequence, an end to obsession. For a people to possess the dignity of their own tragic past becomes sufficient ground for renewal, for turning with new heart to carry on with life. To this decency the authors of the present volume contribute.

1

The Historical Dimensions of the Armenian Question, 1878–1923

Richard G. Hovannisian

The genocide of the Armenian minority in the Ottoman Empire during World War I may be viewed in the context of the broader Armenian Question, which had both internal and international aspects. Indeed, it was to rid themselves of this question and to create a new, homogeneous order that the Turkish dictators organized the deportations and massacres of the Armenian population. Through death and destruction they eliminated the Armenians from most of the Ottoman Empire, including all of the historic Armenian homelands, and radically altered the racial and religious character of the region. An overview of the Armenian Question in the Ottoman Empire should help to place the presentations in the following chapters into perspective.

Although tracing their lineage, according to epical-biblical traditions, to Noah, whose ark was said to have rested on Mount Ararat, the Armenians actually passed through a long era of formation and emerged as an identifiable people sometime around the sixth century before Christ. Their lands lay between the Black, Caspian, and Mediterranean seas, in an area now referred to as Eastern Anatolia and Transcaucasia, on both sides of the current Soviet-Turkish frontier. For the next two thousand years, they were led by their kings, nobles, and patriarchs, sometimes independently and often under the sway of powerful, neighboring empires of the East and West. Located on perhaps the most strategic crossroads of the ancient and medieval worlds, the Armenians managed not only to survive but also to develop a rich, distinctive culture by maintaining a delicate balance between Orient and Occident. Adopting Christianity as the state religion at the turn of the fourth century A.D., however, the Armenians were often persecuted because of their faith by invaders and alien overlords. By the end of the fourteenth century, the last Armenian kingdom had collapsed, the nobility had been decimated in constant warfare, and the Armenian plateau had fallen under foreign subjugation. Most of the country ultimately came under Turkish rule, except for the eastern sector, which came first under Persian and then in the nineteenth century under Russian dominion.

In the Ottoman Empire, which by the seventeenth century pressed to the gates of Vienna, the Armenians were included in a multinational and multireligious realm, but as a Christian minority they had to endure official discrimination and second-class citizenship. Inequality, including special taxes, the inadmissibility of legal testimony, and the prohibition on bearing arms, was the price paid to maintain their religion and sense of community. Down through the centuries, many thousands eventually converted in order to be relieved of these disabilities as well as the sporadic violence that fell most heavily upon the defenseless Armenian peasantry. The *devshirme* or child levy was occasionally imposed, and in many districts in Western Anatolia the Armenians were not allowed to speak their own language except in the recitation of prayers. This is not to say that there were not prosperous merchants, traders, artisans, and professional persons throughout the empire, for it is well known that the minority populations played a most important role in international commerce, as interpreters and intermediaries, and in the highly skilled professions. Nonetheless, most of the Armenian population remained rooted in its historic homeland, becoming, in large part, tenant farmers or sharecroppers under the dominant Muslim feudal-military elite.

Despite their second-class status, most Armenians lived in relative peace so long as the Ottoman Empire was strong and expanding. But as the empire's administrative, financial, and military structure crumbled under the weight of internal corruption and external challenges in the eighteenth and nineteenth centuries, intolerance and exploitation increased. The breakdown of order was accelerated by Ottoman inability to compete with the growing capitalistic system in the West and to modernize and reform. The legal and practical superiority of one element over the other groups continued, and the lavish and uncontrolled spending of the Ottoman court led to even more oppressive taxation, including the infamous method of tax farming, that is, the sale of the privilege to exact as much tax as possible from a particular district in return for an advance lump-sum payment. The wasteful ways of the ruling elite drew the empire into bankruptcy in the 1870s and opened the way for direct European financial supervision, beginning in 1881.

The decay of the Ottoman Empire was paralleled by cultural and political revival among many of the subject nationalities, which were swept by the European winds of romanticism and revolt. The national liberation struggles, supported at times by certain European powers, contributed to Ottoman loss of most Balkan provinces in the nineteenth century and constituted one aspect of the Eastern Question, namely, what was to become of the decrepit empire. The rivalry among the European powers and their economic exploitation of the Ottoman Empire led to efforts to preserve it as a weak buffer state and a lucrative marketplace. The British, in particular, fearing that dissolution of the empire would threaten their mastery of the seas, came to the conclusion that it could be saved only if the worst abuses of government were eliminated and fundamental administrative changes implemented. A growing circle of Ottoman liberals was also persuaded that survival depended on reform. These men became the movers behind the several major reform edicts issued during the so-called *tanzimat* period from 1839 to 1876.[1] Yet time and again the supporters of reform became disappointed and disillusioned in the face of the entrenched vested interests that resisted change. The *tanzimat* era, for all its fanfare, brought virtually no improvement in the daily life of the common person.

Of the various subject peoples, the Armenians perhaps sought the least. Unlike the Balkan Christians, they were dispersed throughout the empire and no longer constituted a majority in much of their historic homelands. Hence, Armenian leaders did not think in terms of separation or independence, but, professing loyalty to the sultan and renouncing any separatist aspirations, they petitioned for the protection of their people and property from corrupt officials and from marauding bands often linked with those officials. It was not inappropriate, therefore, that the Ottoman sultans should have referred to the Armenians as their "faithful community." The Armenians nonetheless also passed through a long period of cultural revival. Thousands of youngsters enrolled in schools established in the nineteenth century by U.S. and European missionaries and hundreds of middle-class youth traveled to Europe for higher education. Many of these men returned home, imbued with the social and political philosophies of contemporary Europe, to engage in teaching, journalism, and literary criticism. Gradually a network of Armenian schools and newspapers spread from Constantinople (Istanbul) and Smyrna (Izmir) to Cilicia, and eventually to many towns in the primitive eastern provinces, that is, Turkish Armenia. As it happened, however, this Armenian self-discovery was paralleled by heightened administrative corruption, economic exploitation, and physical insecurity. It was this dual development—the conscious demand for security of life and property on the one hand, and the growing insecurity of both life and property on the other—that gave rise to the Armenian Question as a part of the larger Eastern Question.

Widespread dissatisfaction with inadequate implementation of the several reform edicts of the *tanzimat* period, the aggravated plight of the Asiatic Christians, and, above all, the severe Turkish reprisals against a rebellious Balkan Christian population brought renewed European pressure on the Sublime Porte [Ottoman government] in 1876. In a maneuver to undermine the international conference summoned to deal with the crisis, Sultan Abdul-Hamid II (1876–1909) promulgated a liberal constitution drafted by sincere advocates of reform.[2] Had the sultan been as sincere in implementing the constitution, it could have removed the major grievances of the subject peoples, the Armenians included. But having warded off the European diplomats, Abdul-Hamid soon suspended the constitution and the parliament for which it had provided. Instead of abating, the tribulations of the Armenians multiplied. Robbery, murder, and kidnapping became commonplace in a land where even the traditional feudal protective system had broken down.

In the aftermath of the Russo-Turkish war of 1877–78, the leaders of the Armenian community, or *millet,* put aside their customary caution and conservatism and appealed to the victorious Russian commander-in-chief to include provisions for the protection of the Armenians in the forthcoming peace treaty.[3] That treaty, which was signed at San Stefano in March 1878, granted independence to Serbia, Montenegro, and Rumania, and autonomy to a large Bulgarian state. No such provision was either sought or executed for the Armenians. On the contrary, the Russians agreed to withdraw their armies from most of Turkish Armenia, while annexing the border districts of Batum, Ardahan, Kars, Alashkert, and Bayazid. The Armenian leaders were not entirely disappointed, however, because Article 16 of the treaty stipulated that Russian withdrawal would be contingent upon the implementation of effective reforms in Turkish Armenia:

> As the evacuation by the Russian troops of the territory which they occupy in Armenia, and which is to be restored to Turkey, might give rise to conflicts and complications detrimental to the maintenance of good relations between the two countries, the Sublime Porte undertakes to carry out into effect, without further delay, the improvements and reforms demanded by local requirements in the provinces inhabited by the Armenians, and to guarantee their security from Kurds and Circassians.[4]

General M. T. Loris-Melikov was to stand firm in Erzerum until this condition was met.

The aftermath of the Treaty of San Stefano is familiar to students of European history. Prime Minister Benjamin Disraeli and especially Foreign Secretary Robert Salisbury believed that the interests of the

British Empire were jeopardized by the treaty. Enlisting the support of other European powers, they intimidated Russia with threats of joint action, not excluding war The outcome was the convening of a European congress in Berlin in mid-1878 to review and revise the treaty. An Armenian delegation also traveled to Berlin with the goal of persuading the six European powers to arrange for a specific Armenian reform program, rather than simply general reforms, past instances of which had proved most disappointing. Using the administrative statute for Lebanon as a model, the Armenians asked that Turkish Armenia be granted a Christian governor, local self-government, civil courts of law, mixed Christian-Muslim militias, voting privileges for all tax-paying adult males, and the allocation of most local tax revenues for local improvements.[5]

The sympathetic expressions of the European diplomats aside, the Berlin congress revised the Treaty of San Stefano in conformity with the guidelines of the British negotiators. Several provinces were taken back from the newly independent and autonomous states in the Balkans, and on the Caucasus frontier the districts of Alashkert and Bayazid were restored to Ottoman rule. Moreover, insofar as Armenian reforms were concerned, the coercive aspect of Article 16 in the Treaty of San Stefano was superseded by the stipulation in Article 61 of the Treaty of Berlin that the Russian armies should withdraw immediately, and that the sultan would simply pledge to take it upon himself to implement the necessary reforms and to report to the European powers collectively about the progress.[6] The effect of the inversion of Article 16 at San Stefano to Article 61 at Berlin was trenchantly caught in the Duke of Argyll's cryptic observation, "What was everybody's business was nobody's business."[7]

As payment for services rendered to the sultan, Great Britain exacted, through secret agreement, control over the strategic island of Cyprus, and Austria-Hungary gained the right to administer Bosnia and Herzegovina, which had been taken back from Serbia. In the eastern provinces, meanwhile, horrified Armenian peasants witnessed the evacuation of Loris-Melikov's army. As had been the case during the Russian withdrawal from Erzerum in 1829, thousands of Armenians departed with the Russian troops to resettle in the Caucasus. Yet, despite the setback, the Armenian religious leaders did not lose hope and declared that they still had faith in the Ottoman government and in its introduction of the necessary reforms. Armenian patriarch Nerses Varzhapetian swore fidelity to the sultan and emphasized that efforts to overcome Armenian misfortunes would be made within the established legal framework of the Ottoman homeland. At a time when several of the Balkan nationalities had won independence, the Armenians still shunned talk of separatism.[8]

The Treaty of Berlin elevated the Armenian Question to the level of international diplomacy, but the Armenians gained no advantage from that status. On the contrary, Kurdish tribesmen, organized and armed by the sultan's government, spread havoc over the eastern provinces, particularly in the districts from which the Russian army had recently withdrawn. Neither the petitions of the Armenian patriarch nor the establishment of more European consular posts in Turkish Armenia helped to improve the situation. European consuls at Kharput, Erzerum, Van, and other interior centers could do little more than relay frequent dispatches describing the rapacious acts to which the Armenians were subjected. For two years the European powers, outwardly cooperating under the joint responsibility of Article 61, issued collective and identic notes reminding the Sublime Porte of its treaty obligations. But by 1881, these powers had become too involved in the scramble for empire elsewhere to worry further about the Armenians. They silently shelved the Armenian Question and turned away from Armenian troubles.[9]

Feeling abandoned and betrayed, a growing number of Armenians began to espouse extralegal means to achieve what they now regarded as the right and moral duty to resist tyrannical rule. Instead of meeting its obligation to protect its subjects, the Ottoman government had become the instrument of exploitation and suppression. Some Armenians came to believe that, like the Balkan Christians, they too would have to organize, perhaps even take arms. Local self-defense groups that had coalesced in the 1880s gradually gave way to several broadly based secret political societies in the 1890s. Still, few among those who called themselves revolutionaries were prepared to expound national independence as a goal. Rather, they sought cultural freedom and regional autonomy, equality before the law, freedom of speech, press, and assembly, unhindered economic opportunity, and the right to bear arms.[10]

Thus, while the patriarch in Constantinople continued supplications to the Sublime Porte, exponents of the new political mentality preached resistance. Under such influence the rugged villagers of the Sassun district in the province of Bitlis refused to continue paying an extortionary protection tax to Kurdish chieftains. In 1894 the Kurds, unable to subdue their former clients, accused Sassun of sedition and appealed to Ottoman officials. Regular Turkish regiments joined the irregular Kurdish Hamidiye cavalry units and, after weeks of siege and combat, forced the Armenians to lay down their arms in return for the promise of amnesty. Instead, however, Sassun was plundered and several thousand Armenians were put to the sword without regard to age or sex. European consuls and

Christian missionaries raised their voices against the outrage, and soon the newspapers of Europe and the United States were again demanding intercession on behalf of the Armenians. After nearly fifteen years of silence, the European powers were drawn back to the Armenian Question, but now only Great Britain, France, and Russia were willing to address the Sublime Porte on the subject. European representatives attached to an Ottoman commission of inquiry reported that the Armenians of Sassun had been forced to take arms for their own protection and that the gratuitous acts of cruelty by the sultan's regular and irregular troops and the irresponsibility of the Ottoman officials and commanders were reprehensible. There had been no rebellion, and even if the facts had proved otherwise, the unbridled, indiscriminate brutality could in no measure be justified.[11]

The Sassun crisis revived the European call for Armenian reforms. In May 1895 a joint British, French, and Russian plan was submitted for the consolidation of the Armenian provinces into a single administrative region, the release of political prisoners and the repatriation of exiles, the making of reparations to the people of Sassun and other victims, the disarming of the Hamidiye corps in time of peace, and the creation of a permanent control commission to oversee the reforms. Diplomatic exchanges continued through the summer and autumn of 1895 until at last, in October, Sultan Abdul-Hamid assented to a reform program based on, but far less inclusive than, that proposed by the three European governments. Once again, a ripple of optimism emanated from Constantinople.[12]

As before, however, European intercession unsustained by force only compounded the troubles of the Armenians. Even as Abdul-Hamid seemed to acquiesce in the reform program in October 1895, the Armenians in Trebizond were in the throes of massacre. In the following months, systematic pogroms swept over every district of Turkish Armenia. The slaughter of between 100,000 and 200,000 Armenians, the forced religious conversion of the population of scores of villages, the looting and burning of hundreds of other settlements, and the coerced flight into exile of countless Armenians were Abdul-Hamid's actual response to European meddling.[13] His use of violent methods was a desperate attempt to preserve the weakening status quo in the face of enormous external and internal challenges to it. In this regard, the major difference between Abdul-Hamid and his Young Turk successors was that he unleashed massacres in an effort to maintain a state structure in which the Armenians would be kept in their place without the right to resist corrupt and oppressive government, whereas the Young Turks were to employ the same tactic in 1915 on a grander scale to bring about fundamental and far-reaching changes in the status quo and to create an entirely new frame of reference that did not include the Armenians at all.

In the years following the calamities of 1894–96, disillusion weighed heavily upon the Armenians, yet some comfort was found in the fact that other elements, too, were organizing against the tyrannical rule of Abdul-Hamid. In Geneva, Paris, and other emigre centers, reformists and revolutionaries of all the Ottoman nationalities conceived programs of change and envisaged a new, progressive government for their common homeland. In 1902 the first congress of Ottoman liberals, attended by Turkish, Armenian, Arab, Greek, Kurdish, Albanian, Circassian, and Jewish intellectuals, convened in Paris and joined in demands for equal rights for all Ottoman subjects, local self-administration, and restoration of the constitution, which had been suspended since 1877. A second congress in 1907 pledged its constituent groups to a united campaign to overthrow Abdul-Hamid's regime by the swiftest means possible and to introduce representative government.[14]

Within the Ottoman Empire itself, Turkish opposition elements, especially among the junior military officers and the faculty of the technical institutes, merged into the Committee of Union and Progress (Ittihad ve Terakki Teshkilati), popularly referred to as the Young Turks. Thereafter, events moved quickly toward confrontation. When Young Turk army officers in Macedonia were about to be exposed by the sultan's agents in 1908, they led their regiments toward Constantinople in a defensive maneuver and, as the mutiny spread, demanded the restoration of the constitution. Lacking loyal units to crush the rising, Abdul-Hamid bowed to the ultimatum in July and acquiesced in the formation of a constitutional monarchy. The Armenians hailed the victory of the army and its Young Turk commanders; at this historic moment manifestations of Ottoman Christian and Muslim brotherhood abounded.[15]

One of the most unexpected and, for the Armenians, most tragic metamorphoses in modern history was the process, from 1908 to 1914, that transformed the seemingly liberal, egalitarian Young Turks into extreme chauvinists, bent on creating a new order and eliminating the Armenian Question by eliminating the Armenian people. European exploitation of Turkish weaknesses contributed to this process. In the immediate aftermath of the Young Turk revolution, Austria-Hungary annexed Bosnia-Herzegovina, Bulgaria asserted full independence, Crete declared union with Greece, and Italy forcibly pursued claims to Tripoli and the Libyan hinterland. The impact of these troubles emboldened Turkish conservative elements to stage a countercoup to restore the sultan's authority. Although the movement was suppressed and Abdul-Hamid was deposed and exiled, the turmoil did not abate without renewed tragedy for the Armenians. Throughout Cilicia, Armenian villages and city quarters were looted and burned and some 20,000 Armenians were massacred. While there was evidence that Young Turk sympathizers, too, had been among those who incited the mobs, the party's leaders moved to placate the Armenians by ascribing the bloodshed to the Hamidian reaction and by conducting public memorial services for Muslim and Christian sons of a common fatherland who had fallen in defense of the revolution.[16]

The abortive countercoup prompted the Young Turk cabinet to declare a state of siege and to suspend normal constitutional rights for the next four years, until 1912. It was during this period that the concepts of Turkism and exclusive nationalism captivated several prominent Young Turks, who began to envisage a new, homogeneous Turkish state structure in place of the enervated and exploited multinational Ottoman Empire.[17] In a new coup in 1913 the ultranationalistic faction of the Young Turk party seized control, and thereafter, until the end of World War I in 1918, the government was dominated by a triumvirate composed of Enver, minister of war; Talaat, minister of internal affairs and subsequently grand vizier; and Jemal, military governor of Constantinople and later minister of the marine.[18]

The Young Turk revolution of 1908 allowed Armenian political parties to emerge from the underground and to operate clubs and newspapers and vie for the parliamentary seats allotted the Armenians. The most influential of those parties, the Dashnaktsutiun, was in fact linked in an alliance with the Young Turks. Despite increasing signs of Turkish extremism, the Dashnaktsutiun resolved to remain loyal during the troubled years preceding the outbreak of World War I. Yet the seeming gains in the postrevolutionary period did little to diminish the hardships of the rural population. Armed marauding bands in the eastern provinces became all the more audacious when the Armenian youth went off to fight for the Ottoman homeland during the Balkan wars of 1912–13. European consuls in the region filled their dispatches with descriptions of the deadly anarchy. In Constantinople the petitions of the patriarch were answered with promises of action, but effectual measures did not ensue.

As a result of renewed international interest in the Armenian Question following the Balkan wars, the European powers once again raised the issue of reforms. Great Britain, France, and Russia on the one hand, and Germany, Austria-Hungary, and Italy on the other, ultimately reached a compromise settlement. Trebizond and the six Turkish Armenian provinces—Erzerum, Sivas, Kharput, Diarbekir, Bitlis, and Van—would be combined into two administrative regions with broad local autonomy, under the guarantee of the European powers and the supervision of inspectors-general selected from citizens of the small European nations. Without detailing the extensive diplomatic correspondence and the final provisions of the compromise plan of February 1914, let it suffice to say that the reform measure was the most comprehensive and promising of all the proposals put forth since the internationalization of the Armenian Question in 1878.[19]

The outbreak of world war in the summer of 1914 jeopardized implementation of the reform program and deeply alarmed Armenian leaders. Should the Ottoman Empire enter the conflict on the side of Germany, the Armenian plateau would become the inevitable theater of another Russo-Turkish war. In view of the fact that the Armenian homelands lay on both sides of the frontier, the Armenians would suffer severely no matter who might eventually win the war. For these reasons, Armenian spokesmen implored their Young Turk associates to maintain neutrality and spare the empire from calamity. When pressured to organize an Armenian insurrection in the Caucasus against Russia, the leaders of the Dashnaktsutiun declined, again urging neutrality but making it known that if war did engulf the region the Armenians would dutifully serve the government under which they lived.[20]

Despite the advice and appeals of the Armenians, the Germanophile Young Turk faction, led by Enver and Talaat, sealed a secret alliance with Germany in August 1914 and looked to the creation of a new Turkish realm extending into Russian Transcaucasia and Central Asia. Turkey's entrance into the war voided the possibility of solving the Armenian Question through administrative reform. Rather, the Young Turk leaders were drawn to the newly articulated ideology of Turkism, which was to supplant the principle of egalitarian Ottomanism and give justification to violent means for transforming a heterogeneous empire into a homogeneous state based on the concept of one nation, one people. Any vacillation that still may have lingered after Turkey's entrance into the war was apparently put aside as the result of the tragic Caucasus campaign, in which Enver Pasha sacrificed an entire army to his militarily unsound obsession to break through to Baku and the Caspian Sea in the dead of winter, as well as the subsequent Allied landings on the Gallipoli peninsula in April 1915 in an abortive maneuver to capture Constantinople and knock Turkey out of the war.[21] The major Turkish military setback and parallel Allied threat to the capital allowed Young Turk extremists to make Armenians the scapegoats by accusing them of treachery and persuading reluctant comrades that the time had come to settle the Armenian Question once and for all. In *Accounting for Genocide*, Helen Fein has concluded: "The victims of twentieth-century premeditated genocide—the Jews, the Gypsies, the Armenians—were murdered in order to fulfill the state's design for a new order. . . . War was used in both cases . . . to transform the nation to correspond to the ruling elite's formula by eliminating the groups conceived of as alien, enemies by definition."[22]

On the night of April 23/24, 1915, scores of Armenian political, religious, educational, and intellectual leaders in Constantinople, many of them friends and acquaintances of the Young Turk rulers, were arrested, deported to Anatolia, and put to death. Then in May, Minister of Internal Affairs Talaat Pasha, claiming that the Armenians were untrustworthy, that they could offer aid and comfort to the enemy, and that they were in a state of imminent nationwide rebellion, ordered their deportation from the war zones to relocation centers—actually the deserts of Syria and Mesopotamia. In fact the Armenians were driven out not only from the war zones but from the width and breadth of the empire, with the exception of Constantinople and Smyrna, where there were many foreign diplomats and merchants. The whole of Asia Minor was put in motion. Armenians serving in the Ottoman armies, who had already been segregated into unarmed labor battalions, were now taken out in batches and murdered. Of the remaining population, the adult and teenage males were, as a pattern, swiftly separated from the deportation caravans and killed outright under the direction of Young Turk officials and agents, the gendarmerie, and bandit and nomadic groups prepared for the operation. The greatest torment was reserved for the women and children, who were driven for weeks over mountains and deserts, often dehumanized by being stripped naked and repeatedly preyed upon and abused. Many took their own and their children's lives by flinging themselves from cliffs and into rivers rather than prolonging their humiliation and suffering. In this manner an entire nation melted away, and the Armenian people were effectively eliminated from their homeland of nearly three thousand years. Countless survivors and refugees scattered throughout the Arab provinces and Transcaucasia were to die of starvation, epidemic, and exposure. Even the memory of the Armenian nation was intended for obliteration; churches and monuments were desecrated, and small children, snatched from their parents, were renamed and farmed out to be raised as Turks.[23]

The Turkish wartime rationalizations for these deeds were roundly refuted by statesmen and humanitarians such as Henry Morgenthau, Arnold Toynbee, James Bryce, Henry Adams Gibbons, René Pinon, Anatole France, Albert Thomas, and Johannes Lepsius.[24] It was not Armenian treachery, Lepsius declared, but the exclusivist nationalism adopted by the Young Turk extremists that lay at the root of the tragedy.

Elimination of the Armenians would avert continued European intervention in the name of a Christian minority and would remove the major racial barrier between the Ottoman Turks and the Turkic peoples of the Caucasus and Transcaspia, the envisaged new realm of pan-Turkish champions.[25] Gibbons described the Armenian massacres as "The blackest page in modern history," and Ambassador Morgenthau wrote: "I am confident that the whole history of the human race contains no such horrible episode as this. The great massacres and persecutions of the past seem almost insignificant when compared to the sufferings of the Armenian race in 1915."[26]

While the decimation of the Armenian people and the destruction of millions of persons in Central and Eastern Europe during the Nazi regime a quarter of a century later each had particular and unique features, historians and sociologists who have pioneered the field of victimology have drawn some startling parallels.[27] The similarities include the perpetration of genocide under cover of a major international conflict, thus minimizing the possibility of external intervention; conception of the plan by a monolithic and xenophobic clique; espousal of an ideology giving purpose and justification to chauvinism, racism, exclusivism, and intolerance toward elements resisting or deemed unworthy of assimilation; imposition of strict party discipline and secrecy during the period of preparation; formation of extralegal special armed forces to ensure the rigorous execution of the operation; provocation of public hostility toward the victim group and ascribing to it the very excesses to which it would be subjected; certainty of the vulnerability of the intended prey (demonstrated in the Armenian case by the previous general massacres of 1894–96 and 1909); exploitation of advances in mechanization and communication to achieve unprecedented means for control, coordination, and thoroughness; and use of sanctions such as promotions and the incentive to loot, plunder, and vent passions without restraint or, conversely, the dismissal and punishment of reluctant officials and the intimidation of persons who might consider harboring members of the victim group.

News of the deportations and massacres evoked expressions of sympathy and outrage in many countries. On May 24, 1915, when the first reports had reached the West, the Allied Powers declared: "In view of this new crime of Turkey against humanity and civilization, the Allied Governments make known publicly to the Sublime Porte that they will hold all members of the Turkish Government, as well as those officials who have participated in these massacres, personally responsible."[28] In December 1916 the *Manchester Guardian* summarized the sentiments of most British leaders: "Another word remains—Armenia—a word of ghastly horror, carrying the memory of deeds not done in the world since Christ was born—a country swept clear by the wholesale murder of its people. To Turkey that country must never and under no circumstances go back."[29] A year later Prime Minister David Lloyd George declared that Mesopotamia would never be restored to Turkish tyranny, adding: "That same observation applies to Armenia, the land soaked with the blood of innocence, and massacred by the people who were bound to protect them."[30] In his war aims, delivered in January 1918, Lloyd George reiterated that "Arabia, Armenia, Mesopotamia, Syria and Palestine are in our judgment entitled to a recognition of their separate national condition."[31] And in August, shortly before the end of the war, he told an Armenian delegation: "Britain will not forget its responsibilities toward your martyred race."[32]

Similar statements were issued in France, as Prime Minister and Foreign Minister Aristide Briand declared in November 1916: "When the hour for legitimate reparations shall have struck, France will not forget the terrible trials of the Armenians, and in accord with her Allies, she will take the necessary measures to ensure for Armenia a life of peace and progress."[33] His successor, Georges Clemenceau, wrote to an Armenian leader in July 1918: "I am happy to confirm to you that the Government of the Republic, like that of Great Britain, has not ceased to place the Armenian nation among the peoples whose fate the Allies intend to settle according to the supreme laws of Humanity and Justice."[34] The Italians, too, expressed determination that the Armenian people would have a secure collective future. Prime Minister Vittorio Orlando declared: "Say to the Armenian people that I make their cause my cause."[35]

In the United States, incredulity and indignation were the reactions to the Turkish atrocities. The country rallied to assist the "Starving Armenians" through an outpouring of private charity. Until the Ottoman government broke diplomatic relations with the United States in April 1917, U.S. officials tried to assist the Armenian survivors as best they could. In the wake of the massacres, leaders of both parties and of all branches of government pledged themselves to the goal of caring for the survivors and restoring them to their ancestral lands. One of President Wilson's Fourteen Points for peace read: "The Turkish portions of the present Ottoman Empire should be assured a secure sovereignty, but the other nationalities which are now under Turkish rule should be assured an undoubted security of life and an unmolested opportunity of autonomous development."[36] This statement reflected a recommendation by the United States Inquiry, a special commission charged with the formulation of a U.S. peace program: "It is necessary to free the subject races of the Turkish Empire from oppression and misrule. This implies at the very least autonomy for Armenia and the protection of Palestine, Syria, Mesopotamia and Arabia by the civilized nations."[37]

The chain of events caused by the world war, the deportations and massacres, and the revolutions in Russia disrupted the lives not only of the more than two million Turkish (Western) Armenians but also of the other half of the nation, the Russian (Eastern) Armenians. One and three-quarter million Armenians lived across the frontier from the Ottoman Empire in the Caucasus region, which had been under Russian dominion for a century. Several hundred thousand Turkish Armenian refugees had fled into this area during the war years. Refugees and native inhabitants alike were caught up in the Russian revolutions of 1917, which imperiled the Caucasus front and cut the region from central Russia because of the civil war that engulfed the country. At this seemingly opportune moment, Enver Pasha again pursued his plan to seize Baku. Ignoring the advice and admonition of his German allies, he launched an offensive into the Caucasus in the spring of 1918, now bringing death and destruction to the Russian Armenians. It was in the midst of this powerful Ottoman campaign that the three main peoples of the Caucasus, the Georgians, Azerbaijanis, and Armenians, gave up attempts at collaboration and looked to their own individual salvation. The Georgians, acquiring German protection, and the Azerbaijanis, welcoming Turkish assistance, declared their independence from Russia in May 1918, leaving Armenian leaders no choice but to try to save the small unoccupied portion of Russian Armenia by declaring independence of the territory around Erevan. The Armenian republic was the smallest and weakest of the three Caucasian states and lacked the minimal requirements for a viable existence, yet it managed to hold out until the end of the world war opened whole new vistas before the Armenian people.[38]

The surrender of the Ottoman Empire and the flight of the Young Turk leaders in October 1918 evoked thanksgiving and hope among the Armenian survivors. The prospect of compatriots returning to the homeland from all over the world, some refugees and survivors of the genocide, and others longtime exiles from the days of Abdul-Hamid, excited imaginations. Every Allied Power was pledged to a separate autonomous or independent existence for the Armenians in their historic lands. A small republic had already taken form in the Caucasus and now gradually expanded as the Turkish armies withdrew from the area. There were, of course, major obstacles to its incorporation of Turkish Armenia because the population had been massacred or driven out and the Turkish army still controlled the region. In drawing up the Mudros Armistice, British negotiators had required Turkish evacuation of the Caucasus but gave up their initial intent to demand also the clearance of Turkish Armenia, although they reserved for the Allies the right to occupy any or all of the region in case of disorder, an option never exercised. Nonetheless, to the Armenians and to an international legion of supporters and sympathizers, it seemed that the crucifixion of the nation would be followed by a veritable resurrection.

When the Paris Peace Conference convened in January 1919, one of the first decisions taken was that "because of the historical mis-government by the Turks of subject peoples and the terrible massacres of Armenians and others in recent years, the Allied and Associated Powers are agreed that Armenia, Syria, Mesopotamia, Palestine and Arabia must be completely severed from the Turkish Empire."[39] During this immediate postwar period, the new Ottoman government conceded that the Young Turk leaders, now fugitives, had perpetrated criminal acts against both the Christian and Muslim populations of the empire. Military court-martial proceedings were brought against the principal organizers of the Armenian genocide, with verdicts of death in absentia handed down on Enver, Talaat, Jemal, and Dr. Nazim. The logical continuation of proceedings against the hundreds of officials who had participated in the Armenian annihilation did not occur, however, because of subsequent developments in Anatolia. Nonetheless, in pleading the case of the defeated empire at the peace conference in June 1919, the grand vizier and chief Turkish representative admitted that there had occurred "misdeeds which are such as to make the conscience of mankind shudder forever."[40] In reply, the Allied Powers drew attention to the fact that Turkey's willful and inhuman pursuit of the war "was accompanied by massacres whose calculated atrocity equals or exceeds anything in recorded history." Any attempt to escape punishment would be rejected, for "a nation must be judged by the Government which rules it, which directs its foreign policy, which controls its armies."[41]

Sent out from Paris in the summer of 1919 as the chief of a fact-finding mission to Anatolia and the Caucasus, U.S. Major General James G. Harbord collected a large corpus of evidence regarding the massacres and saw with his own eyes the desolation caused by the genocide. At the end of his investigation, Harbord reported:

> Massacres and deportations were organized in the spring of 1915 under definite system, the soldiers going from town to town. The official reports of the Turkish Government show 1,100,000 as having been deported. Young men were first summoned to the government building in each village and then marched out and killed. The women, the old men, and children were, after a few days, deported to what Talaat Pasha called "agricultural colonies," from the high, cool, breeze-swept plateau of Armenia to the malarial flats of the Euphrates and the burning sands of Syria and Arabia. . . . Mutilation,

violation, torture and death have left their haunting memories in a hundred beautiful Armenian valleys, and the traveler in that region is seldom free from the evidence of this most colossal crime of all the ages.[42]

Throughout 1919 and 1920 the Western powers remained publicly committed to the establishment of a united Armenian state combining the Russian Armenian and the Turkish Armenian provinces, with an outlet on the Black Sea. The Allied leaders hoped that the United States would accept a League of Nations mandate over the projected state, just as Britain and France were to assume supervisory control over several Arab provinces to be severed from the Ottoman Empire. Yet, wishes alone were not enough to organize an autonomous Armenian state, repatriate several hundred thousand refugees, and provide the resources for the defense and development of the state. While all the Allies advocated a free Armenia, none was willing to commit the requisite resources to make that goal a reality. The United States, under domestic pressure for rapid demobilization and recoiling into "splendid isolation," declined the Armenian mandate, while Great Britain and France, trying to preserve the rights acquired in their secret wartime pacts relating to the Near East, concentrated their energies on the Arab provinces, where they intended to impose a long-range presence. Rivalries flared repeatedly among the Allies over the spoils of war and zones of influence, thereby contributing to the long delay in drafting the Turkish peace settlement.[43]

While the victors in war negotiated the treaties with the defeated European powers and tried to outmaneuver one another in decisions affecting many parts of the world, a Turkish Nationalist movement took form, aimed at the preservation of the territorial integrity of Anatolia and the rejection of an imperialist and colonialist settlement. Directed by Mustafa Kemal, the Nationalists gained momentum at the end of 1919, winning over much of the remaining Turkish army, and created a countergovernment at Angora (Ankara) in the spring of 1920. To impress the Armenians and the Allies with the seriousness of their intent, the Nationalists attacked the French garrison at Marash in January and killed or drove out most of the Armenians who had repatriated to the city under French and British auspices. Thereafter, the Nationalists besieged many other cities and towns in Cilicia, where approximately 150,000 Armenians had returned in 1919. At the same time, Turkish emissaries, including former Young Turk leaders, sought the assistance of Soviet Russia, offering to incite Islamic peoples against Great Britain and to join forces against the common enemies in the West. During the summer of 1920 the first shipment of Soviet gold reached Anatolia.[44]

Under these circumstances, the Allies began to retreat in Armenian matters. Arguing that the formation of a greater Armenia was impossible without the participation of the United States, the Allies early in 1920 cut the projected state nearly in half by planning the union of the Russian Armenian republic with parts of the provinces of Van, Bitlis, and Erzerum, with an outlet to the sea through Trebizond. To soften the impact of the retreat, the Allies extended de facto recognition to the existing republic, which, despite its fluid borders, landlocked location, crush of refugees, and famine conditions, had made significant organic progress and had expanded to the former Russo-Turkish frontier. The Republic of Armenia increasingly became the focal point of hopes and aspirations for a united national homeland.[45]

At long last, in August 1920, nearly two years after the end of the war, the Treaty of Sèvres was imposed upon the Ottoman Empire and signed by the sultan's representatives.[46] Imperialistic in its financial and economic clauses, the treaty was regarded as a compromise in relation to the Armenian Question. Turkey recognized the freedom and independence of the Armenian republic and renounced all rights over those portions of Van, Bitlis, Erzerum, and Trebizond that were to be included in the new united state. All religious conversions since the beginning of the world war were nullified, and the family or religious community of kidnapped or lost persons could claim and search for such persons through a mixed commission. The Turkish government would assist in the recovery of women and children who had been sequestered in Muslim households, would cooperate in furnishing information and seeking the extradition of persons guilty of war crimes and massacres of Armenians, and would accept nullification of the notorious abandoned properties law, which had made the Ottoman state the beneficiary of all Armenian goods and properties having no living owners or legal heirs. In view of the fact that thousands of Armenian families had perished in their entirety, the law had rewarded the Young Turk government with enormous wealth as a corollary of genocide.

The Treaty of Sèvres offered the Armenians a solution to a question that had cost the lives of half their nation and the devastation of their religious, political, cultural, economic, and social infrastructure. Execution of the treaty, however, would require direct Allied involvement. Every Allied leader knew that the Armenians had been decimated and would need a period of support to take possession of the lands awarded them and to restore and rehabilitate the survivors. As it happened, however, no power was willing to shoulder the moral and material responsibilities. Allied armies did occupy Egypt, Palestine, Syria, Mesopotamia, and parts of Anatolia, but no troops could be spared for the Armenians, who were to be left to their own devices.

In order to break the Treaty of Sèvres and obviate the menace of an independent Armenia, in September 1920 Mustafa Kemal ordered the Turkish armies to breach the frontier and crush the existing Armenian republic in the Caucasus. The Allied Powers looked on with a mixture of distress and resignation as the Turkish armies advanced into the heart of the republic and in December forced the Armenian government to repudiate the terms of the Sèvres settlement, renounce all claims to Turkish Armenia, and even to cede the former Russian Armenian districts of Kars, Ardahan, and Surmalu, including Mount Ararat, the symbolic Armenian mountain. One of the ironies of the postwar era was that of all the defeated powers Turkey alone expanded its boundary, and this only on the Caucasus front at the expense of the Armenians. Desperate and forlorn, the crippled Armenian government had no choice other than to save what little territory was left by opting for Soviet rule and seeking the protection of the Red Army.[47]

By the beginning of 1921, the prospect of a free and independent Armenia had vanished. All Turkish Armenia and a part of Russian Armenia had been lost, several hundred thousand refugees were barred from ever returning to their native districts, and Armenians who had repatriated to Cilicia and western Asia Minor were again driven into exile, this time permanently. When the Turkish armies pushed the Greek forces into the Aegean Sea and burned the city of Smyrna in 1922, the Armenian presence in Turkey, except for Istanbul, was virtually eliminated.[48] The Allied Powers looked on with some embarrassment, but already two of them had moved to win favor with the new rulers of Turkey, even engaging in the secret sale of arms. Military, commercial, and colonial circles in the West exerted strong pressure to attain a rapprochement with Turkey, expressing all the while their undisguised disdain for weak and dependent subject peoples.

The effective Turkish response to the Treaty of Sèvres motivated the Allied governments to seek a normalization of relations with Mustafa Kemal. The Turkish hero, too, was ready to make peace. Dispatching envoys both to Moscow and London to gain greater leverage in the negotiations, Mustafa Kemal pushed the Allies toward a drastic revision of the treaty. He was not disappointed. During the Lausanne conferences in 1923, the Western diplomats acceded to most of the Turkish Nationalist program, despite their sundry protests and face-saving gestures. The British delegates tried to salvage something for the Armenians by urging the Turks to provide them a national home or foyer within the confines and under the suzerainty of Turkey, but the Turkish representatives understood well that no one was prepared to use anything more than words on behalf of the Armenians and therefore adamantly refused to yield. The absolute Turkish triumph was reflected in the fact that in the final versions of the Lausanne treaties neither the word *Armenia* nor the word *Armenian* was to be found. It was as if an Armenian Question or the Armenian people themselves had never existed. The Allies recognized the new frontiers of Turkey, including the annexations in the East and a revised southern boundary that left a string of cities from Aintab to Urfa and Mardin within Turkey.[49]

The Lausanne treaties marked the international abandonment of the Armenian Question. When their case had first been internationalized in 1878, the Armenians had taken hope, but to no avail. If in 1878 they were deprived of fundamental rights and the security of life and property, in 1923 they no longer even existed in their ancestral lands. The intervening years had brought repeated bloodshed and flight, and culminated in a genocide representing the most irreversible tragedy in their turbulent three-thousand-year history. Genocide had become the solution to the Armenian Question. It cleared the country of its largest Christian minority and laid the basis for the Republic of Turkey, which continued on a course of achieving increased homogeneity despite resistance from Kurds and other non-Turkish Muslim peoples.

The Armenian survivors were condemned to a life of exile and dispersion, subjected to inevitable acculturation and assimilation on five continents and facing an indifferent and even hostile world that preferred not to remember. For many years, it seemed as though the genocide had been forgotten by all except the Armenians themselves, as efforts to draw attention to unrequited wrongs failed to reach into high political places. In time, a number of foreign scholars and politicians began to rationalize the Armenian calamity as a sad but perhaps inevitable step toward the formation of modern Turkey. This naive and self-serving attitude was already manifest in the 1950s when a professor at Princeton University wrote: "Had Turkification and Moslemization not been accelerated there [in Anatolia] by the use of force, there certainly would not today exist a Turkish Republic, a Republic owing its strength and stability in no measure to the homogeneity of its population, a state which is now a valued associate of the United States."[50]

Several more recent writers and the Turkish government itself have transformed rationalizations into denials, asserting that there was neither genocide nor even wholesale deportations and massacres.[51] Yet, the ferment created by the perpetration of genocide with impunity is not easily dissipated and, despite the passage of time and concerted efforts to make the Armenian Question a nonissue, new generations have been stirred to demand that the world community address the problem. They insist that without action to close and eventually heal the raw wounds of the Armenian holocaust, current deliberations and resolutions concerning the prevention and punishment of the crime of genocide may become only hollow words.

Notes

1. See, for example, Roderic H. Davison, *Reform in the Ottoman Empire, 1856–1876* (Princeton: Princeton University Press, 1963); A. Schopoff, *Les Réformes et la protection des Chrétiens en Turquie, 1673–1904* (Paris: Plon-Nourrit, 1904); Edouard Engelhardt, *La Turquie et le tanzimat,* vol. 1 (Paris: Cotillon, 1882); Bernard Lewis, *The Emergence of Modern Turkey* (London: Oxford University Press, 1961).

2. Great Britain, Parliament, House of Commons, Sessional Papers, 1877, vol. 112, command 1739, Turkey no. 16, *Reports by Her Majesty's Diplomatic and Consular Agents in Turkey respecting Conditions of the Christian Subjects of the Porte, 1868–1875;* Sessional Papers, 1876–77, vol. 91, c. 1641, Turkey no. 2, *Correspondence respecting the Conference at Constantinople and the Affairs of Turkey, 1876–1877;* Sessional Papers, 1877, vol. 91, c. 1738, Turkey no. 15, *Further Correspondence respecting the Affairs of Turkey,* and vol. 92, c. 1806, Turkey no. 25, *Further Correspondence. . . . ;* Great Britain, Foreign Office, *British and Foreign State Papers,* 1875–76, vol. 68, 683–98, "Constitution de l'Empire Ottoman, promulguée le Zilhidjé 1293 (11/23 Décembre 1876)," and vol. 68, 1114–1207, "Protocols of Conferences between Great Britain, Austria-Hungary, France, Germany, Italy, Russia, and Turkey . . . , Constantinople, December 1876–January 1877."

3. Leo [A. Babakhanian], *Hayots hartsi vaveragrere* [Documents on the Armenian question] (Tiflis, 1915), pp. 56–58.

4. Great Britain, Sessional Papers, 1878, vol. 83, c. 1973, Turkey no. 22, *Preliminary Treaty of Peace between Russia and Turkey Signed at San Stefano 19th February/2nd March, 1878,* and c. 1975, Turkey no. 23, *Maps Showing the New Boundaries under the Preliminary Treaty between Russia and Turkey Signed at San Stefano.*

5. Leo, *Hayots hartsi vaveragrere,* pp. 63–69; Gabriel Lazian, *Hayastan ev hai date (vaveragrer)* [Armenia and the Armenian question (documents)] (Cairo: Houssaper, 1946), pp. 86–88.

6. Great Britain, Sessional Papers, 1878, vol. 83, c. 2083, Turkey no. 39, *Correspondence relating to the Congress of Berlin with Protocols of the Congress,* and c. 2108, Turkey no. 44, *Treaty between Great Britain, Germany, Austria, France, Italy, Russia, and Turkey for the Settlement of Affairs in the East, Signed at Berlin.* See also W. N. Medlicott, *The Congress of Berlin and After* (London: Methuen, 1938).

7. Duke of Argyll [George Douglas Campbell, 8th Duke], *Our Responsibilities for Turkey* (London: J. Murray, 1896), p. 74.

8. Leo, *Hayots hartsi vaveragrere,* pp. 113–33; A. O. Sarkissian, *History of the Armenian Question to 1885* (Urbana: University of Illinois Press, 1938), pp. 89–90.

9. For documents relating to conditions after the Treaty of Berlin and to the diplomatic notes and correspondence about the introduction of reforms in the Armenian provinces, see, for example, Great Britain, Sessional Papers, 1878, vol. 81, c. 1905, Turkey no. 1; 1878–79, vol. 79, c. 2204, Turkey no. 53, and c. 2205, Turkey no. 54, vol. 80, c. 2432, Turkey no. 10; 1880, vol. 80, c. 2537, Turkey no. 4, vol. 81, c. 2574, Turkey no. 7, and c. 2611, Turkey no. 9, vol. 82, c. 2712, Turkey no. 23; 1881, vol. 100, c. 2986, Turkey no. 6. See also *British and Foreign State Papers*, 1877–78, vol. 69, 1313–47, and 1880–81, vol. 72, 1196–1207.

10. See Louise Nalbandian, *The Armenian Revolutionary Movement* (Berkeley and Los Angeles: University of California Press, 1963); Mikayel Varandian, *H. H. Dashnaktsutian patmutiun* [History of the Armenian Revolutionary Federation], vol. 1 (Paris: Navarre, 1932).

11. France, Ministère des Affaires Etrangères, *Documents diplomatiques: Affaires arméniennes; Projets de réformes dans l'empire Ottoman, 1893–1897* (Paris: Imprimerie Nationale, 1897); Great Britain, Sessional Papers, 1895, vol. 109, c. 7894, Turkey no. 1, pt. 1, *Events at Sassoun and Commission of Inquiry at Moush*, and pt. 2, c. 7894-1, *Commission of Inquiry at Moush: Procès-verbaus and Separate Depositions*. See also E. M. Bliss, *Turkey and the Armenian Atrocities* (Boston: H. L. Hastings, 1896); Victor Bérard, "La Politique du Sultan," *La Revue de Paris* (December 15, 1896):880–89.

12. Great Britain, Sessional Papers, 1896, vol. 95, c. 7923, Turkey no. 1, *Correspondence respecting the Introduction of Reforms in the Armenian Provinces of Asiatic Turkey;* France, *Affaires arméniennes*, nos. 43, 57; Germany, Auswärtiges Amt, *Die grosse Politik der europäischen Kabinette, 1871–1914* (40 vols.; Berlin: Deutsche Verlagsgesellschaft für Politik und Geschichte, 1922–27), vol. 9, nos. 2184–89, 2203–12, vol. 10, nos. 2394–2444; Schopoff, *Les Reformes et la protection des Chrétiens en Turquie*, pp. 475–526.

13. For reports and diplomatic correspondence relating to the Armenian massacres of 1895–96, see, for example, Great Britain, Sessional Papers, 1896, vol. 95, c. 7927, Turkey no. 2, vol. 96, c. 8108, Turkey no. 6, and c. 8273, Turkey no. 8, and 1897, vol. 101, c. 8305, Turkey no. 3; France, *Affaires arméniennes*, nos. 116–235, and *Supplément, 1895–1896* (Paris: Imprimerie Nationale, 1897), no. 1–178; Germany, *Grosse Politik*, vol. 10, nos. 2410–76 *passim*, and vol. 12, nos. 2883–2910, 3065–3113 *passim*. Of the hundreds of books and eyewitness accounts relating to the massacres, see, for example, Johannes Lepsius, *Armenia and Europe* (London: Hodder & Stoughton, 1897); Georges Clemenceau, *Les Massacres d'Arménie* (Paris: n.p., 1896).

14. Ernest E. Ramsaur, Jr., *The Young Turks* (Princeton: Princeton University Press, 1957), pp. 65–76, 124–29; Paul Fesch, *Constantinople aux derniers jours d'Abdul-Hamid* (Paris: M. Riviere, 1907), pp. 366–76.

15. Ramsaur, *The Young Turks*, pp. 130–39; Feroz Ahmad, *The Young Turks* (Oxford: Clarendon Press, 1969), pp. 1–13; Charles R. Buxton, *Turkey in Revolution* (London: T. F. Unwin, 1909), pp. 55–73.

16. For findings of the Armenian member of the inquiry commission sent to Cilicia, see Hakob Papikian, *Adanayi egherne* [The Adana calamity] (Constantinople: Kilikia, 1919). See also Duckett Z. Ferriman, *The Young Turks and the Truth about the Holocaust at Adana in Asia Minor, during April, 1909* (London: n.p., 1913); Georges Brèzol, *Les Turcs ont passé là: Receuil de documents sur les massacres d'Adana en 1909* (Paris: L'Auteur, 1911);

René Pinon, *L'Europe et la Jeune Turquie* (Paris: Perrin, 1911); M. Seropian, *Les Vêpres ciliciennes* (Alexandria: Della Roca, 1909).

17. See Uriel Heyd, *Foundations of Turkish Nationalism: The Life and Teachings of Ziya Gökalp* (London: Luzac, 1950), esp. pp. 71–81, 104–48. See also Arnold J. Toynbee, *Turkey: A Past and a Future* (New York: George H. Doran, 1917), pp. 15–40; Victor Bérard, *La Mort de Stamboul* (Paris: A. Coller, 1913), pp. 259–398.

18. Ahmad, *The Young Turks,* pp. 92–120; Wilhelm Feldmann, *Kriegstage in Konstantinopel* (Strassburg: K. J. Trübner, 1913), pp. 106–71.

19. See Roderic H. Davison, "The Armenian Crisis, 1912–1914," *American Historical Review* 53 (April 1948):482–504; Russia, Ministerstvo Inostrannykh Del, *Sbornik diplomaticheskikh dokumentov: Reformy v Armenii* (Petrograd: Gosudarstvennaia Tipografiia, 1915); Germany, *Grosse Politik,* vol. 38, nos. 15283–15434 *passim; British Documents on the Origins of the War, 1898–1914,* ed. G. P. Gooch and Harold Temperley (11 vols.; London: H.M.S.O., 1926–38), vol. 10, pt. 1 *passim;* Leo, *Hayots hartsi vaveragrere,* pp. 342–57.

20. V. Minakhorian, *1915 tvakane* [The year 1915] (Venice: St. Lazarus, 1949), pp. 66–71. See also Johannes Lepsius, *Der Todesgang des armenischen Volkes* (Potsdam: Tempelverlag, 1930), pp. 178–79.

21. W.E.D. Allen and Paul Muratoff, *Caucasian Battlefields* (Cambridge: Cambridge University Press, 1953), pp. 240–84; N. Korsun, *Sarykamishskaia operatsiia na kavkazskom fronte mirovoi voiny v 1914–1915 godu* (Moscow: Gosudarstvennoe Voennoe Izdatel'stvo, 1937). See also Winston Churchill, *The World Crisis* (2 vols.; New York: Scribner's, 1929), vol. 2, *1915;* Trumbull Higgins, *Winston Churchill and the Dardanelles* (New York: Macmillan, 1963).

22. Helen Fein, *Accounting for Genocide* (New York: Free Press, 1979), pp. 29–30.

23. For archival sources and published studies on the Armenian genocide, see Richard G. Hovannisian, *The Armenian Holocaust: A Bibliography Relating to the Deportations, Massacres, and Dispersion of the Armenian People, 1915–1923* (Cambridge, Mass.: Armenian Heritage Press, 1980).

24. For Turkish rationalizations, see, for example, Ahmed Rustem Bey, *La Guerre mondiale et la question turco-arménienne* (Berne: Staempfli, 1918); Turkey, *Aspirations et agissements révolutionnaires des comités arméniens avant et après la proclamation de la constitution ottomane* (Constantinople: n.p., 1916).

25. Lepsius, *Todesgang,* pp. 215–29. See also Toynbee, *Turkey,* pp. 20–27, 30–31.

26. Henry Morgenthau, *Ambassador Morgenthau's Story* (Garden City, N.Y.: Doubleday, Page, 1918), pp. 321–22.

27. See especially Vahakn N. Dadrian, "The Structural-Functional Components of Genocide," in *Victimology,* vol. 3, ed. I. Drapkin and E. Viano (Lexington, Mass.: D. C. Heath, 1974), and "The Common Features of the Armenian and Jewish Cases of Genocide," in *Victimology,* vol. 4, ed. I. Drapkin and E. Viano (Lexington, Mass.: D. C. Heath, 1975).

28. Richard G. Hovannisian, "The Allies and Armenia, 1915–18," *Journal of Contemporary History* 3, no. 1 (1968):147.

29. *Manchester Guardian,* 29 December 1916, p. 4.

30. Great Britain, Parliament, House of Commons, *The Parliamentary Debates,* 5th series, 1916, vol. 100, col. 2220.

31. Carnegie Endowment for International Peace, Division of International Law, *Official Statements of War Aims and Peace Proposals, December 1916 to November 1918* (Washington, D.C.: Carnegie Endowment, 1921), p. 231.

32. *Armenia's Charter* (London: Spottiswoode, Ballantyne, 1918), p. 9.
33. *Le Temps,* 7 November 1918.
34. *Armenia's Charter,* pp. 14–15.
35. Archives of Republic of Armenia Delegation to the Paris Peace Conference (now housed in Boston, Mass.), File 344/1, *H. H. Hromi Nerkayatsutschutiun ev Italakan Karavarutiune, 1918* [Republic of Armenia Rome Mission and the Italian Government, 1918].
36. U.S. Department of State, *Papers Relating to the Foreign Relations of the United States, 1918,* Supplement 1: *The World War,* 2 vols. (Washington, D.C.: G.P.O., 1933), vol. 1, 16.
37. Ibid., 1919: *The Paris Peace Conference,* 13 vols. (Washington, D.C.: G.P.O., 1942–47), vol. 1, 52.
38. See Richard G. Hovannisian, *Armenia on the Road to Independence, 1918* (Berkeley and Los Angeles: University of California Press, 1967).
39. U.S. Department of State, *Paris Peace Conference,* vol. 3, 795.
40. Ibid., vol. 4, 509.
41. Ibid., vol. 6, 688–89; Great Britain, Foreign Office, *Documents on British Foreign Policy,* 1st series, ed. W. L. Woodward et al., 23 vols. to date (London: H.M.S.O., 1947–81), vol. 4, 645–46.
42. U.S. Congress, Senate, 66th Cong., 2d sess., Senate Document no. 266, Major General James G. Harbord, *Conditions in the Near East: Report of the American Military Mission to Armenia* (Washington, D.C.: G.P.O., 1920), p. 7.
43. See Richard G. Hovannisian, *The Republic of Armenia,* vol. 1 (Berkeley, Los Angeles, London: University of California Press, 1971).
44. See Richard G. Hovannisian, "Armenia and the Caucasus in the Genesis of the Soviet-Turkish Entente," *International Journal of Middle East Studies* 4 (April 1973):129–47.
45. See Richard G. Hovannisian, *The Republic of Armenia,* vol. 2 (Berkeley, Los Angeles, London: University of California Press, 1982); Levon Marashlian, "The London and San Remo Conferences and the Armenian Settlement," *Armenian Review* 30, nos. 3–4 (1977):227–55, 398–414.
46. The Treaty of Sèvres is included in Great Britain, Foreign Office, *British and Foreign State Papers,* 1920, vol. 113, 652–776.
47. Richard G. Hovannisian, "Caucasian Armenia between Imperial and Soviet Rule: The Interlude of National Independence," in *Transcaucasia: Nationalism and Socialism,* ed. Ronald G. Suny (Ann Arbor: University of Michigan Press, 1983), pp. 277–92.
48. See Marjorie Housepian, *The Smyrna Affair* (New York: Harcourt Brace Jovanovich, 1966).
49. See France, Ministère des Affaires Etrangères, *Recueil des actes de la Conférence de Lausanne* (6 vols.; Paris: Imprimerie Nationale, 1923); Great Britain, Foreign Office, *British and Foreign State Papers,* 1923, vol. 117, 543–639.
50. Lewis V. Thomas and Richard N. Frye, *The United States and Turkey and Iran* (Cambridge: Harvard University Press, 1951), p. 61.
51. See, for example, Stanford J. Shaw and Ezel Kural Shaw, *History of the Ottoman Empire and Modern Turkey,* vol. 2 (Cambridge: Cambridge University Press, 1977), esp. pp. 311–17, 322–24; *Setting the Record Straight on Armenian Propaganda against Turkey* (Washington, D.C., 1982); Turkey, Prime Ministry, Directorate General of Press and Information, *Documents on Ottoman Armenians* (2 vols.; Ankara, 1982–83).

2

The Turkish Genocide of Armenians, 1915–1917

Leo Kuper

Though the crime of genocide is ancient, the concept itself is relatively new, and definitions vary with the purposes and with the perspectives of the analysts. Some emphasize the central role of the state, in contrast to the United Nations definition, which deliberately excluded reference to the general involvement of the state in genocide.[1] Definitions vary, too, in the nature and scope of acts conceived as genocide. The most exclusive conception finds its model in the Holocaust, in which the intent was that of total annihilation, and its effect the destruction of the biological basis for continued communal existence. Others are more inclusive, providing a basis for the comparative analysis of the mass destruction of racial, ethnic, or religious groups, but rendering it difficult to draw the line between genocide and what might be described as pogroms or communal massacres.

The UN definition of the crime is inclusive enough to encompass the genocides of colonization, the annihilation of indigenous groups, the destruction of "stranger groups" cast in the role of hostages to their host societies, the large-scale massacres resulting from struggles for a measure of self-determination, or for separation, or for power, as well as the Holocaust and the genocides in time of war.

The definitions, then, include, in addition to the UN definition, centrally planned state-organized murder, committed with the intent of totally eliminating a racial, ethnic, or religious group;[2] a structural and systematic destruction of one of these groups by a state bureaucratic apparatus;[3] an extensive massacre usually carried out by the state, whose principal aim or policy is the elimination of a communal group from the social structure;[4] and at a folk level of definition, the extermination, or the systematic extermination, of a national, racial or religious group.

43

I assume the UN definition is the international legally accepted definition because it is contained in the UN Convention on the Prevention and Punishment of the Crime of Genocide, ratified by ninety-two states. It reads as follows:

> In the present Convention, genocide means any of the following acts committed with intent to destroy, in whole or in part, a national, ethnical, racial or religious group, as such:
>   a) Killing members of the group;
>   b) Causing serious bodily or mental harm to members of the group;
>   c) Deliberately inflicting on the group conditions of life calculated to bring about its physical destruction in whole or in part;
>   d) Imposing measures intended to prevent births within the group;
>   e) Forcibly transferring children of the group to another group.

The core of this definition, the intent to destroy a national, ethnic, racial, or religious group by killing members of the group, or by deliberately inflicting on the group conditions of life calculated to bring about its physical destruction, would be a common element in most, if not all, definitions of genocide.

However, the precise definition of genocide is not significant in the present case. Whatever tenable definition is applied to the massacres of Armenians in World War I, they would clearly constitute genocide. The most extreme form of genocide in its merciless commitment to total extermination is represented by the Holocaust. But even then, the Turkish massacres are often coupled with the Holocaust. Thus Dawidowicz, in a book devoted to the Holocaust, and preoccupied with the unique experience of Jews as a people chosen for total extinction, comments that the Turkish massacres of Armenians "in their extent and horror most closely approximated the murder of the European Jews. The once unthinkable 'Armenian Solution' became, in our time, the achievable 'Final Solution', the Nazi code name for the annihilation of the European Jews."[5]

Toynbee had earlier referred to the view that the twentieth century had initiated a new process in genocide, committed in cold blood by the deliberate fiat of the holders of despotic political powers with the utilization of modern technology and organization, and exemplified by the massacres of Armenians, and more effectively by the massacres of the European Jews.[6] A similar conception is to be found in Arlen.[7] Fein, in an influential book devoted essentially to the Holocaust, includes the massacres of Armenians with those of Jews and Gypsies in her category of "modern premeditated genocide."[8] Melson describes the destruction of Armenians in 1915 and of Jews during World War II as the quintessential genocides of our era.[9] And other authors might also be cited as advancing a conception of forms of genocide in which the massacres of Armenians and Jews and Gypsies are closely related.

From a comparative perspective, a remarkable feature of the Turkish genocide of Armenians was its immediate documentation by the accounts of eyewitnesses and of contemporary analysts. The convergence of accounts from different areas and by different witnesses, and the eradication of the geographic and historic presence of the Armenians from their traditional homelands establish the general pattern and provide overwhelming testimony to the commission of the crime of genocide.

Whether the genocide be traced back to the decree in February 1915 for the disarming of Armenians, or to the first deportations on 8 April, the ensuing massacres became immediately known to the outside world.[10] Already on 24 May 1915, the Entente nations (Britain, France, Russia) charged the Ottoman government with massacres of Armenians over a wide area, and declared that they would hold all the members of the Turkish government personally responsible as well as those officials who had participated in the massacres.[11] Morgenthau, U.S. ambassador in Constantinople, reports that in April 1915 he was suddenly deprived of the privilege of using cipher for communicating with U.S. consuls, and that the most rigorous censorship was also applied to letters:

> Such measures could mean only that things were happening in Asia Minor which the authorities were determined to conceal. But they did not succeed. Though all sorts of impediments were placed on traveling, certain Americans, chiefly missionaries, succeeded in getting through. For hours they would sit in my office and, with tears streaming down their faces, they would tell me of the horrors through which they had passed. Many of these, both men and women, were almost broken in health from the scenes which they had witnessed. In many cases they brought me letters from American consuls, confirming the most dreadful of their narrations and adding many unprintable details.[12]

Morgenthau made repeated, but unsuccessful, representations to leading members of the Turkish government. Dr. Johannes Lepsius, a most nobly dedicated and courageous man, whom Morgenthau describes as a high-minded Christian gentleman, representative of German missionary interests, had investigated the earlier massacres of 1895–96 and published his account of them. He now arrived in Constantinople, in July 1915, to carry out further investigations.

Back in Germany, he bore witness to the new waves of massacres, and the following year he published his report, a highly confidential report because he did not wish to embarrass his government in its relations with its Turkish ally. It seems, however, to have been widely disseminated before the German censors formally prohibited the printing and distribution of further copies.[13] In England, in July 1916, Viscount Bryce submitted to the secretary of state for foreign affairs massive documentation of the massacres. These documents, edited by Arnold Toynbee, and consisting largely of eyewitness accounts from neutral witnesses, from consular representatives, missionaries, nurses in the Red Cross, German subjects, and survivors, were published later in the year as a government Blue Paper, with a preface by Viscount Bryce and an historical account by Toynbee. And quite apart from the many diplomatic dispatches, and parliamentary debates, and the wide concern in missionary circles, there was the agitation in the European and U.S. press.

These early documents convey some of the horror of this great catastrophe. They relate the events with immediacy, and with an emotional involvement, drained from later, scholarly writings. And in presenting this brief description, I shall rely appreciably on these accounts.

The major preliminary step was the disarming of Armenians, first the soldiers serving in the Turkish army, and then the civilian population.

In the early part of 1915, the Armenian soldiers in the Turkish army were reduced to a new status. Up to that time most of them had been combatants, but now they were all stripped of their arms and transformed into workmen. Instead of serving their country as artillerymen and cavalrymen, these former soldiers now discovered that they had been transformed into road labourers and pack animals. Army supplies of all kinds were loaded on their backs, and, stumbling under the burdens and driven by the whips and bayonets of the Turks, they were forced to drag their weary bodies into the mountains of the Caucasus. Sometimes they would have to plough their way, burdened in this fashion, almost waist high through snow. They had to spend practically all their time in the open, sleeping on the bare ground—whenever the ceaseless prodding of their taskmasters gave them an occasional opportunity to sleep. They were given only scraps of food; if they fell sick they were left where they had dropped, their Turkish oppressors perhaps stopping long enough to rob them of all their possessions—even of their clothes. If any stragglers succeeded in reaching their destinations, they were not infrequently massacred. In many instances Armenian soldiers were disposed of in even more summary fashion, for it now became almost the general practice to shoot them in cold blood. In almost all cases the procedure was the same. Here and there squads of 50 or 100 men would be taken, bound together in groups of four, and then marched out to a secluded spot a short distance from the village. Suddenly the sound of rifle shots would fill the air, and the Turkish soldiers who had acted as the escort would sullenly return to camp. Those sent to bury the bodies would find them almost invariably stark naked, for, as usual, the Turks had stolen all their clothes. In cases that came to my attention, the murderers had added a refinement to their victims' sufferings by compelling them to dig their graves before being shot. . . .

Dreadful as were these massacres of unarmed soldiers, they were mercy and justice themselves when compared with the treatment which was now visited upon those Armenians who were suspected of concealing arms. Naturally the Christians became alarmed when placards were posted in the villages and cities ordering everybody to bring their arms to headquarters. Although this order applied to all citizens, the Armenians well understood what the result would be, should they be left defenseless while their Moslem neighbours were permitted to retain their arms. In many cases, however, the persecuted people patiently obeyed the command; and then the Turkish officials almost joyfully seized their rifles as evidence that a 'revolution' was being planned and threw their victims into prison on a charge of treason. Thousands failed to deliver arms simply because they had none to deliver, while an even greater number tenaciously refused to give them up, not because they were plotting an uprising, but because they proposed to defend their own lives and their women's honour against the outrages which they knew were being planned. The punishment inflicted upon these recalcitrants forms one of the most hideous chapters of modern history. Most of us believe that torture has long ceased to be an administrative and judicial measure, yet I do not believe that the darkest ages ever presented scenes more horrible than those which now took place all over Turkey. Nothing was sacred to the Turkish gendarmes; under the plea of searching for hidden arms, they ransacked churches, treated the altars and sacred utensils with the utmost indignity, and even held mock ceremonies in imitation of the Christian sacraments. They would beat the priests into insensibility, under the pretense that they were the centres of sedition.[14]

There follow descriptions of atrocities inflicted.

Then came deportations, accompanied in the early stages by the culling of Armenian leaders. Throughout the country, the government arrested and deported the elite, the educated, the deputies, the publicists, the writers, the poets, the jurists, the advocates, the notaries, the civil servants, the doctors, the merchants, the bankers, and all those with substantial means and influence. Lepsius comments that this measure was presumably designed to deprive Armenians of leadership and representation, so that the deportations might be completed without public clamor and without resistance.[15]

The deportations were countrywide. Constantinople (in which Lepsius reports that some 10,000 were deported), Smyrna, and Aleppo were spared the mass deportations of Armenians. The deportations were carefully timed, moving from one region to another. Morgenthau describes the destination for the deportations as the dreary, desolate waste of the Syrian desert and the Mesopotamian valley.[16] And he writes that if the Turks had undertaken such a deportation in good faith, it would have represented the height of cruelty and injustice, but that in fact they never had the slightest intention of reestablishing the Armenians in this new country. They knew that the great majority would never reach their destination and that those who did would either die of thirst and starvation, or be murdered by "wild Mohammedan desert tribes." The deportations really represented a new method of massacre. "When the Turkish authorities gave the orders for these deportations, they were merely giving the death warrant to a whole race; they understood this well, and, in their conversations with me, they made no particular attempt to conceal the fact."

There was variation in the pattern of the deportations. Some latitude was allowed local authorities, and there were a few officials who resisted the deportations, but they were mostly removed from office, or rendered ineffective by the activities of the local branches of the ruling party. In areas of strategic significance, because of proximity to the advancing Russians, the military authority, with the help of the local Kurds, carried out an extermination of the civilian populations.[17] In some areas, the movement more nearly corresponded to a genuine deportation; and the men would be spared. There were areas in which the women might be bullied into conversion to Islam; in others, conversion might be disallowed; or the women might be massacred like the men. And there were differences in the use of torture and in the disposal of Armenian property.[18]

Toynbee describes the common pattern of the deportations, starting with a call from the public crier that male Armenians forthwith present themselves at the government building. This was the usual procedure, though in some cases, the warning was given by the soldiers or gendarmes slaughtering every male Armenian they encountered in the streets. When the men arrived, "they were thrown without explanation into prison, kept there a day or two, and then marched out of the town in batches, roped man to man. . . . But they had not long to ponder over their plight, for they were halted and massacred at the first lonely place on the road. . . . the women and children were not disposed of by straightforward massacre like the men. Their destiny under the Government scheme was not massacre but slavery or deportation." Usually after a few days, the women and children, and the remnant of men who, through sickness, infirmity, or age, had escaped the general fate of their sex, were ordered to prepare themselves for deportation. For the women, the alternative of conversion to Islam (if available) could only be ratified by immediate marriage to a Muslim, and the surrender of children to be brought up as true Muslims. "Deportation was the alternative adopted by, or imposed upon, the great majority."[19]

The former Italian consul-general at Trebizond gives this agonized account of his suffering as a helpless spectator of the deportation from that town:

> It was a real extermination and slaughter of the innocents, an unheard-of thing, a black page stained with the flagrant violation of the most sacred rights of humanity, of Christianity, of nationality. The Armenian Catholics, too, who in the past had always been respected and excepted from the massacres and persecutions, were this time treated worse than any—again by the orders of the Central Government. There were about 14,000 Armenians at Trebizond—Gregorians, Catholics, and Protestants. They had never caused disorders or given occasion for collective measures of police. When I left Trebizond, not a hundred of them remained.
>
> From the 24th June, the date of the publication of the infamous decree, until the 23rd July, the date of my own departure from Trebizond, I no longer slept or ate; I was given over to nerves and nausea, so terrible was the torment of having to look on at the wholesale execution of these defenceless, innocent creatures.
>
> The passing of the gangs of Armenian exiles beneath the windows and before the door of the Consulate; their prayers for help, when neither I nor any other could do anything to answer them; the city in a state of siege, guarded at every point by 15,000 troops in complete war equipment, by thousands of police agents, by bands of volunteers and by the members of the 'Committee of Union and Progress'; the lamentations, the tears, the abandonments, the imprecations, the many suicides, the instantaneous deaths from sheer terror, the sudden unhingeing of men's reason, the conflagrations, the shooting of victims in the city, the ruthless searches through the houses and in the countryside; the hundreds of corpses found every day along the exile road; the young women converted by force to Islam or exiled like the rest; the children torn away from their families or from the Christian schools, and handed over by force to Moslem families, or else placed by hundreds on board ship in nothing but their shirts, and then capsized and drowned in the Black Sea and the River Deyirmen Deré—these are my last ineffaceable memories of Trebizond, memories which still, at a month's distance, torment my soul and almost drive me frantic.[20]

While in the southeastern districts of the zone immediately threatened by the Russian advance, there were outright massacres of the population, in the northwestern districts of the frontier zone, the semblance of deportation was preserved, but deportation served merely as a cloak for massacre.[21] As for the convoys of exiles, they were little more than death caravans. The long journey on foot inflicted terrible physical sufferings. "Yet," Toynbee writes, "these were the least part of their torture; far worse were the atrocities of violence wantonly inflicted upon them by fellow human beings." And he describes the mobbing by Muslim peasants with the connivance of the gendarmes assigned to the convoys; the outrages against the women; the massacres of the old men and the boys, and of women, too, by Kurds and *chettes* (brigands recruited from the public prisons) and gendarmes.

> It depended on the whim of the moment whether a Kurd cut a woman down or carried her away into the hills. When they were carried away their babies were left on the ground or dashed against the stones. But while the convoy dwindled, the remnant had always to march on. The cruelty of the gendarmes towards the victims grew greater as their physical sufferings grew more intense; the gendarmes seemed impatient to make a hasty end of their task. Women who lagged behind were bayoneted on the road, or pushed over precipices, or over bridges. The passage of rivers, and especially of the Euphrates, was always an occasion of wholesale murder. . . . The lust and covetousness of their tormentors had no limit. The last survivors often staggered into Aleppo naked; every shred of their clothing had been torn from them on the way. Witnesses who saw their arrival remark that there was not one young or pretty face to be seen among them, and there was assuredly none surviving that was truly old. . . .

As for those who were transported by rail from the metropolitan districts and the railway zone, "the sum of their suffering can hardly have been less." They were packed in cattle trucks; they were turned out into the open to wait for days or even weeks for rolling stock; in breaks in the railway line, they were forced across the mountains on foot; they died by the thousands of hunger, exposure, and epidemics "in the vast and incredibly foul concentration camps" which grew up along the route. "The portion of them that finally reached Aleppo were in as deplorable a condition as those that had made the journey on foot from beginning to end." And they were finally marooned with the other exiles in the worst, and most remote, districts at the disposal of the government, "with neither food, nor shelter, nor clothing, and with no able-bodied men among them to supply these deficiencies by their labour and resource."[22]

Of the conditions of these camps, Lepsius quotes a most heartrending account by an American eyewitness, from which I have taken the following excerpt:

> It is impossible to render an image of the horrible impressions I received on my journey through the dispersed camps along the Euphrates river. I travelled on the right-hand bank of the stream. To speak of 'camps' is actually not possible.
>
> The major portion of these miserable people brutally driven from home and land, separated from their families, robbed of everything they owned

and stripped of all they carried underway, have been herded like cattle under the open skies without the least protection against heat and cold, almost without clothing, and were fed very irregularly, and always insufficiently. Exposed to every change in weather, the glowing sun in the desert, the wind and rain in spring and fall, and the bitter cold in winter, weakened through extreme want and their strength sapped by endless marches, deplorable treatment, cruel torture and the constant fear for their lives, those that had some shreds of their strength left dug holes at the banks of the river to crawl into them.

The extreme few who managed to salvage some clothes and some money and who are in a position to purchase some flour are considered fortunate and rich people. Fortunate are those, too, who could obtain a few watermelons or a sick and skinny goat from the nomads in exchange for the same weight in gold. Everywhere one only sees pale faces and emaciated bodies, wandering skeletons conquered by disease and surely soon victims of starvation.

When the measures to transport the entire population into the desert were adopted, no appropriations were made for any kind of nourishment. On the contrary, it is obvious that the government pursued a plan to let the people die of starvation. Even an organized mass-killing such as during the times when liberty, equality, and fraternity had not yet been proclaimed in Constantinople, would have been a much more human measure, since it would have saved these miserable people from the horrors of hunger and the slow death and the excruciating pains of tortures so fiendish that the most cruel of the Mongols could not have imagined them. But a massacre is less constitutional than death by starvation. Civilization is saved!

What remains of the Armenian nation, scattered along the banks of the Euphrates, consists of old men, women, and children. Men of middle age and younger people, as far as they had not been slain, are scattered over the roads of the country where they smash stones or do other labors for the Army in the name of the state.[23]

The concern of the Great Powers seemed more sincere, and the commitment to the Armenian cause more serious, than in the past. The Treaty of Sèvres (August 1920) provided for the recognition of Armenia as a free and independent state. It imposed on Turkey the obligation to ensure equality of treatment for racial, religious, or linguistic minorities and to facilitate to the greatest extent possible the return to their homes, and the reestablishment in their businesses, of the Turkish subjects of non-Turkish race who had been forcibly driven out after January 1914 by fear of massacre or other pressure. There were Turkish trials of some of those involved in the massacres and the Ittihadist triumvirate of World War I were put on trial and sentenced to death in absentia.[24] Carzou, in Un Génocide exemplaire: Arménie 1915, reprints the judgments of the courts relating to murder and massacre in three areas, and these are entirely consistent with the eyewitness accounts.[25]

But this is where the retribution and restitution ended. The trials were of little significance save as confirmations of observers' accounts. And as to the provisions of the Treaty of Sèvres, they were swept aside in the predatory rivalries of the victors, in their unwillingness to assume a mandate over Turkish Armenia, in the Turkish-Armenian war, in the aftermath of the Russian revolution, in the Turkish-Soviet Treaty of Friendship and the Turkish-Greek war, in further massacres of Armenians, and in the growth of Turkish nationalism and the resurgence of its military power. In the result, the Treaty of Lausanne in July 1923 makes provision for the rights of minorities to equality of treatment, but for the rest, it ignores the earlier commitments to the Armenians.

Thus ends the Armenian presence in Turkey, reduced from a population of about 2 million to less than 25,000 at the present time.

Genocide is preeminently a government crime, and governments can hardly be expected to plead guilty. The German case is unusual, with its radical change of government, and its acceptance of responsibility for genocide in a massive and continuing program of reparations. The more usual, perhaps invariable response, particularly if the same government continues in power, is to deny responsibility, first on the ground that there was in fact no genocide, and second by the contention that the victims were themselves the guilty parties and responsible for the loss of life they sustained.

The denial of genocide in the Armenian case includes in part a battle of statistics, based on Turkish estimates of the Armenian population at the time as not more than 1.3 million, thereby greatly reducing the number of those who perished. This is in contrast to the figures cited by Hovannisian of between 1.5 million and 2 million Armenians in Turkey,[26] or the estimate by the American Committee for Armenian and Syrian Relief of a prewar Armenian population of 1.8 million. Arlen writes that "it is possible to say, not precisely but with a general respect for accuracy and plausibility, that in the course of the 1915–1916 massacres and deportations close to one million Armenians—more than half the Armenian population of Turkey—disappeared; which is to say, were killed, outright by police or soldiers, or by roadside massacres, or by forced marches, or by starvation, or by sickness, or by conditions in the concentration camps."[27] But the magnitude of the crime of genocide is hardly reduced if the number of victims is, say, 200,000. The statistical argument must therefore by complemented by such assertions as that the deaths were the result "not only of the transportation but also of the same conditions of famine, disease, and war action that carried away some 2 million Muslims at the same time" and that the army had been given orders to care for the protection and needs of the Armenians during their march and in their new wartime settlements.[28]

As for the second theme, that of the victims as their own executioners, there is the attempted justification that the deportations were a wartime measure, rendered necessary, so the argument runs, by the disloyalty of the Armenians, who were accused of supporting the country's enemies.[29] Now the Armenians were divided between Russian and Turkish territory, and Russian Armenians served in the Russian army as Turkish Armenians served in the Turkish. There were also volunteer Armenian units assisting the Russians, the British, and the French, and there would seem to be no doubt of the sympathies of the Turkish Armenians for the European powers to whom they had turned in the past for protection against Turkish rule. But there is substantial evidence, advanced by both Toynbee and Lepsius, against the thesis of Turkish-Armenian disloyalty. And even if this had been true, it would have been argument for the disarming of Armenian soldiers and their conversion into labor battalions, or their internment with other able-bodied Armenians, but no argument for massacres of the men, nor for deportation of the women and children, the aged and infirm, by long incredibly arduous forced marches, nor for the choice of desolate wastes as the destination of the survivors of the death caravans. The whole plan of the deportations, and the testimony of eyewitnesses are clear evidence of an exterminatory intention to so reduce the Turkish-Armenian population as to dispose of the Armenian Question once and for all. There is as little credibility in this line of Turkish defense as in the defense of the Burundi government that in its slaughter of Hutu (variously estimated as between 100,000 and 200,000) it was punishing, though admittedly with some understandable excesses, only those guilty of massacres and planned genocide against the Tutsi.[30]

The Turkish government's denial of the genocide is aggressively pursued in the attempt to expunge it from historical memory. This is notwithstanding the overwhelming contemporary testimony to the crime, and past historical indications of a genocidal threat in the relations of the Turkish rulers to their Armenian subjects. As we look back on events during the period of the disintegration of the Turkish Empire, it seems clear that there were early warning signals of this threat of genocide, and that it was deeply rooted in the structure of the Ottoman Empire, in the history of Turkish-Armenian relations, and in the involvement of outside powers in the affairs of the empire.

There had been a long, if intermittent and convoluted, involvement of outside powers in the treatment of Armenians and other Christians under Turkish rule. The Treaty of Paris (1856), at the conclusion of the Crimean War, had incorporated guarantees for internal reforms in the

Ottoman Empire. A generation later, following the Russian-Turkish War, the occupation of many settled Armenian areas by the Russians, and representations by the Armenian Patriarchate for protection of Ottoman Armenians, the Treaty of San Stefano (1878) imposed on the Sublime Porte the obligation "to carry out, without further delay, the ameliorations and reforms demanded by local requirements in the provinces inhabited by the Armenians, and to guarantee their security against the Kurds and Circassians." When this treaty was revised by the Treaty of Berlin, the reforms previously guaranteed to Russia alone were guaranteed to the European nations (Great Britain, Austria-Hungary, France, Germany, Italy, and Russia), with power to superintend their application.[31]

These provisions proved ineffective. In 1894, there was the massacre of Sassun, an old-style city massacre of Armenian men, women, and children by regular Turkish units and the irregular Hamidiye (Kurdish) cavalry, in reprisal for the refusal to pay a tribute to Kurdish chieftains and for rebellious resistance. Under pressure from European powers following riotous and bloody disturbances attendant upon an Armenian demonstration in Constantinople, the sultan signed the Program of Reforms, which also proved illusory. "Even before the promulgation of the reform act of October 1895, massacres had begun in Trebizond. In the following months, the Armenian Plateau met with the same fate. Abdul-Hamid's actual response to European meddling was the extirpation of between one and two hundred thousand Armenians during 1895–1896."[32] And the same writer records the disillusionment as "once again, the nations of Europe, now involved in the struggle for empire, turned away from the tragedy to which they had contributed." It was not until some five years after the Adana massacres of 1909 that the European powers finally imposed on the Ottoman government an agreement for reforms, and for procedures to ensure their implementation, which seemed to promise relief. But these were set aside with Turkey's participation in World War I. And the way was now cleared for the final solution of genocide.

Toynbee, in his discussion of the evolution of the bureaucratic and technological genocides of the twentieth century, describes the massacres at the instigation of the Sultan Abdul-Hamid II at the end of the nineteenth century as amateurish and ineffective compared with the largely successful attempt to exterminate the Ottoman Armenians during World War I, and the latter in turn as less effective than the German genocide of the European Jews, "since the general level of technological and organizational efficiency in Germany during the dozen years of the Nazi regime was considerably higher than it had been in Turkey during the ten years of the CUP regime."[33] Arlen writes to similar effect that the entire production of the Armenian genocide of 1915 was based on the imperfectly utilized but definitely perceived capacities of the modern state for politically restructuring itself, which were made possible by the engines of technology. In due course,

> Hitler's Germany was to perfect the process of railway deportation and to develop the gas chamber and the crematoria, and Lenin's and Stalin's Russia was to evolve further the institutions of the concentration camp and secret surveillance. . . . But in virtually every modern instance of mass murder, beginning, it appears, with the Armenians, the key element— . . . which has raised the numerical and psychic levels of the deed above the classic terms of massacre—has been the alliance of technology and communications.[34]

The Sultan Abdul-Hamid's massacres do not appear to have been all that amateurish and ineffective. They had limited objectives, being designed as a sort of ambassadorial note to the European powers to refrain from intervention in the domestic affairs of Turkey, and a most bloody warning to the Armenians themselves against seeking the intercession of these powers on their behalf or aspiring to autonomy. They also took a somewhat different form from the later genocide in the sense that they were perpetrated on the spot without resort to such devices as the death caravans of the deportation. Lepsius, in *Armenia and Europe,* in which he reports his investigations in 1896, describes how massacres were announced by a bugle call or other signal and called off at an appointed time (though there was variability in this), and he shows the concentrated nature of the massacres, particularly evident in the tabular statement of occurrences in Asia Minor in 1895, prepared by the Committee of Delegates from the six embassies and included by Lepsius in an appendix.[35] But whether or not the sultan's massacres were relatively ineffective, and however much they differed in the immediacy and concentrated nature of their occurrence, they employed many of the same elements as the 1915 genocide, serving somewhat as a pilot project for the later genocide. The organizational base was found in the provincial and local administration, with its officials, its military, and its police.

There was similar use made of social forces, generated from the plural structure of the society, and hostile to the Armenians, so that the slaughter had some appearance of spontaneous action by mobs of Turkish peasants and townsmen, and by plundering and massacring bands of Kurds and Circassians. Religious hatreds played their part, with terrible atrocities against priests, the desecration and destruction of churches, and forced conversions. Even the actions of the European nations described by Lepsius as "a fine piece of moral scene-painting behind which political intrigue wished to hide" resemble the later abandonment of the Armenians to the disastrous consequences of Great Power involvement in their affairs.[36]

The extreme vulnerability of the Armenian minority, and its selection as a target for genocide by the Turkish rulers as they became involved in the cataclysmic conflicts of World War I, rested on the superimposition of differences in structure and culture, and of issues of conflict with considerable historical depth. The system of administration had served to maintain, perhaps even to enhance, the ethnic and cultural distinctiveness of the Armenians. The *millet* was a unit of Turkish administration, conferring, on the basis of religious affiliation, appreciable autonomy in spiritual matters, in the maintenance of schools, and in the exercise of certain limited judicial functions. The effect, in the case of the Armenian subjects of the Turkish Empire was a convergence of political, ethnic, religious, and cultural differentiation, too deep-rooted to be effaced by such reforms as were introduced.

To these differences must be added occupational differentiation. It is quite often referred to in the literature, sometimes in the pejorative characterization of Armenians as a "mercantile race," whatever that may mean. It is the same characterization as that applied to Jews, or to Chinese in Southeast Asia, or to Indians in East Africa, or to Lebanese in West Africa, and seems to be used as a justification for murder, as if this quality in the victim transmuted massacre to justifiable homicide. In the case of the Armenians, it is true that they were active in commerce, a not unusual reaction where subjects are largely denied advancement to positions of leadership in government and warfare. Lepsius writes that the Armenians controlled 60 percent of imports, 40 percent of exports, and at least 80 percent of the commerce in the interior.[37] But some 80 percent were peasants, and the remainder were not only merchants but members of the liberal professions and artisans, to the extent that the U.S. consul at Aleppo reported that in the areas evacuated there was no longer, with some exceptions, a single mason, smith, carpenter, potter, tentmaker, weaver, shoemaker, jeweller, pharmacist, doctor, advocate, not a single person belonging to the liberal professions or engaged in some craft.[38] Yet there was sufficient involvement of Armenians in commerce for this to serve as a source of grievance and as an issue for manipulation.

The administrative framework for the mosaic of peoples who composed the Turkish Empire also served to maintain the distinctiveness of other groups. In the eastern provinces, nomadic Kurdish tribesmen maintained a state of feud with the settled Armenian communities that they periodically ransacked.[39] Abdul-Hamid had used the Kurds as an irregular force of cavalry against the Armenians in the 1895–96 massacres. In the turbulent history of these areas, there had been many forced movements of population, following the vicissitudes of war, and these had left their bitter residue of antagonistic memories. Of special significance were the many Muslim refugees from previous upheavals (the Shaws cite a figure of over 1 million for the period 1878–97), and more immediately from the Balkan wars and the new Christian regimes of Bulgaria, Serbia, and Greece.[40] All these divisions offered a base for the mobilization of social forces murderously hostile to the Armenians.

The division and conflicts between subject groups operated within the wider context of the overriding conflicts in Turkish-Armenian relations. It is difficult to estimate the power of the major cleavage of religion. There were areas, as we have seen, in which the Muslim inhabitants or the officials were quite opposed to the deportations, and the Turkish leaders of the Committee of Union and Progress were not themselves religious fanatics. But nevertheless, their declaration that the country was engaged in a holy war in the defense of Islam was deliberately designed to inflame religious passion; and the participation of the Turkish populace in the deportations and the pillage and the massacres, the desecration of churches, the atrocities against priests, the forced conversions all point to the persistence of ancient religious hatreds. The long history of the intervention of foreign nations on behalf of the Christian subjects of the Ottoman Empire arose out of, and was superimposed on, this fundamental religious cleavage. But this concern of the outside powers was anything but purely benevolent; it was associated with, and no doubt appreciably motivated by, predatory interests in the dismemberment of the Turkish Empire, already far advanced. Engaged in a highly destructive conflict, initiated by disastrous campaigns, the Turkish rulers were now driven from the high hopes with which they had entered the war, to the desperate defense of their borders and dissolving empire. Under these circumstances, and driven by an extreme and exclusive nationalism, the anxiety lest the Armenians revolt became the conviction that they were disloyal, and the warrant for their genocide.[41]

The provincial and local administrations provided, as we have seen, the organizational base for the genocide. The presence of local branches of the Committee of Union and Progress, the "many-headed hydra" of the Young Turk Clubs, greatly enhanced the effectiveness of this administrative structure. These branches became the catalysts of genocide, exerting pressure where necessary on reluctant officials, inflaming the hatreds of the populace with tales of Armenian treachery and atrocity, and in general activating the genocidal process. There was some variability by reason of the dependence on local initiative and the variation in such conditions as proximity to the Russian front; and there was some appearance of spontaneity, given a great reliance on the action of mobs and predatory bands. But the countrywide distribution of the destruction of Armenian communities, the timing, the general pattern were the product of a central administrative plan. It proceeded, however, appreciably by indirection, that is to say, not by massacres from the center but by setting in motion the genocidal process as a low-cost operation with extensive reliance on local social forces.

Notes

1. See, for example, Helen Fein, *Accounting for Genocide* (New York: Free Press, 1979), p. 7. My discussion of the Armenian genocide is based on a chapter in my book, *Genocide,* published in the United Kingdom by Penguin Books and in the United States by Yale University Press in 1982.
2. Ibid.
3. Irving Louis Horowitz, *Genocide: State Power and Mass Murder* (New Brunswick, N.J.: Transaction Books, 1976), p. 18.
4. See Robert Melson's chapter in this volume.
5. Lucy Dawidowicz, *The Holocaust and the Historians* (Cambridge: Harvard University Press, 1981), p. 20.
6. Arnold J. Toynbee, *Experiences* (London: Oxford University Press, 1969), pp. 241–42.
7. Michael J. Arlen, *Passage to Ararat* (New York: Farrar, Straus & Giroux, 1975), pp. 243–44.
8. Fein, *Accounting for Genocide,* p. 7.
9. See Melson's chapter in this volume.
10. Arnold J. Toynbee, ed., *The Treatment of Armenians in the Ottoman Empire, 1915-1916* (London: H.M.S.O., 1916), p. 638; Johannes Lepsius, *Deutschland und Armenien, 1914-1918: Sammlung diplomatischer Aktenstücke* (Potsdam: Tempelverlag, 1919), pp. 10–11, gives the end of March 1915 as the date for commencement of the deportations and December 1914 as the date for the calling in of arms in Zeitun, Cilicia.
11. Richard G. Hovannisian, *Armenia on the Road to Independence* (Berkeley and Los Angeles: University of California Press, 1967), pp. 51–52.
12. Henry Morgenthau, *Ambassador Morgenthau's Story* (Garden City, N.Y.: Doubleday, Page, 1918), pp. 327–28.
13. See the preface by Pinon (1919) to *Le Rapport secret du Dr. Johannès Lepsius* (Paris: Payot, 1918); Ulrich Trumpener, *Germany and the Ottoman Empire, 1914-1918* (Princeton: Princeton University Press, 1968), pp. 227, 240.
14. Morgenthau, *Ambassador Morgenthau's Story,* pp. 302–5.
15. Lepsius, *Deutschland und Armenien,* p. 29.
16. Morgenthau, *Ambassador Morgenthau's Story,* pp. 308–9.
17. Toynbee, *The Treatment of Armenians in the Ottoman Empire,* p. 640.
18. Ibid., p. 653.
19. Ibid., pp. 640–41.
20. Ibid., pp. 291–92.
21. Ibid., pp. 646–47.
22. Ibid., pp. 642–45.

23. Dickran H. Boyajian, *Armenia: The Case for a Forgotten Genocide* (Westwood, N.J.: Educational Book Crafters, 1972), pp. 117–24. The report is contained in Lepsius, *Deutschland und Armenien.*
24. Richard G. Hovannisian, *The Republic of Armenia*, vol. 1 (Berkeley, Los Angeles, London: University of California Press, 1971), pp. 419–20.
25. Jean-Marie Carzou, *Un Génocide exemplaire: Arménie 1915* (Paris: Flammarion, 1975), pp. 233–46.
26. Hovannisian, *Road*, pp. 34–37.
27. Arlen, *Passage to Ararat*, p. 240.
28. Stanford J. Shaw and Ezel Kural Shaw, *History of the Ottoman Empire and Modern Turkey*, vol. 2 (Cambridge: Cambridge University Press, 1977), pp. 315–16.
29. An extreme version of the Turkish case will be found in Shaw and Shaw, *History of the Ottoman Empire*, vol. 2. See also the critique of this version by Richard G. Hovannisian, "The Critic's View: Beyond Revisionism," *International Journal of Middle East Studies* 9 (August 1978):379–88.
30. See Leo Kuper, *The Pity of It All* (Minneapolis: University of Minnesota Press, 1977), ch. 5.
31. Louise Nalbandian, *The Armenian Revolutionary Movement: The Development of Armenian Political Parties Through the Nineteenth Century* (Berkeley and Los Angeles: University of California Press, 1967), pp. 27–28.
32. Hovannisian, *Road*, p. 28.
33. Toynbee, *Experiences*, pp. 241–42.
34. Arlen, *Passage to Ararat*, pp. 243–44.
35. Johannes Lepsius, *Armenia and Europe* (London: Hodder & Stoughton, 1897), pp. 280–331. A summary by Lepsius of his analysis of the organization and course of the massacres is given on pp. 58–61, 76–85.
36. Ibid., p. 92.
37. Johannes Lepsius, *Le Rapport secret du Dr. Johannès Lepsius . . . sur les massacres d'Arménie* (Paris: Payot, 1918), pp. 328, 277–79.
38. Ibid., p. 280.
39. Arlen, *Passage to Ararat*, p. 172.
40. Shaw and Shaw, *History of the Ottoman Empire*, vol. 2, pp. 238–39.
41. See the discussion by Robert Melson in this volume of the role of the exclusive nationalism of the Young Turk regime in the genocide.

3

Provocation or Nationalism: A Critical Inquiry into the Armenian Genocide of 1915

Robert Melson

I am a soldier [the nation] is my commander
I obey without question all its orders
With closed eyes I carry out my duty.
—Ziya Gökalp

Surely one of the most salient and deplorable features of our era is its history of massacre and genocide. Millions of innocent noncombatants have been slaughtered by states, mostly their own, usually in the name of preposterous worldviews. Among the most terrible of these catastrophes—caused by human intervention, not by natural forces—have been the widespread massacres of Ottoman Armenians in 1894-96 and again in 1915. Indeed, the violence that was visited upon the Armenians in 1915 has been called the first modern genocide, and it is with this event that we are here concerned.[1]

Our aim in this essay is to raise three questions: What happened? Why did it happen? And what might be learned from the Armenian case that might shed some light on others as well? Given the complexity of the problem, the answers that this essay will suggest must necessarily be tentative. Within the perspectives of political science, relying on the work of historians and scholars in other disciplines, the best one can hope for is more or less convincing, more or less credible formulations.

Against a number of historians who have argued that the reason for the genocide derives from Armenian provocations, in this essay we suggest that the reason may be found in the context of Armenian-Turkish relations and in the motives and worldview of the Committee of Union and Progress, the ruling party of the time. If there was a necessary condition for the genocide, it may have derived from the military and political disasters of 1908-1915 that isolated the Armenians and stimulated Turkish nationalism. It was this newly experienced nationalism that not only transformed Turkish identity but changed as well the image of the Armenians from that of a loyal *millet* into that of a threatening and alien minority. In that sense it can be said that disaster and ideology estranged Armenians from Turks and made them available for extermination.

The discussion that follows is divided into four parts. The first is a brief synthesis of some of the evidence pertaining to the Armenian genocide. The second critically examines the thesis that alleges that the genocide stemmed from the provocations of the victims themselves. The third proposes an explanation that includes the independent motives, the worldview, and the situation of the Committee of Union and Progress preceding the killings. The fourth suggests some parallels between the Armenian genocide and other cases, especially the Holocaust of European Jews.

The Genocide

Many scholars who are concerned with the Young Turks and the Committee of Union and Progress (CUP), which led the revolution of 1908 against Sultan Abdul-Hamid II and which directed Turkey from 1908 to 1918, would agree with Davison's judgment that although it failed in the short run, "In the long run, it not only transmitted to the future the progress made in the preceding hundred years, but also contributed to the institutional, ideological, and social development that underlay the emergence of the modern Turkish nation and Turkish republic."[2] In this essay, since we are not concerned with the salutary effects that the Young Turks might have had on Turkish progress but with their effects on the Armenians, it can be said without hesitation that the Young Turk regime, especially in its later phases, was an unmitigated disaster for the Armenian people.[3] Significantly, it was the Committee of Union and Progress, headed by Talaat Pasha, minister of the interior, and Enver Pasha, minister of war, that was responsible for the deportations leading to the genocide of 1915.

So many years after the tragedy, a detailed recapitulation of the genocide remains to be written, and one of the best sources in a Western language is still Toynbee.[4] Relying explicitly on that account, we shall briefly describe in this first section of our paper the course of events constituting the genocide of 1915. It should be noted, however, that there exists a sharp controversy pertaining to the motives of the actors, the extent of the destruction, and the actual course of events.[5] Within this limited space, it is impossible to resolve all such quarrels, some of which are tendentious in the extreme. Indeed, the best we can do here is to make note of the controversy and steer the reader to accounts that differ from our own. In the next two sections, however, we shall take up the controversy directly in the hope of clarifying some of the issues.

The killings began in the spring of 1915 with the deportation of the total Armenian population from the *vilayets* or provinces of the East to the Syrian desert at Aleppo in the south. Portents of what was to come, however, became apparent by February 1915, when Armenian troops serving with the Ottoman forces were disarmed, demobilized, and grouped into labor battalions. Concurrently, the Armenian civilian population was also disarmed, with each community required to produce a specified number of weapons. Indeed, the search for weapons became an occasion to destroy the local leadership. When community leaders were not able to come up with the required number they were arrested for withholding arms; when they did come up with the required number they were arrested for conspiring against the government.

The deportations were coordinated between Talaat Pasha's Ministry of the Interior, which was in charge of the civilian population, and Enver Pasha's Ministry of War, which was in charge of the disarmed labor battalions. On 8 April 1915, when the deportations commenced from Zeitun and other population centers, the Armenian labor battalions were rounded up by troops of the regular army and massacred.[6]

As to the deportations, these began with the killing of the able-bodied men and the deporting of the remainder. Toynbee summarizes the process as follows:

On a certain date in whatever town or village it might be . . . the public crier went through the streets announcing that every male Armenian must present himself forthwith at the Government Building. In some cases the warning was given by the soldiery or gendarmerie slaughtering every male Armenian they encountered in the streets . . . but usually a summons to the Government Building was the preliminary stage. The men presented themselves in their working clothes. . . . When they arrived, they were thrown without explanation into prison, kept there a day or two, and then marched out of the town in batches, roped man to man, along some southerly or southeasterly road. They were starting, they were told, on a long journey—to Mosul or perhaps to Baghdad. . . . But they had not long to ponder over their plight, for they were halted and massacred at the first lonely place on the road. The same process was applied to those other Armenian men . . . who had been imprisoned during the winter months on the charge of conspiracy or concealment of arms. . . . This was the civil authorities' part. . . .[7]

Except for Bitlis, Mush, and Sassun, where the total population was marked out for extermination by the army, presumably because these population centers were close to Van, the women and children and the surviving men in other population centers were deported.

As columns of defenseless Armenians were marched through towns and villages they would be set upon again and again, sometimes by brigands but more often by Turkish or Kurdish villagers.[8] The gendarmerie from the Ministry of the Interior, which was ostensibly there to "protect" the deportees, far from discouraging such attacks, joined in the violence.[9]

With the deserts beyond Aleppo as their final destination, Toynbee draws the following pattern in the timing of the deportations:

> The months of April and May were assigned to the clearance of Cilicia; June and July were reserved for the east; the western centres along the railway were given their turn in August and September; and at the same time the process was extended, for completeness' sake, to the outlying Armenian communities in the extreme southeast. It was a deliberate, systematic attempt to eradicate the Armenian population throughout the Ottoman Empire, and it has certainly met with a large measure of success.[10]

An extensive massacre or genocide always leads to a controversy over the number of victims. Those who would deny it minimize the number; those who would affirm it maximize the number. Clearly no precise measures can be cited. To gauge the extent of the destruction, Toynbee estimates the predeportation population, the number who escaped the deportations, and the number who perished during the deportations.

If one takes the Armenian Patriarchate figures as a bench mark, the mid-nineteenth century Armenian population in the Ottoman Empire was 2.5 million. Presumably due both to emigration and massacre it became 2.1 million by 1914. Toynbee, however, is more conservative. Suggesting that the Patriarchate figures may be inflated, he averages these with the Ottoman census figures, which claimed that the Armenian population of the day was 1.1 million. This gives him a predeportation figure of 1.6 million (the average of 2.1 and 1.1).[11]

Toynbee estimates that some 600,000 Armenians escaped the deportations. Among these were 182,000 who fled as refugees into the Russian Caucasus, and 4,200 who fled into Egypt. Significantly, he points out that the Armenian populations of Smyrna and Constantinople were not deported, and nominally at least, Armenian Catholics, Protestants, and converts to Islam were also not deported. But, "It is impossible to estimate the numbers in these categories . . . for the conduct of the authorities in respect of them was quite erratic."[12]

Toynbee estimates that the number of refugees plus the populations of Smyrna and Constantinople who escaped the deportations was 350,000, and the number of non-Apostolic (Gregorian) Armenians, plus converts to Islam, plus those who may have escaped in hiding was 250,000. This gives him a figure for the number who escaped or were spared at 600,000.[13]

Combining the predeportation figure with the figure of those who escaped gives Toynbee 1 million Armenians who were deported.[14] Of these he estimates some 50 percent perished due to massacre or other causes:

> A large combined convoy, for instance, of exiles from Mamouret-ul-Aziz and Sivas, set out from Malatia 18,000 strong and numbered 301 at Viran Shehr, 150 at Aleppo. In this case, however, the wastage appears to have been exceptional. We have one similar instance of a convoy from Harpout which was reduced on the way to Aleppo from 5,000 to 213, a loss of 96 percent; but in general the wastage seems to fluctuate, with a wide oscillation, on either side of 50 percent.

This should give Toynbee a figure of some 500,000 who perished, but this he revised upward and suggests a final figure of 600,000.

> We can sum up this statistical enquiry by saying that, as far as our defective information carries us, about an equal number of Armenians in Turkey seem to have escaped, to have perished, and to have survived deportation in 1915; and we shall not be far wrong, if, in round numbers, we estimate each of these categories at 600,000.[15]

Toynbee's description and analysis stops with the winter of 1915 and the spring of 1916, by which time the bulk of the Armenian population had been killed or deported. As valuable as it is, this work cannot take into account what subsequently happened to the deportees in 1916 nor can it take into account the Armenians who were deported from some of the major urban areas after 1916.[16] Thus, Aram Andonian's translator notes:

> Three great massacres took place after 1916. . . . Men, women, and children from Constantinople and the surrounding district, from the Anatolian railway line and Cilicia, were driven into the desert, where they met people from the six Armenian provinces and from the shores of the Black Sea, but this latter contingent consisted only of women, girls and boys of seven and under, as every male over seven had been slaughtered. All these were the victims of the three massacres. The first massacre was that of Res-ul-Ain, in which 70,000 people were killed; the second took place at Intilli, where there were 50,000 people assembled, most of them working on a tunnel of the Baghdad Railway; and the third, which was the most fearful of all,

at Der Zor, where Zia Bey slaughtered nearly 200,000 Armenians. . . .
These figures only give the numbers of people killed by massacre. If we
add to their numbers the victims of misery, sickness and hunger, especially
in Res-ul-Ain and Der Zor, the number of Armenians who were slain or
died in the desert will exceed a million.[17]

Leaving out further killings of Armenians such as occurred in Smyrna
in 1922, after the conclusion of World War I and after the demise of
the CUP, we are still left with close to 1 million people killed. This
amounts to nearly half of the Armenian population if we take the
Patriarchate figures, and more than half if we take Toynbee's estimate
for the initial population. The figure of about 1 million killed is independently arrived at by Johannes Lepsius.[18]

Unlike the massacres of 1894-96, where the connection between Sultan
Abdul-Hamid II and the violence had to be constructed on conclusive
but nonetheless circumstantial evidence, in the case of the deportations
the orders were clearly given by the CUP headed by Talaat and Enver.[19]
Indeed when the U.S. ambassador, in trying diplomatically to intercede
on behalf of the Armenians, attempted to separate the mass killings of
the Armenians from the real intentions of the CUP, he was rebuffed by
no less a figure than Enver Pasha:

> In another talk with Enver I began by suggesting that the Central Government
> was probably not to blame for the massacres. I thought this would not be
> displeasing to him.
>
> "Of course, I know that the Cabinet would never order such terrible things
> as have taken place," I said. "You and Talaat and the rest of the Committee
> can hardly be held responsible. Undoubtedly your subordinates have gone
> much further than you have ever intended. I realize that it is not always
> easy to control your underlings."
>
> Enver straightened up at once. I saw that my remarks, far from smoothing
> the way to a quiet and friendly discussion, had greatly offended him. I
> had intimated that things could happen in Turkey for which he and his
> associates were not responsible.
>
> "You are greatly mistaken," he said. "We have this country absolutely
> under our control. I have no desire to shift the blame on to our underlings
> and I am entirely willing to accept the responsibility myself for everything
> that has taken place. The Cabinet itself has ordered the deportations. I am
> convinced that we are completely justified in doing this owing to the hostile
> attitude of the Armenians toward the Ottoman Government, but we are
> the real rulers of Turkey, and no underling would dare proceed in a matter
> of this kind without our orders."[20]

Adding shading to an already sinister picture, no sooner had the Armenian population been physically removed or liquidated and replaced by a Turkish or Kurdish one, than all symbolic, cultural traces of the former inhabitants such as churches and place names were destroyed and eradicated. It was as if the Committee of Union and Progress had wanted to obliterate even the memory of Armenian existence.

In contemporary Turkey, as Michael Arlen remarked: "The Armenian connection" has been erased, "as though by an act of will."[21] It is not only the extent of the destruction, it is this "act of will," this desire to wipe the slate clean, that convinces us that genocide was perpetrated against the Armenians. The question that needs to be raised is, "Why?"

The Provocation Thesis

A number of influential historians continue to argue that the reason for the Armenian genocide derives from Armenian provocations, that is, from the intolerable threat that the Armenians presented to Turkey and to the Committee of Union and Progress. A most succinct and influential statement of the provocation thesis is that of Bernard Lewis.[22] We have chosen to focus on his explanation because it both attempts to be fair and is part of what has become a classic study of the history of modern Turkey. Other explanations that rely on the provocation thesis may be more verbose and more strongly felt but they are not more convincing.

Referring to the rise of Armenian nationalism in the latter half of the nineteenth century, Lewis points out:

> For the Turks, the Armenian movement was the deadliest of all threats. From the conquered lands of the Serbs, Bulgars, Albanians, and Greeks, they could, however reluctantly, withdraw, abandoning distant provinces and bringing the Imperial frontier nearer home. But the Armenians, stretching across Turkey-in-Asia from the Caucasian frontier to the Mediterranean coast, lay in the very heart of the Turkish homeland—and to renounce these lands would have meant not the truncation, but the dissolution of the Turkish state. Turkish and Armenian villages, inextricably mixed, had for centuries lived in neighbourly association. Now a desperate struggle between them began—a struggle between two nations for the possession of a single homeland, that ended with the terrible holocaust of 1915, when a million and a half Armenians perished.[23]

For Lewis, then, the matter of the Armenian genocide seems to be a clear-cut case of two nationalisms in conflict. Armenians were a Christian, national minority living, unfortunately for them, on both sides of the Turkish-Russian border. Like the other minorities of the Ottoman Empire they came to be caught up in the nationalism of the nineteenth and early twentieth centuries. Hence, like the Serbs, Bulgars, Albanians, and Greeks they might have been expected to want to secede. Whereas the secession of the latter nationalities might have been a blow to the power and prestige of the Ottoman state, the secession of Armenia would spell its demise, for the Armenians lived in the very heartland of Turkey. Thus Armenians posed a deadly threat. Presumably Lewis does not advise genocide in cases such as this, indeed he refers to the Armenian genocide as a "holocaust" in clear allusion to the Jewish genocide and cites a figure of a million and a half dead, which one presumes to be based on the Armenian Patriarchate statistics. The problem with the Lewis analysis does not lie in its insensitivity to the moral issue. The problem with the Lewis analysis is that it moves too easily by analogy from Turkish nationalism to that of the Armenians and, paradoxically, argues for a historical treatment that ignores Armenian history.

Let us consider his assumptions one at a time: to say that there were two nations locked in a desperate struggle for the possession of a single homeland without adding qualifying remarks is to impute a level of equality of force and self-consciousness that is unwarranted by any evidence. Clearly, without knowing more about the situation, one would be under the impression that the Armenians, like the Turks, were in possession of a government, of an army, or of some other centralizing, directing agency representing a monopoly of legitimate forces. One would also expect them to be armed and in some way powerful. The truth of the matter is that the Armenians were not united under a single agency, even under a single political party, and they certainly did not have any army or a police force either to conquer the Turks or to defend themselves. Beyond an assumption of equality of power, the "two-nations-same-land" argument assumes that Armenian national sentiment was somehow symmetric or equivalent to Turkish national sentiment. That there was Turkish nationalism can be assumed from Lewis's work itself. That it had not as yet found its proper boundaries in the manner of Kemal Ataturk is something else again, but that it existed in the manner of Ziya Gökalp and that it had broken with Islam and Ottomanism are Lewis's major point. That such an evolution or transformation of identity and ideology occurred for the Armenians as well, however, is to beg the question, What was Armenian nationalism? How did it differ from fealty to the millet? What boundaries and powers did it claim for itself? And how did it differ from other nationalisms, including Turkish, in the disintegrating Ottoman Empire?

Finally, to state that "for the Turks the Armenian movement was the deadliest of all threats" is to be ambiguous in the extreme. What is meant? Is it meant that the Turks *perceived* the Armenians to be a deadly threat? Or is it meant that the Armenians were *in fact* a deadly threat? If the first is meant, there can be no quarrel. Talaat and Enver have themselves clearly stated that they feared the Armenians as a deadly threat to the integrity of Turkey. Indeed, given the drastic situation of the Young Turks, where the secession of minorities was joined to military defeat on a large scale, one might assume that their perceptions and judgments were not clear. The question remains, however, whether their fear of the Armenians rose out of the actions and capabilities of the Armenians or whether it rose out of other sources including their own desperate situation and their newfound faith in Turkish nationalism?

In addressing oneself to the reality of the Armenian threat—Were Armenians the threat that the Young Turks thought they were?—it is important to make clear what time and which Armenians one is talking about. Two Armenian political parties, the Hnchakist and the Dash-naktsutiun, especially following the massacres of 1894-96, were in league with the Young Turks and therefore may have been a threat to the regime of Abdul-Hamid—a point that has been touched on elsewhere.[24]

As to being a threat to the Young Turks themselves, neither the Armenian population as a whole nor any of its parties was either a threat or seen to be a threat in 1908 when the "revolution" first broke out. Quite the contrary, Armenians took great satisfaction in the victory of the army and its CUP commanders, as well they might. The downfall of the sultan and the restoration of the constitution of 1876 was everything and more that they and their parties such as the Dashnaks had hoped for. Their long years of active participation in the liberal wing of the Young Turk movement had finally borne fruit, and Lewis himself writes of the enthusiasm of the hour: "The long night of Hamidean despotism was over: the dawn of freedom had come. The constitution had once again been proclaimed and elections ordered. Turks and Armenians embraced in the streets."[25] One assumes, therefore, that in 1908 Armenians as a whole and Dashnaks in particular were not a "deadly threat" to the Ottoman Empire and were not perceived to be such. What intervened that might have made them seem to be a deadly threat?

Though it is questionable that the regime should be blamed for the Adana massacres of 1909, where it is estimated that fifteen to twenty thousand Armenians perished, these massacres plus the increasing harshness of the CUP and the continuing insecurity of Armenian peasants in the face of Kurdish depredations did strain relations between the Young Turks and the Armenians. As one of the more careful scholars of the period notes:

Armenian disillusionment sprang from the massacres of 1909, the so-called "Cilician Vespers," in Lesser Armenia for which the Young Turks must bear a goodly share of responsibility. More lasting troubles came with Kurd depredations in Greater Armenia. . . . Wandering Kurds or *Muhajirs* had seized the lands of many Armenians who had been massacred or had fled in 1895. When some of the refugees returned in 1908, the Kurds would not restore the lands. . . . From 1909 on there was what the French vice-consul in Van described as real war between the two peoples.[26]

The Armenian response was to ask for greater autonomy in internal matters and for greater government protection against Kurdish depredations. The precariousness of the Armenian situation was taken note of by Russia, which in 1912 once more reopened the Armenian Question. Since Britain and Russia had come to terms in 1907 by concluding the Eastern settlement, Russia once more felt the temptation to expand her influence. Here it found some support among the Armenian leadership in the National Assembly, which wanted to use Russia as leverage against the CUP. Russian moves were checked by Hans von Wangenheim the German ambassador, but by 8 February 1914, an accord was reached between the powers and the CUP that called for the appointment of European inspectors-general in the eastern *vilayets* whose duties were in large part to oversee intercommunal relations.[27]

One can only imagine the sense of humiliation and rage felt by the Turkish nationalists at this proposed interference. Nevertheless, even at this late date, it cannot be said that there ensued a "struggle between two nations." For the Armenians were not struggling to destroy the Turks, nor were they even struggling to secede or to join Russia. As Davison notes: "The peasant mass was not very vocal. Higher classes of Ottoman Armenians wished rather for a regenerated and orderly Turkey and thought that autonomy would be possible only within Turkey and not under Russian domination."[28] Turning to the Dashnaks, easily the leading Armenian party, which by 1907 claimed for itself a membership of 165,000, Davison writes: "Their program was essentially one of reform within the Ottoman Empire. They did not believe that Russian occupation would bring them more freedom."[29] On the contrary, continues Davison, they did believe that "a complete separation of Armenia from Turkey was ethnographically and geographically impossible." Indeed, as late as 1913 when the CUP had become more authoritarian and intolerant, "on the whole Dashnaksouthium [*sic*] seems not yet to have favored separatism or Russian occupation, but to have pursued a policy of waiting and pressure for reform and autonomy."[30] If in the prewar period Armenians came to be seen as a deadly threat, it was not necessarily because of anything they did or did not do. The perception of threat did not emanate only from changes in the object. Could it have been engendered by changes in the context in which the object was perceived or in changes that the perceiving subject experienced?

Provocation and Scapegoating

The provocation thesis argues that something in the actions or demeanor of the victim causes the perpetrator, the provoked party, to react with violence. The causal connection, though not explicit, assumes a flow from the victim to the perpetrator, from the provocateur to the provoked. If the Armenians had behaved differently, if they had acted less threateningly, the Committee of Union and Progress would not have decided on genocide in 1915. If there had been fewer Jewish communists, or bankers or department store owners, or journalists or beggars, there would have been no Holocaust.

The principal weakness of the provocation thesis is that it neglects the independent predispositions, perceptions, and actions of the perpetrators. It may be that Mr. A killed Mr. B because Mr. B taunted him, but it also may be that Mr. A killed Mr. B because he wanted to rob Mr. B or because A hated B or even because he mistook B for C. Indeed, taking a clue from gestalt psychology we know that a perception of an object not only depends on the object itself but depends as well on the context in which the object is perceived and depends on the predispositions of the perceiver. Thus if A found B threatening it may be that A was paranoic or it may be that he saw B in a threatening context.

To argue against the provocation thesis does not at all imply that the victim was a pure scapegoat whose motives and actions played no role in the violence. It is to argue that both the perpetrator and victim and their relations must be examined for a complete explanation.

Turkish Disaster and Armenian Genocide

We come closer to the truth of why the Armenians were seen as a deadly threat, leading to genocide, when we move away from the intentions and alleged provocative actions of the victims and examine, on the one hand, the context of Armenian-Turkish relations, and on the other hand, the experiences and views of the perpetrators. Both the context of relations and the views of the CUP were drastically altered when between 1908 and 1915 the Young Turks were not able to stem further defeat in battle or the secession of minorities.[31] The retreat of the empire from Europe to Anatolia was nothing less than a military and political disaster for the Turks, but it was a disaster that had even more serious consequences for the Armenians. Not only did the retreat isolate this minority, thereby making it more conspicuous, it produced a crucial shift from Ottoman pluralism to narrow Turkish nationalism in the ideological perspective and worldview of the ruling party. These two consequences, we propose, gave rise to the view that the Armenians were a deadly threat to which a deadly response seemed appropriate.

Turning first to the disasters on October 5, 1908, some three months after the Young Turk revolution, Bulgaria proclaimed her complete independence, and on October 6, 1908, Austria annexed Bosnia and Herzegovina, which she had occupied since 1878. Due to the rapaciousness of the Great Powers and the weakness of Turkish arms, the empire was to experience still greater losses: in 1911, the Italians captured Libya, and the next year the Balkan states effectively eliminated Turkey from Europe.

Out of a total area of approximately 1,153,000 square miles and from a population of about 24 million, by 1911 the Turks had lost about 424,000 square miles and 5 million people. By 1913, when Talaat and Enver were already in power, the Ottoman government had lost all of its European territory except for a strip to protect the straits of Istanbul itself. As Feroz Ahmad has noted, "The significance of these losses is difficult to exaggerate."[32]

Of profound significance for the Armenians was the fact that the loss of the European provinces, in effect, destroyed the multinational and multireligious character of the Ottoman Empire. The Greeks and then the Balkan Christians had seceded, leaving the Armenians as the last of the great Christian minorities still under Ottoman rule. Moreover, the Armenians were not just any minority. Though they had experienced the full measure of Ottoman contempt for dhimmis and infidels—tolerance did not mean equality under the empire[33]—they had throughout the nineteenth century undergone a process of social, economic, cultural, and political development that has been called a renaissance.[34] It has been proposed elsewhere that it was this social mobilization that was a contributing factor to the massacres of 1894-96 under the regime of Abdul-Hamid.[35] Our suggestion is that the sultan's regime committed or tolerated the massacres not as a measure to exterminate the Armenians but to teach them a lesson, to keep them in their assigned place in the millet system, to abort their renaissance, and to restore an old order.

The coming of the Young Turks with their emphasis on renewal and modernization seemed like a new opportunity to the Armenians and they invested their energies in the new regime. Ironically and tragically for them, however, by 1912, as the new regime became increasingly less tolerant and more nationalistic, the very aptitude of the Armenians for modernization must have made them appear as a threat to the CUP.

In sum, the disastrous loss of territory and population that the empire experienced between 1908 and 1912 isolated the Armenians, made them more salient and exposed than they wished to be. Meanwhile, their ongoing social mobilization challenged Turkish and Muslim supremacy. But this was not all.

It should be kept in mind that after the Turkish disasters the bulk of the Armenian population was not located just anywhere in the remaining Ottoman regions. The great mass of Armenian peasants lived in eastern Anatolia, an area claimed to be the heartland of Turkey, bordering on Russia, Turkey's traditional enemy. Beyond that a sizable Armenian population lived across the border in Russia itself. Here there were parties that evinced irredentist sentiments. Even a benign regime devoted to pluralism might under these circumstances cast an uneasy glance in the direction of the Armenians. But, by 1912, certainly by 1915, the Young Turks were not particularly benign, nor were they dedicated to pluralism.

Had the Young Turks clung to the ideology of Ottomanism, which made legitimate the presence of minorities among them, military disaster and transformations in the geopolitical context need not automatically have produced a corresponding change in Armenian-Ottoman relations. But, as Lewis has noted, the Young Turks themselves, partly in response to the crisis of 1908-12, were to experience and help to engender a radical change in identity and ideology that came to replace Ottomanism with nationalism. Indeed, he begins his masterful work by noting:

"The Turks are a people who speak Turkish and live in Turkey." At first glance this does not seem to be a proposition of any striking originality, nor of any revolutionary content. Yet the introduction and propagation of this idea in Turkey, and its eventual acceptance by the Turkish people as expressing the nature of their corporate identity and statehood, has been one of the major revolutions of modern times, involving a radical break with the social, cultural, political traditions of the past.[36]

The point that he makes here and that he develops so ably throughout his book is that the heirs of the Ottoman Empire, the Young Ottomans, the Young Turks, Kemal Ataturk himself, had to preside over a major revolution in perception and identity as well as in politics in order to create a modern Turkey. It is my contention that the genocide of the Armenians, the first genocide of our modern era, was at one and the same time a product of this nationalist revolution and a stage in its development.

Ottomanism and Pan-Islam

To understand Turkish nationalism and how it might have helped to engender genocide, we need briefly to contrast it with two competing orientations that lost out. These were Ottomanism and Pan-Islam.

During the *tanzimat,* the nineteenth century reform period, when it seemed that the millet system could still be adapted to the exigencies of empire, the dominant ideology was Ottomanism, whose tenets were embodied in the reform constitution of Midhat Pasha.[37] Ottomanism had hoped to maintain the integrity of the empire by allowing greater autonomy to the minority millets and by introducing certain liberal reforms and rights that were to be used equally by all Ottomans regardless of religion and national origin. It will be recalled that under Abdul-Hamid, Ottomanism had to go underground where it found its supporters among the minorities such as the Armenian Dashnaks and in the liberal wing of the Young Turk movement led by Prince Sabahaddin. With the overthrow of the sultan, Ottoman liberalism and pluralism came into its own for a brief period, but its success was short-lived. It was abandoned by some of the minorities who preferred self-determination over its profferred autonomy and protofederalism. Above all it was undermined, as we have noted, by the crushing military defeats that pared the empire down to the Anatolian core. In a sense, except for the Armenians, these defeats solved the minority problem by excising most of the minorities from the empire. But by eliminating the minorities, such defeats at the same time undermined the very *raison d'être* for the doctrine of Ottomanism and gave rise to two competing orientations, which were Pan-Islam and Turkish nationalism.

One should bear in mind that Abdul-Hamid had already been unsuccessful in his attempts to preserve the empire by making appeals to Pan-Islam. After 1908, however, Pan-Islam once again came into vogue, but with the successful revolt and secession of Muslim nationalities especially in Albania and Macedonia, the hope that Islam could serve as a basis for imperial unity was seriously undermined. Still later it was to be dashed by the Arab revolt. As Davison has noted, "The crowning blow to Pan-Islamism was the wartime attitude of the Arabs within the Ottoman domains. . . ." When the Arabs, on the side of Britain, began to attack their Turkish rulers, it became clear that "Islamic unity was a mirage, and Pan-Islam was worthless as a political doctrine."[38] Having abandoned Ottomanism and Pan-Islamism by 1914, the Young Turks increasingly turned to Turkish nationalism.

Integral Nationalism

Though it was to be Mustafa Kemal who would finally nail down the boundaries of the Turkish state, thereby defining the territorial and social scope of Turkish nationalism, in the first instance this ideology took the form of a rather nebulous doctrine, a kind of Pan-Turkism called Turanism.[39] According to this belief system, ardently adhered to by Enver Pasha until his end, all Turkic-speaking peoples share a common culture and should be unified into a political entity. Since Turkic-speaking peoples were present as far afield as the Russian Caucasus, Central Asia, Kazan, and the Crimea, in theory Turanism aspired to a size rivaling that of the Ottoman Empire but without that empire's annoying minority problems. In practice Turanism had little chance of succeeding, but its primary result was to "increase a sense of Turkishness among Ottoman Turks."[40] By the same token it was to decrease the sense that minorities such as the Armenians had a right to exist in the newly valued entity.

As expressed in the thought of Ziya Gökalp, "the father of Turkish nationalism," and in some of the public statements of Talaat and Enver, Turkish nationalism had close parallels to the ideology of organic or integral nationalism enunciated by such figures as Herder and Fichte in continental Europe.[41] In its rejection of minority rights and individual liberties implicit in liberal nationalism, and in its glorifying the ascriptive and "primordial sentiments" of the majority group, it had certain affinities to *Volkism* and racism as well.[42]

Classifying Turkish nationalism under the rubric of "integral nationalism" does not imply that European movements and ideologies were imported by some kind of ideational processes unrelated to the very real political and military conditions of Turkey. Far from it. As we have seen, the Turkish crisis, especially after 1911, gave rise to a felt need for a new direction, a new ideology, and a new identity, which came to be satisfied by a homegrown nationalism. Indeed, in the case of Ziya Gökalp it was neither Herder nor Fichte who were influential, but Durkheim! More precisely it was Gökalp's reading of Durkheim and his adapting Durkheim to the political landscape that proved to be seminal.

It should be noted that when the Young Turk revolution first took power in 1908, in addition to the integral nationalism that was to succeed, there did exist another tendency, namely, that of liberal nationalism led by Prince Sabahaddin. That it failed in holding onto power set the conditions for the Armenian genocide; that it existed, however, indicates that this catastrophe was not a foregone conclusion in 1908.

Gökalp

To illustrate how integral nationalism came to be used in the Turkish context, it may be instructive to quote from Ziya Gökalp, about whom Heyd, his intellectual biographer, has noted, "He laid in his writings the foundation of the national and modern state which was eventually established by Mustafa Kemal."[43] Beyond his intellectual influence on Talaat and Enver, when the CUP took power Gökalp was a member of the Central Council and was designated to investigate the conditions of minorities, especially the Armenians. Heyd notes rather cryptically, "A considerable part of his suggestions were accepted by the Party and carried out by its Government during the First World War."[44] In 1919, when the Allied forces entered Constantinople, he was arrested together with other members of the Committee of Union and Progress. When he was placed on trial for his part in the genocide,

> Gökalp denied that there had been any massacres, explaining that the Armenians had been killed in a war between them and the Turks whom they had stabbed in the back. He admitted, however, without hesitation that he had approved of the expulsion of the Armenians. The Military Court sentenced him and his friends to be exiled from the country.[45]

In trying to assess the consequences of Gökalp's thought, Heyd notes without irony: "The Turkish Republic tried to achieve Gökalp's ideal of a homogeneous Turkish nation. The majority of the Greek population was exchanged against the Turks, and the bulk of the Armenians left Turkey gradually."[46]

According to the doctrine of integral nationalism, one familiar to most students by now, the primary units of historical and political action are not social and economic forces such as classes, nor for that matter are they dynasties or heroic personalities. They are nations. In all essentials unchanged from time immemorial, such nations have their origins in a dim but glorious past, a Golden Age. Since the beginning, the history of nations, and hence the history of humankind, is one of ceaseless struggle of one nation over another for power and territory, with the result that in some cases nations become militarily defeated—usually through inner corruption or treachery—wherein they run the risk of being physically eliminated. But, their elimination, or rather their temporary submergence, can also be accomplished by the stifling of the national culture and the national language.

For his part Gökalp saw in the Turkish past, not in the Ottoman past, a Golden Age that predated the coming of Islam. He gloried in the military exploits of such "Turkish" conquerors as Attila, Jenghis

Khan, and Timur Babur. He contrasted their times with the weakness and decadence of the present. He emphasized the national affinities between Turks and such ancient peoples as the Scythians, Sumerians, and Hittites, among whom he found the same moral qualities that distinguished the Turks from other peoples. These were "open handed hospitality, modesty, faithfulness, courage, uprightness. . . . Especially praiseworthy was their attitude to the peoples subdued by them. Strong as was their love for their own people . . . they did not oppress other nations."[47] He lamented, however, that "the sword of the Turk and likewise his pen have exalted the Arabs, Chinese, and Persians. He has created a history and a home for every people. He has deluded himself for the benefit of others."[48] In a poem, Gökalp wrote,

> We succeeded in conquering many places
> But spiritually we were conquered in all of them.[49]

According to Heyd, Gökalp defined the nation as

> a society consisting of people who speak the same language, have had the same education and are united in their religious, moral and aesthetic ideals—in short, those who have a common culture and religion.[50]

On the surface this definition is innocuous enough, but in the context of Ottoman pluralism, on the basis of religion, history, and descent it excludes Armenians as well as other minorities from the newly valued Turkish entity. "Greeks, Armenians and Jews who lived in Turkey were Turks only in respect of citizenship but not of nationality . . . they would remain a foreign body in the national Turkish state."[51] For Gökalp, as for all integral nationalists, the nation is not merely an analytic construct but a basic principle of moral action. As Heyd notes, "replacing the belief in God by the belief in nation," for Gökalp, "nationalism had become a religion."[52] Simply put, the good without limit is the good of the nation and for its sake all is permissible.

> I am a soldier it is my commander
> I obey without question all its orders
> With closed eyes I carry out my duty.[53]

Given Gökalp's identification of the good with the good of the nation and given his exclusion of Armenians from the nation, it follows that he excluded Armenians from his moral concerns. It should be noted that this kind of integral nationalism was quite distinct from Ottomanism, which not only accorded minorities a place in the empire but also defined certain moral and political responsibilities of the ruling classes toward them and toward all millets. A once recognizable, if not valued, community under the old Ottoman regime, from the novel perspective of integral nationalism, Armenians came to be regarded as a group of strangers. In this sense it might be said that Gökalp's formulations aided in the estrangement of Turks from Armenians and set the stage for their destruction.

That in the minds of Talaat and Enver the Armenians were fully a stranger group beyond the moral ken can be seen readily from conversations recorded by the U.S. ambassador, Henry J. Morgenthau, when he tried to intervene on behalf of the Armenians. Thus when at the height of the deportations and the killings Morgenthau inquired of Talaat why the supposedly disloyal Armenians could not be separated from those who had remained loyal, Talaat replied: "We have been reproached for making no distinction between the innocent Armenians and the guilty; but that was utterly impossible, in view of the fact that those who were innocent today might be guilty tomorrow."[54] In an even more chilling passage that reveals Talaat's attitude, Morgenthau recalls:

> One day Talaat made what was perhaps the most astonishing request I had ever heard. The New York Life Insurance Company and the Equitable Life of New York had for years done considerable business among the Armenians. . . . "I wish," Talaat now said, "that you would get the American life insurance companies to send us a complete list of their Armenian policy holders. They are practically all dead now and have left no heirs to collect the money. It of course all escheats to the State. The Government is the beneficiary now. Will you do so?"[55]

The ambassador refused, but how astonishing was the change from the traditional Muslim and Ottoman view of the Armenians as "people of the book," as the "most loyal millet" who had a vital role to play even under Abdul-Hamid, to that of Talaat, in which the Armenians had become so alien that, even in death, their sole function was to be exploited for their money.

Lewis's insight that the idea "the Turks are a people who speak Turkish and live in Turkey" had profound consequences for Turks can now be expanded to include profound consequences for non-Turks, especially Armenians, as well. For a transformation of identity in the majority group implies a change in how this group views minorities. Once Turks became Turks, nationalists like Gökalp, Talaat, and Enver saw Armenians in a new, fresh light, not as an ancient millet but as strangers who did not belong among them. Moreover, these strangers were seen as part of a dangerous context: They were the last of the Christian minorities—the others has seceded—who still remained within the newly valued boundaries; there had been national stirrings among them; and in the midst of war, it was said that they favored the Russian side. No wonder Armenians were seen as a "deadly threat."

The genocide of the Armenians, we believe, should be understood not as a response to "Armenian provocations" but as a reaction to Turkish disasters and a stage in the Turkish national revolution. As many historians have noted, that revolution was successful in creating a new Turkey, but it came close to destroying an ancient people in the process.

Conclusion

In this conclusion we would like to summarize briefly the major points of this essay and to draw certain parallels from the Armenian case to other cases such as the Holocaust of European Jews.

In contrast to several historians who have argued that the reason for the Armenian genocide of 1915 derives from the provocative behavior of the victims themselves, we have proposed that in addition to inquiring into the activities of the Armenians, it is also important to consider the context of Armenian-Turkish relations and the motives of the Turkish state.

It was noted that the context of Armenian-Turkish relations was dangerous for this minority because there was an Armenian population on both sides of the Russo-Turkish border, because the Armenians were the last of the Christian millets that had not seceded from the Ottoman Empire, and because for more than a century preceding the genocide they had experienced a period of ethnic renewal and growing self-confidence. Taken together, these factors increased the saliency of the Armenians and made them seem threatening at a time when Turkey was on a collision course with Russia.

Such a context of relations may have led even a secure and pluralist regime to view the Armenians with some suspicion, but as has been pointed out, the CUP was neither secure nor pluralist. Quite the contrary. After a sequence of military and political disasters, by 1912 leading members of the CUP had become radical Turkish nationalists who rejected Ottoman pluralism and who came to view the Armenians not only as threatening but as alien. Hence, from the embattled and exclusivist perspective of the CUP, the Armenians had to be eliminated.

We would suggest that four factors preceding the Armenian genocide may be at work in other cases as well. First, the victimized group is a communal minority that was tolerated but was by no means considered as equal to the majority. Indeed, it was a communal group that had historically experienced some persecution and contempt at the hands of the larger society. Second, despite this history—or perhaps because of it—for some years preceding the genocide, the group that will come to be victimized adapts with relative success to the modern world and undergoes progress in the social, economic, cultural, and political spheres. This social mobilization creates new tensions between this minority and segments of the majority who find its progress to be both illegitimate and threatening to the old order, which was based on inequality. Third, the victimized group comes to be identified, either geographically or ideologically, with the enemies of the larger society and state. This identification may be real or may be imputed to the minority, but a link is established between an external and an internal threat. Fourth, the larger society and the state experience a series of significant military and political disasters that undermine their security and worldview.

Together these factors allow for the emergence of an ideology that links the crisis of the state and the majority to the social mobilization or progress of the minority and to its outside connections with the state's enemies. The progress of the minority is seen as having been gained at the expense of the majority and the targeted group is blamed for the disasters engulfing the state and the larger society. In the grip of its new ideology the state radically redefines its identity and decides to eliminate the offending communal group from the social structure.

It is this fateful convergence of a minority's renaissance and its connections to the outside world with the majority's disasters, fear of external aggression, and transformation of ideology and identity that seems to us to be at the core of both the Armenian and Jewish genocides. Once the state has become convinced that a minority is alien and that it is a deadly threat to its existence, by administrative fiat or by legalistic means it geographically segregates the targeted group and disintegrates it from the social structure. By means of propaganda and reeducation it supplants a worldview that was more or less tolerant of the minority with one that is chauvinistic and that blames the minority for the disasters of the larger society. Once the minority has been socially segregrated and culturally alienated and the instruments of destruction have been readied, the state waits for an opportunity to eliminate the offending minority from the social structure.

It is no accident that the opportunity for both the Armenian and Jewish genocides appeared in the context of a general war. Wartime conditions heighten feelings of threat, permit administrative measures that would not be tolerated otherwise, and provide a cover from external interference and condemnation.

It is suggested that with some adaptation the process described above fits the Armenian and Jewish cases and may be pertinent to state-sponsored domestic genocide in general. In other cases in which a settler regime confronts a technologically less advanced or "primitive" people, where from the first the targeted groups are seen as existing outside the social and moral order of the perpetrators, the genocidal process may be simpler. In such cases, like for example, the Achés of Paraguay, neither the state nor society needs to demolish a worldview that had once tolerated the prospective victims.[56]

Notes

1. The term *genocide* was first coined and used by Raphael Lemkin in 1944 to refer to the partial or total destruction of a nation or an ethnic group. The concept recurs in the indictment of the major German war criminals at Nuremberg in 1945. Most recently and significantly the term has been used by the United Nations in its Convention on Genocide, which was approved by the General Assembly on December 9, 1948. An insightful discussion of the concept and of the efforts of the UN to apply the Genocide Convention is provided by Leo Kuper in *Genocide: Its Political Uses in the Twentieth Century* (New Haven and London: Yale University Press, 1982). A trenchant critique of the too casual use of terms such as *genocide* and *holocaust* is provided by Lucy S. Dawidowicz in *The Holocaust and the Historians* (Cambridge: Harvard University Press, 1981). Yehuda Bauer suggests that the term *holocaust* be reserved for instances of extermination. In his view the Armenian genocide of 1915 is one such instance. See Yehuda Bauer, "The Place of the Holocaust in Contemporary History," in *Studies in Contemporary Jewry,* ed. Jonathan Frankel (Bloomington: Indiana University Press, 1984), pp. 201–24.
2. Roderic H. Davison, *Turkey* (Englewood Cliffs, N.J.: Prentice-Hall, 1968), p. 109.
3. For precursors and background to the Young Turks, see Serif Mardin, *The Genesis of Young Ottoman Thought* (Princeton: Princeton University Press, 1962); Bernard Lewis, *The Emergence of Modern Turkey* (Oxford: Oxford University Press, 1961); Feroz Ahmad, *The Young Turks* (Oxford: Clarendon Press, 1969); Ernest E. Ramsaur Jr., *The Young Turks* (Beirut: Khayats, 1965).
4. Arnold J. Toynbee, "A Summary of Armenian History up to and including 1915," in *The Treatment of Armenians in the Ottoman Empire: Documents Presented to Viscount Grey of Fallodon, Secretary of State for Foreign Affairs* (London: H.M.S.O., 1916), pp. 591–653. For recent accounts that complement the Toynbee study, see Richard G. Hovannisian, *Armenia on the Road to Independence* (Berkeley and Los Angeles: University of California Press, 1967); Christopher J. Walker, *Armenia: The Survival of a Nation* (London: Croom Helm; New York: St. Martin's Press, 1980). For insightful attempts to set the Armenian genocide in a sociological framework, consider especially Vahakn N. Dadrian, "The Structural and Functional Components of Genocide: A Victimological Approach to the Armenian Case," in *Victimology,* ed. Israel

Drapkin and Emilio Viano (Lexington, Mass.: D. C. Heath, 1975), and "A Theoretical Model of Genocide with Particular Reference to the Armenian Case," *Armenian Review* 31 (1979):115–36. For a discussion and critique of the Dadrian approach, see Kuper, *Genocide,* pp. 40–56, and Irving Louis Horowitz, *Genocide: State Power and Mass Murder* (New Brunswick, N.J.: Transaction Books, 1977), pp. 45–48. For a useful bibliography on the Armenian genocide, consider Richard G. Hovannisian, *The Armenian Holocaust: A Bibliography Relating to the Deportations, Massacres, and Dispersion of the Armenian People, 1915–1923* (Cambridge, Mass.: Armenian Heritage Press, 1980).

5. Among writers who disagree with the Toynbee description or interpretation are Stanford J. Shaw and Ezel Kural Shaw, *History of the Ottoman Empire and Modern Turkey,* vol. 2, *Reform, Revolution, and Republic: The Rise of Modern Turkey, 1808–1975* (Cambridge: Cambridge University Press, 1977); William L. Langer, *The Diplomacy of Imperialism* (New York: Alfred A. Knopf, 1935); and Bernard Lewis, *The Emergence of Modern Turkey.* For a critique of the Shaws' approach, see Hovannisian, "The Critic's View: Beyond Revisionism," *International Journal of Middle East Studies* 9 (August 1978):337–86. For a reply, see Stanford J. and Ezel K. Shaw, "The Authors Respond," ibid., pp. 386–400. See also Gwynne Dyer, "Turkish 'Falsifiers' and Armenian 'Deceivers': Historiography and the Armenian Massacres," *Middle Eastern Studies* 12 (1976):99–107. For a critique of Dyer, consider Gerard J. Libaridian, "Objectivity and the Historiography of the Armenian Genocide," *Armenian Review* 31 (Spring 1978):79–87.

6. Toynbee, "A Summary of Armenian History," p. 640.

7. Ibid.

8. Especially in the eastern *vilayets,* some of the Muslim villagers themselves had been driven out of Russia. This is an important point because it might shed some light on the motives of these villagers. See Hovannisian, *Armenia,* p. 13, and Shaw and Shaw, *Reform, Revolution, and Republic,* p. 203.

9. Toynbee, "A Summary of Armenian History," p. 643. Consider as well the testimony of survivors such as Kerop Bedoukian, *The Urchin: An Armenian's Escape* (London: J. Murray, 1978), pp. 34–35. Compare such accounts with the following from the Shaws, *Reform, Revolution, and Republic,* p. 315: "Specific instructions were issued for the army to protect the Armenians against nomadic attacks and to provide them with sufficient food and other supplies to meet their needs during the march and after they were settled . . . the Armenians were to be protected and cared for until they returned to their homes after the war." It should be noted that this description is given without any discussion of disconfirming evidence, including that of Toynbee above.

10. Toynbee, "A Summary of Armenian History," p. 648.

11. Ibid., p. 649. In a private correspondence, Professor Alan Fisher of Michigan State University has suggested that the Ottoman census may have underestimated the total population of whatever group because the census counted number of households only. Thus the 1.1 million figure that Toynbee uses may be low, both because of the Ottoman desire to underestimate the size of the Armenian *millet* and because of the reasons cited by Fisher.

12. Ibid. That there were categories of Armenians who were spared the deportations and the massacres was a point stressed by Professor Yehuda Bauer in "Unique

and Universal: Some General Problems Arising out of Holocaust Research," an undated mimeographed publication from Hebrew University. He used the point to suggest that the Armenian genocide was less inclusive than that suffered by the Jews under the Nazis. Later Bauer changed his mind, referring to both events as "holocausts." See Bauer, "The Place of the Holocaust in Contemporary History." Moreover, Aram Andonian, in *The Memoirs of Naim Bey* (London: Hodder & Stoughton, 1920), suggests that a significant part of the population of Constantinople was not spared, and we know from Marjorie Housepian, *The Smyrna Affair* (New York: Harcourt Brace Jovanovich, 1966), that the population of Smyrna was massacred in 1922. Neither of these facts was available to Toynbee, who in this work was acquainted with reports no later than the spring of 1916.

13. Toynbee, "A Summary of Armenian History," p. 650.
14. Ibid.
15. Ibid., p. 651.
16. In his later works such as *The Western Question in Greece and Turkey* (London: Constable, 1922) and *Acquaintances* (London: Oxford University Press, 1967), Toynbee was to repudiate some of his own denunciations of the Young Turk regime, and like Bernard Lewis, *The Emergence of Modern Turkey*, he came to see why the CUP felt threatened by Armenian self-determination. Nevertheless, he never denied the validity of his earlier findings: "In Turkey . . . in 1915 . . . the deportations were deliberately conducted with a brutality that was calculated to take the maximum toll of lives *en route*. This was the CUP's crime; and my study of it left an impression on my mind that was not effaced by the still more cold-blooded genocide, on a far larger scale, that was committed during the Second World War by the Nazis" (*Acquaintances*, pp. 241–42). For an interesting discussion of Toynbee's position regarding the Armenian genocide, see Norman Ravitch, "The Armenian Catastrophe," *Encounter* 57 (1981):69–84.
17. Aram Andonian, *The Memoirs of Naim Bey* (London: Hodder & Stoughton, 1920; second reprinting, Armenian Historical Research Association, 1965), pp. xiii–xiv.
18. Johannès Lepsius, *Le Rapport secret sur les massacres d'Arménie* (Paris: Payot, 1918; reprint 1966). Dickran Boyajian, in *Armenia: The Case for a Forgotten Genocide* (Westwood, N.J.: Educational Book Crafters, 1972), p. 287, and others dispute the 1 million figure and suggest that 1.5 million Armenians perished. It may be suggested that this higher figure reflects all of the victims from 1915 to 1923.
19. Robert Melson, "A Theoretical Inquiry into the Armenian Massacres of 1894–1896," *Comparative Studies in Society and History* 24 (1982):481–509.
20. Henry Morgenthau, *Ambassador Morgenthau's Story* (Garden City, N.Y.: Doubleday, Page, 1918), pp. 351–52.
21. Michael J. Arlen, *Passage to Ararat* (New York: Ballantine Books, 1975), p. 201.
22. Lewis, *The Emergence of Modern Turkey.*
23. Ibid., p. 356.
24. Melson, "Theoretical Inquiry into the Armenian Massacres," pp. 481–509.
25. Lewis, *The Emergence of Modern Turkey*, pp. 210–11.
26. Roderic H. Davison, "The Armenian Crisis, 1912–1914," *American Historical Review* 53 (1948):482.

27. Hovannisian, *Armenia,* pp. 38–39.
28. Davison, "The Armenian Crisis," p. 483.
29. Ibid., p. 484.
30. Ibid., pp. 484–85.
31. Ahmad, *The Young Turks.*
32. Ibid., p. 153.
33. Roderic H. Davison, "Turkish Attitudes Concerning Christian-Muslim Equality in the Nineteenth Century," *American Historical Review* 60 (1953-54):844–64.
34. Hovannisian, *Armenia,* p. 1.
35. Melson, "A Theoretical Inquiry into the Armenian Massacres," pp. 505–9.
36. Lewis, *The Emergence of Modern Turkey,* p. 1.
37. Roderic H. Davison, *Reform in the Ottoman Empire, 1856–1876* (Princeton: Princeton University Press, 1963).
38. Davison, *Turkey,* p. 117.
39. For works on Pan-Turkism and Turanism, see, among others, Ahmed Emin, *Turkey in the World War* (New Haven: Yale University Press, 1930), pp. 87–100; Alexander Henderson, "The Pan-Turanian Myth Today," *Asiatic Review* (January 1945):88–92; Gotthard Jäschke, "Der Freiheitkampf des türkischen Volkes," *Die Welt des Islams* 14 (1932):6–21; Jacob M. Landau, *Pan-Turkism in Turkey* (London: C. Hurst, 1981). For a discussion relating "Pan" movements to racism, and in the European context to anti-Semitism, see Hannah Arendt, *The Origins of Totalitarianism* (New York: Meridian Books, 1958).
40. Davison, *Turkey,* p. 112.
41. Salwyn J. Schapiro, *The World in Crisis* (New York: McGraw-Hill, 1950), pp. 134, 136–37; Anthony D. Smith, *Theories of Nationalism* (London: Duckworth, 1971), p. 16.
42. George Mosse, *The Crisis of German Ideology: The Intellectual Origins of the Third Reich* (New York: Grosset & Dunlap, 1964).
43. Uriel Heyd, *Foundations of Turkish Nationalism: The Life and Teachings of Ziya Gökalp* (London: Luzac, 1950), p. 29.
44. Ibid., p. 36.
45. Ibid., p. 37.
46. Ibid., p. 132.
47. Ibid., p. 113.
48. Ibid., p. 111.
49. Ibid.
50. Ibid., p. 63.
51. Ibid., p. 132.
52. Ibid., p. 57.
53. Ibid., p. 124.
54. Morgenthau, *Ambassador Morgenthau's Story,* p. 336.
55. Ibid., p. 339.
56. Eric R. Wolf, "Killing the Achés," in *Genocide in Paraguay,* ed. Richard Arens (Philadelphia: Temple University Press, 1976.)

4

Determinants of Genocide:
Armenians and Jews as Case Studies

R. Hrair Dekmejian

*Nous en sommes venus au temps où l'humanité
ne peut plus vivre avec, dans sa cave, le
cadavre d'un peuple assassiné.*
—Jean Jaurès

The comparative study of genocide has never been a popular subject among social scientists, despite the awesome frequency of the incidence of genocide.[1] The "here-and-now" philosophy of modern mass society is against the remembrance of things past, especially when these involve tragedies. Consequently, the study and commemoration of specific genocidal events is left to the individual ethnic communities that have been their victims, and axiomatically, the victims of one genocide display little empathy for the victims of another.

Yet the practice of mass extermination has been a universal phenomenon, with a cyclical dialectic that seems to follow certain inexorable "laws" of social dynamics. Therefore, the determination of the objective conditions under which genocides occur should be a priority item in interdisciplinary research.

The Comparative Study of Genocide

The logic of comparative inquiry necessitates the identification of commonalities as well as differences between specific situations. Only through comparative analysis can one develop theories of general validity and applicability. In order to understand a particular genocidal event better, it is imperative that one examine other instances of mass annihilation.

The objectives of this essay are (1) to propose a preliminary conceptual framework for the comparative study of nineteenth- and twentieth-century genocides, and (2) to illustrate its theoretical utility by analyzing two case studies, the Jewish Holocaust (1939-45) and the Armenian massacres (1915-22). The present conceptual approach makes no claim to universal applicability, particularly in relation to genocidal situations in preindustrial societies. Nor is it possible to generalize extensively from the Jewish and Armenian experiences to other cases of genocide.

Throughout history the violent victimization of ethnic collectivities—racial, linguistic, religious, tribal—has assumed different configurations in terms of scope, methods, intensity, motivation, catalysts, and other variables. Indeed, the annals of history recount numerous acts of mass violence, massacres and pogroms resulting from wars, deportations, ethnic conflicts, and religious strife. With the emergence of the European nation-states, several new factors came into play that coalesced during the nineteenth century to set the stage for twentieth-century genocide, a form of mass extermination that might be considered *sui generis* in certain of its characteristics. In contrast to the massacres of earlier historical epochs, twentieth-century genocidal phenomena have been conditioned by the ever-expanding penetrative capabilities of supernationalist ruling elites, who possess unique instrumentalities of mass extermination. These distinctive features include (1) organizational specificity; (2) planning, programming, and timing; (3) bureaucratic efficiency and comprehensiveness; (4) technological capability; and (5) the ideological imperative.

The above characteristics constitute the necessary conditions for killing on a mass scale virtually unprecedented in history. The confluence of these organizational, political, and technological factors makes the contemporary instances of genocide somewhat different from their historical antecedents. The differences include the scale, speed, and efficiency of human destruction and its systematic implementation through impersonal bureaucratic rationality. Significantly, all five characteristics were present in the Armenian and Jewish cases. At the level of execution, the task is basically organizational—a bureaucratic function, fully rationalized and routinized. Alongside or inside the regular party and state bureaucracies, special cadres are organized for the purpose of planning and programming the logistics of recruitment, transportation, and annihilation of large groups of people. Ideological commitment, coupled with bureaucratic efficiency, creates a compulsion toward comprehensiveness in the achievement of goals within a specified time; hence the speed and magnitude of human destruction.

It should be noted that the foregoing attributes of genocide are the consequences of the modernization of the state machinery. Yet, their combined impact would not be so massive without an additional factor: technological capability. Indeed, it is technological modernization that makes it possible for the bureaucratic network to maximize its efficiency, not only in the methods of mass killing but also in providing effective communications and transport over long distances. An ideologically conditioned organizational network, armed with technology, creates a totalitarian environment from which there is little opportunity for the victims to escape.

The Ottoman Turkish and Nazi German milieux both meet the foregoing criteria. In the Armenian case, the apparatus of the Young Turk party—Ittihad ve Terakki Cemiyeti—was instrumental in planning and executing the massacre of 1.5 million people. The decision to massacre the Armenians of the Ottoman Empire was taken in secret by the party's Central Committee, Merkezi Umumi. The execution of the plan started in April 1915, at a time when Turkey had already entered the war as an ally of Germany and Austro-Hungary, which effectively blocked any intervention by the Allied Powers on the Armenians' behalf. As a neutral power, only the United States could play a role; however, Ambassador Henry Morgenthau's persistent efforts to stop the massacres were rejected by the Ottoman government. Specific orders were communicated to provincial party headquarters by cipher telegrams. Under the leadership of Dr. Behaeddin Shakir, the organization known as Teshkilati Mahsuse— the Special Organism—was charged with the task of coordinating the execution of the plan, bypassing "inefficient" provincial *valis* (governors) and local party officials. To assure maximum efficiency in the deportations and massacres, two other instrumentalities were used: The Butcher Battalions (*Kassab Taburu*) and the Terrorist Irregulars (*Chete*).[2]

The parallels between the Turkish and German cases are remarkably striking. The Young Turks used the completed segments of the Berlin-Baghdad railway in Anatolia, beyond which the victims were made to leave the cattle cars to join the masses of Armenian deportees traveling on foot in death marches into the Syrian desert. In technological terms, Nazi Germany was far more advanced than Ottoman Turkey. The Third Reich's highly developed railroad network was used to transport the Jews to the gas chambers, the ultimate in technological efficiency. The inspiration and the overall plan for the genocide had the personal imprint of the Fuehrer. By 1939 the process of extermination had already begun. Once again, as in the Armenian case, timing was crucial; it was made to coincide with the onset of World War II, thereby preventing any effective outside initiative to stop the destruction of European Jewry. The specific organizations charged with the implementation of the plan included the Schutzstaffel (defense echelons), as well as the Einsatzgruppen (mobile killing squads), the Totenkopfverbände (death's head units), and other state and party organizations. This technocratic apparatus of the totalitarian state functioned with deadly efficiency in carrying out its assigned objectives, the murder of 6 million Jews, in addition to Poles and other East Europeans.[3]

The Ideological Imperative

The above-mentioned instrumentalities of mass murder do not explain the human motivation to perform genocide. The fundamental question concerns the dynamics of how mass murder becomes a public policy of overriding priority.

In the contemporary nation-state setting, it is difficult, if not impossible, for any government to undertake the wholesale extermination of a large portion of its citizenry without public support or at least acquiescence. Even in authoritarian states, major policies of high priority cannot be promulgated, much less executed, without an official justification or explanation. Both in the Ottoman and German cases, the *raison d'être* to perform genocide was embedded in the official ideologies espoused by the respective political elites, i.e. Pan-Turanism and National Socialism.

Ideologies that not only condone but specifically prescribe genocidal "solutions" are reflective of serious social discontinuities and crises in society. To analyze the anatomy of genocide, the process by which ideological prescriptions are translated into public policy, it is necessary to examine the crisis milieu and its interaction with the political leadership. In the final analysis, the political elite functions as the ultimate executioner as it succeeds in unifying theory and practice in the very act of genocide.

Crisis Milieux and Pathological Leadership

We may hypothesize that the convergence of three catalytic factors—societal, ideological, and governmental—produces a genocidal outcome in the context of deep and pervasive social crisis, which generates psychological pathologies affecting both the masses and the elite. This crucial coincidence of elite and mass psychopathology finds its theoretical expression in the official ideology, and its practical expression in genocide. An examination of the Ottoman and Nazi milieux demonstrates that, at the pregenocidal phase, both societies were experiencing intense crises—social, political, and economic—all of which were related to deeper psychological disorientations, i.e. a pervasive crisis in identity among Turks and Germans.

By combining the theoretical insights of Weber and Erikson, it is possible to explain the social-psychological dynamics of the two crisis situations.[4] In the Turkish case, the empire had experienced progressive territorial contraction after its defeat at Vienna in 1683. Caught between the conquering imperialism of the European powers and the secessionist nationalism of its ethnic minorities, the empire faced the threat of extinction during the nineteenth century. Consequently, the Ottoman ruling elite's faith in the superiority of its creed began to decline as the leadership drifted toward a reluctant and disjointed experimentation with Westernization. The trend toward reformist liberalism was aborted by Sultan Abdul-Hamid II, who prorogued the newly elected parliament in 1877 and reverted to Pan-Islamism and sultanic despotism, which led to the massacre of 200,000 Armenians in 1894-96. The Young Turk (Ittihad) Revolution of 1908 marked a return to constitutional life, which, however, did not prevent the Adana massacres in 1909, in which 30,000 Armenians perished. Meanwhile, the Ittihad government continued to suffer defeats in North Africa and the Balkans, amid threats of European intervention and increasing internal pressure for reforms not only from the Armenians but also from Arabs, Kurds, and other ethnic groups. In these circumstances of crisis, a new group of young radicals rose to positions of prominence in the Ittihad party and the government itself. These men wanted to arrest the deterioration of the empire and to preside over its rejuvenation. By 1914, the Ittihadist elite had synthesized a "package" of solutions that included adherence to a new ideology—Pan-Turanism—and the forging of an alliance with Germany. The German "connection" would provide Turkey with military, technical, and economic aid to strengthen itself, in addition to protection against its European enemies. This rapprochement with Germany and the consequent increase of the German presence in the empire, exercised a powerful influence on the formation of the ideology and policies of the Ittihad party. In the German Reich, the Ittihad elite saw a most worthy model of emulation for building a militarily powerful and internally united Turkish state. It was no accident that the Ittihad leadership adopted the ideology of Pan-Turanism (Pan-Turkism), which was a replica of Pan-Germanic super-nationalism mixed with heavy doses of European authoritarian and racist thought. In searching for a "teutonic" mythology of the German variety, the Pan-Turanists attempted to revive and recreate a pre-Ottoman and pre-Islamic Turkish past in Central Asian lands, which they called Turan. Thus, the advocates of Pan-Turanism envisaged the creation of an exclusively Turkish superstate based on the Ottoman Empire that would unite all the Turkic peoples of European Russia, the Caucasus, and Central Asia.[5] The application of Pan-Turanism in the Ottoman Empire stressed total social homogenization through Turkification and/or outright extermination; hence the decision to massacre *all* the Armenians—in Interior Minister Talaat Pasha's telegraphic message, "Without heeding the dictates of one's conscience, all the Armenians—women, children, invalids—must be eliminated."[6]

Only Germany, as Turkey's senior partner in the alliance, possessed the power to stop the massacres; this it refused to do. Instead, less than a quarter-century after the Armenian massacres, Germany itself presided over the victimization of the Jews, although with greater bureaucratic efficiency and technological virtuosity. Once again, the catalysts of genocide in Germany were singularly analogous to those found in the Ottoman Empire.

As a reaction to the Napoleonic conquests, Prussia had emerged as the unifier of the German people during the nineteenth century. Being a late modernizer, the Prussian state resorted to "pressure-cooker" development to catch up with its more advanced French and British adversaries. This effort was undertaken in the context of an increasingly shrill nationalist ideology, which was reinforced by victory in the Franco-Prussian War (1871). Consequently, the defeat of German arms in World War I was injurious to the supernationalistic aspirations of the populace. The Germans' sense of national dignity was further eroded by the Versailles Treaty, which imposed heavy reparations, ceilings on German rearmament, the dismemberment of the empire, and the territorial contraction of Germany itself. These factors, combined with the depression, provided the backdrop of crisis that in its deeper roots was a crisis in German identity. Such circumstances of turmoil are marked by legitimacy crises and mass alienation from the dominant ideologies and institutions, which in the German case included the Weimar Republic and Christianity. The vacuum of values and identities was soon filled by the ideology of National Socialism.

Despite Hitler's unique role as the supreme ideologue of National Socialism, this ideology was firmly rooted in the Prussian past. By proclaiming the inherent superiority of the German race, it provided for various "racial" categories of *Untermenschen* (subhumans), among which were the "non-Aryan" Jews, who were expressly tagged for extermination. Indeed, Hitler probably intended the physical destruction of the Jews long before his seizure of power. By 1935, the Nuremberg racial laws were passed, and increasingly Jews were stripped of their economic and political rights and became stateless persons.

As in the Turkish case, some Germans opposed Hitler's "Final Solution." Yet it was clearly impossible effectively to implement such a large-scale operation without public acquiescence and participation in both the Turkish and German cases. Ironically, Pan-Turanism and National Socialism became immensely popular ideologies among average Turks and Germans, respectively, by virtue of chiliastic content and promises of utopia.

The Crucial Interaction

The key elements for a genocidal outcome may well exist in different social situations without necessarily producing genocide. The missing factor—the crucial catalyst—is the elite and its pathological commitment to the total destruction of a particular "race." Hence, the quintessential question: What are the psychosociological determinants of genocidal leadership?

Erikson's psychological theories, combined with the notion of marginality, offer some plausible answers. Six sequential propositions may be advanced:

1. *Identity Crisis.* Situations of social turmoil that are characterized by pervasive crises of identity provide the necessary conditions for the emergence of a new elite which promotes radical ideologies of socio-political change.
2. *Marginality.* In the aggregate, the social background attributes of the elite is marked by substantial marginality vis-à-vis the society, culture, and institutions. Since marginality is the dominant characteristic of the members of the new elite, their identity crisis becomes even more pronounced than that of the general population.
3. *New Identity.* To compensate for their marginality and tenuous identities, the new elites will embrace extremist ideologies and become "true believers" by assuming a new identity in its most rigid form.
4. *Projection of Patienthood.* In the midst of the crisis milieu, the members of the new elite will project their "individual patienthood to the level of a universal one" and try to solve for all what they could not solve for themselves.
5. *Patienthood of the Masses.* The projection of the elite's collective patienthood through radical ideologies will succeed only if wide segments of society are psychologically receptive and instrumentally supportive. This situation could occur only when there is a pathological "fit" between the elite's identity crisis and that of the masses.
6. *Medium of Salvation.* In compensation for their feelings of past deprivation, the elite and its supporters proceed to identify specific "undesirable" groups, who become scapegoats to blame. Ultimately, the resolution of the elite's identity crisis and that of the nation is achieved through a "medium of salvation"—the act of genocide. Thus, the extermination of specific groups constitutes the ultimate compen-

sation for the deprived marginals, as well as the reaffirmation of their newly found identity.

This six-phase conceptualization of the social-psychological evolution of the elite provides the framework within which it functions as the crucial catalyst to trigger the genocidal process. The evidence from the Armenian and Jewish experiences illustrates the striking parallels between the roles of Ittihadist and Nazi elites.

The Turkish Case

The emergence of the Ittihad elite, particularly its Pan-Turanist wing, was a direct consequence of the social and political crises besetting the Ottoman Empire. In the face of heightening ethnic nationalism among the subject peoples of the empire, the Turks were beginning to develop their own nationalism by late nineteenth century. The unifying power of Islam was in decline, as shown by the manifestation of separatist sentiments among the Arab Muslims—the largest ethnic component of the empire. Therefore, in their desperate efforts to save the "Sick Man of Europe," the Ittihad leaders were working within the framework of their newly emerging sense of Turkishness and its extremist projection, Pan-Turanism.

A plausible case can be made to show that the assumption of a Turkish identity often lacked genealogical depth in the case of a substantial number of Ittihadist leaders. The significant point is the pervasive marginality of the Young Turk party apparatus, particularly of its leading personalities. Not only was Turkish nationalism a new faith, having recently emerged with an identity separate from the Islamic-Ottoman ethos, but also many Ittihad leaders were themselves recent converts to Turkism. Indeed, a close examination reveals several distinct dimensions of marginality.

It has been observed that some prominent members of the Young Turk party came from "obscure" origins.[7] A significant number belonged to the middle and lower-middle classes. Another index of marginality concerned the ethnic and geographical diversity of the Ittihadist elite. The top party cadre can be divided into two groups: (1) the ideologues who provided the rational justification for the party's social-political activities in the context of Pan-Turanism, and (2) the political functionaries who converted ideology into public policy in the form of massacres. The party's four ideologues were Ziya Gökalp, a Kurd from Diarbekir; Yusuf Akcura, a Kazan Tatar from Russia; and Ali Husseinzade and Ahmet Agayev, both Azeris from Baku. The last three were instrumental in introducing Pan-Turanism into the Ottoman Empire as an ideology directed against the Russian Empire, which dominated their homelands. Among the top party functionaries were Interior Minister Talaat Pasha (Bulgarian Gypsy); Treasury Minister Javid Bey (Dönme—an Islamized syncretic Jew); Grand Vizier Said Halim Pasha (Albanian prince from Egypt); and Minister of War Enver Pasha (Cherkez/Albanian). Three other functionaries, Dr. Nazim, Dr. Behaeddin Shakir, and Midhat Shükrü, came from obscure Balkan origins to become members of "The Committee of Three"—the triumvirate that coordinated the implementation of the massacres through the Teshkilati Mahsuse, a force of 12,000 specially recruited from imprisoned criminals.

These marginals, along with others who had newly found their own Turkishness, were transformed into true believers in the ideology of Pan-Turanism. The secret minutes of the party's meetings in 1911 and 1913, no less than the elite's ciphered telegraphic orders in 1915, indicate their pathological mind-sets, the totality of their goals, and their sense of duty and the "necessity" of their mission of genocide. To compensate for their social-psychological marginality and to resolve their identity crises, the Young Turks projected their individual and collective patienthood upon Ottoman society. This tragic projection, the resolution of the Turks' identity crisis, called for a medium of salvation—the massacre of the Armenian people.

The German Case

The epicentric role of Adolf Hitler in the Jewish Holocaust had no parallel in the Armenian massacres. In organizing the Armenian genocide, the Ittihadist elite functioned collectively; in a neat division of labor, its intellectuals developed a genocidal ideological framework and its functionaries carried out the plan. In the Nazi case, Hitler personally succeeded in bridging the gap between theory and practice: he provided an ideology of Jewish extermination while pursuing an abiding personal concern in its implementation with the help of the Nazi elite.

Aside from his special role, however, Hitler shared many of the attributes of marginality that characterized the Nazi elite. This has been convincingly demonstrated by Lerner, Pool, and Schueller in a far-ranging statistical analysis of biographical data derived from the *Fuehrerlexicon* of 1934. Most striking was geographical marginality; a large number of Nazi leaders were *Volksdeutsch,* born in peripheral areas in and outside Germany (e.g. Hitler, Rosenberg, Hess, Rohm, Göering, and Kaltenbrunner). They also manifested marginality in their family backgrounds and occupations; a significant number of Nazi leaders had had erratic life histories.[8] Like their déclassé Ittihadist counterparts, they were "plebeians on the make" who had failed to "make it" until joining the Nazi party. Such an elite of marginal elements, angrily seeking to compensate for their perceived past deprivations, needed to settle a "personal account on a large scale." As the charismatic embodiment of the Nazi elite's pathology, Adolf Hitler personified in himself all the salient attributes of marginality—genealogical, ethnic, social, and psychological—and successfully projected them onto his society.[9] Having internalized their Fuehrer's message and ideology, a significant portion of Germans also came to share his plans for the "Final Solution." Thus, psychologically, the Germans became a nation of marginals in their leader's image, in quest of a super-reaffirmation of their collective identity, which propelled them toward conquest and genocide. As a medium of salvation, the Holocaust was therapy for the demented souls of the Nazi elite, the definitive resolution of their identity crisis.

Distinctive Attributes

Despite the remarkable similarities between the Jewish and Armenian cases, there are several differences that can be discerned from the historical record. To a great extent these differences flowed from the developmental disparity between the Ottoman and Nazi societies. Indeed, Nazi Germany was in a far more advanced stage of modernization than the Ottoman Empire. Bureaucratic efficiency was the hallmark of the Third Reich, especially in its efficacious "organization of technology, and the technology of organization."[10] In contrast, the Young Turks were novices in planning and organizing for genocide; nor were their "physical plant" and instrumentalities of death a match to the sophistication of the Nazis. Yet even the relative crudeness and primitiveness of Young Turkish cadres and technology proved adequate to achieve a substantial portion of their objectives.

Another dissimilarity issued from the perceptual differences of the two victimizers vis-à-vis their victims. The Jews were perceived as a racial and economic threat. The Armenians were seen as a potential economic and political danger threatening the establishment of the projected Pan-Turkic state; in Talaat Pasha's response to Morgenthau, "Those who were innocent today might be guilty tomorrow." A further perceptual difference was the Nazi notion of Jewish racial inferiority, in sharp contrast to the Young Turk view of Armenian elitism. Finally, a large portion of the Armenian victims were the indigenous inhabitants of historic Armenia under Ottoman rule, in contrast to the diasporic situation of European Jewry.

Universality of the Genocidal Moment

In view of the complexity of human affairs, no two historical moments can be perfectly alike. Yet the Armenian and Jewish experiences with genocide show certain distinct similarities, which could be salient in the comparative study of other genocidal milieux. It appears that genocides occur in those historical moments of crisis when powerful social, political, psychological, and technological determinants come together in a complex interaction presided over by pathological elites. Equally manifest is the universality of genocidal solutions in different societal contexts. Neither the victims (i.e. Armenians and Jews) nor the victimizers (i.e. Turks and Germans) hold a perpetual monopoly over their respective roles. Genocide is a part of the human condition. Any national collectivity is capable of becoming the victim *or* the victimizer—an awesome potentiality of the crisis environment of our time. The growing instability of the modern nation-state system in the midst of increasing poverty, interethnic conflict, and religious revivalism could well produce the necessary preconditions for genocide in the last two decades of the twentieth century and beyond. Hence the overwhelming imperative not to forget the genocides of the past. Only through the careful analysis of the anatomy of genocide—the convergence of complex social forces leading to the perverse catharsis of systematic mass carnage—will it be possible to diagnose impending genocidal situations. The study and remembrance of massacres of Jews, Armenians, Bengalis, and others should transcend the quest for vengeance and compensation. The vast majority of the criminal participants were never punished; and nothing in the material realm could possibly erase the consequences of these colossal crimes. Yet if humankind is to survive, it is essential that future generations work to disprove Hitler's assertion: "Who still talks nowadays of the extermination of the Armenians?"[11] The raising of the level of public consciousness may be the only sure psychological antidote to the genocidal syndrome. At the level of political action, the prevention of genocide must become a universal priority, second only to the prevention of nuclear war.

Notes

1. Notable exceptions of comparative studies on genocide include Irving Louis Horowitz, *Taking Lives: Genocide and State Power* (New Brunswick, N.J.: Transaction Books, 1980); Leo Kuper, *Genocide: Its Political Use in the Twentieth Century* (New Haven: Yale University Press, 1982).
2. Detailed accounts of the Armenian massacres are found in Great Britain, *The Treatment of Armenians in the Ottoman Empire,* ed. Arnold Toynbee

(London: H.M.S.O., 1916); Helen Fein, "The Armenians: An Example of Genocide," in *Accounting for Genocide* (New York: Free Press, 1979); Henry Morgenthau, *Ambassador Morgenthau's Story* (Garden City, N.Y.: Doubleday, Page, 1918); Johannes Lepsius, *Deutschland und Armenien, 1914-1918: Sammlung diplomatischer Aktenstücke* (Potsdam: Tempelverlag, 1919); André Mandelstam, *La Société des Nations et les Puissances devant le problème arménien* (Paris: A. Pedone, 1926); Jean-Marie Carzou, *Un Génocide exemplaire: Arménie 1915* (Paris: Flammarion, 1975); Yves Ternon, *Les Arméniens: Histoire d'un Génocide* (Paris: Le Seuil, 1977); Gérard Chaliand and Yves Ternon, *Le Génocide des Arméniens* (Paris: Editions Complexe, 1980); Ulrich Trumpener, *Germany and the Ottoman Empire, 1914–1918* (Princeton: Princeton University Press, 1968); Stanley Kerr, *The Lions of Marash* (Albany: State University of New York Press, 1973).

3. On the Holocaust, see *Encyclopedia Judaica*, vol. 8 (Jerusalem: Keter Publishing House, 1972); Raul Hilberg, *The Destruction of the European Jews* (Chicago: Quadrangle Books, 1961); Richard L. Rubenstein, *The Cunning of History* (New York: Harper & Row, 1975); Leon Poliakov, *The Arian Myth* (London: Sussex University Press, 1974); Norman Cohn, *Warrant for Genocide* (New York: Harper & Row, 1966). On the relationship of German social crisis, Nazi ideology, and the rise of Hitler, see Fred Weinstein, *The Dynamics of Nazism* (New York: Academic Press, 1980).

4. H. H. Gerth and C. Wright Mills, trans., *From Max Weber: Essays in Sociology* (New York: Oxford University Press, 1946), pp. 78–79; Erik Erikson, *Identity, Youth and Crisis* (New York: Norton, 1968), pp. 9-19; and *Young Man Luther* (New York: Norton, 1958), pp. 13-14.

5. On the ideology of Pan-Turkism, see Charles Warren Hostler, *Turkism and the Soviets* (London: G. Allen & Unwin, 1957); Jacob M. Landau, *Pan-Turkism in Turkey: A Study of Irredentism* (London: C. Hurst, 1981); Zarewand, *United and Independent Turania* (Leiden: Brill, 1971).

6. Melvanzade Rifat, *Türkiye inkilabinin iç yüzü* (Aleppo: Waqt, 1929); Johannes Lepsius, *Bericht über die Lage des armenischen Volkes in der Türkei* (Potsdam: Tempelverlag, 1916).

7. See Hostler, *Turkism and the Soviets*, pp. 142-49.

8. Harold Lasswell and Daniel Lerner, eds., *World Revolutionary Elites* (Cambridge: M.I.T. Press, 1965).

9. In certain situations, nonmarginal "establishment" elites might also display genocidal propensity.

10. I am indebted to Professor I. L. Horowitz for this insightful formulation.

11. See *New York Times*, 24 November 1945, p. 7. See also, U.S. Chief Counsel for the Prosecution of Axis Criminality, *Nazi Conspiracy and Aggression*, vol. 7 (Washington, D.C.: G.P.O., 1946), p. 753. For other references by Hitler to the Armenian massacres, see Edouard Callic, ed., *Secret Conversations with Hitler*, trans. Richard Barry (New York: John Day, 1971), p. 81.

5

What Genocide? What Holocaust? News from Turkey, 1915–1923: A Case Study

Marjorie Housepian Dobkin

During the annihilation of the Turkish Armenians in 1915–16, an act now called genocide, the United States media (periodicals as well as newspapers) gave extensive coverage to what was then called the Armenian "extermination." In that age before broadcasting, almost every literate American learned from these sources that the Turkish government was systematically liquidating every Armenian man, woman, and child in the land, outside the cities of Smyrna and Constantinople, both of which had large foreign communities.

The media also predicted Turkish leaders would pay dearly after the war for what were called "unprecedented crimes" and "crimes against humanity." Powerful testimony also came from German eyewitnesses, some so upset that they left Turkey and even Germany. Johannès Lepsius, a German clergyman, after going to Turkey to investigate, returned so shaken that he published and secretly distributed all he had seen before his government learned what he had done.[1] Word of his testimony leaked out, however. Protestant missionaries in Turkey, virtually all American, were also eyewitnesses whose reports made the news regularly. The American missions had some 551 elementary and high schools, eight colleges, and countless dispensaries serving Armenians and some Greeks.[2] The missionaries had gone to Turkey in the 1830s and quickly discovered that under Quranic law conversion from Islam meant death. Yet they stayed, convinced, as one of their historians wrote, that Armenian Christians converted to a more evangelical denomination would ultimately be their best missionaries as they were "native to the soil."[3] In the years before World War I, joining the Foreign Service either for God or flag was the fashionable thing to do after graduating from the trend-setting

Ivy League schools. This meant great interest in the news about missionaries, and hence about Armenians.

Primary Sources

I have studied closely the *New York Times* and its monthly magazine *Current Events,* very popular at the time. I have also looked through enough reports from other newspapers (*New York Herald Tribune, Boston Herald, Chicago Tribune,* and such magazines as *Literary Digest, Atlantic Monthly, Nation, Outlook*) to note that the *Times* coverage was not exceptional.

The genocide began with the arrest of all Armenian community leaders in Constantinople on the night of 24 April 1915. By December the *Times* alone had published over 100 articles in increasingly vivid detail. The majority were featured in the first six pages, about half on the first three. Reading these articles shows the extent to which they tell the story and constitute a primary source of the genocide. They began tentatively in late April 1915. Armenian deaths were news, but not a novelty. The massacre of about 200,000 in 1895-96 had been well reported, though without anyone in Turkey (besides the Armenians) having suffered any consequences.

March, April, and May headlines on "Renewed Massacres of Armenians" vied with news of sporadic resistance and a pitifully few, isolated, and unsuccessful attempts at retaliation.[4] But from August to the end of the year the reports became increasingly ominous. "Armenian Horrors Grow—Massacres Greater Than Under Abdul Hamid!" (6 August);[5] "Armenians Are Sent to Perish in Desert" (18 August), with subhead "Turks Accused of Plan to Exterminate Whole Population."[6] On 27 August was the headline "Turks Depopulate Towns of Armenia," and subhead "Traveller Reports Christians of Great Territory Have Been Driven From Homes."[7] On 5 September: "1,500,000 Armenians Starve."[8] A smaller piece on 3 September had indicated that the Turks had massacred all the Armenians of Ismid.[9] As the *Times* observed, Ismid is fifty-six miles from Constantinople, and nowhere near the Russian frontier, where Turkey claimed Armenians were aiding and abetting the enemy and thus provoking the "deportations"—the euphemism for genocide. (It is true that Armenians who were residents of Russia were fighting with the *Russian* army against Turkey. This is a distinction Turkey has never made—then or now.)

The Germans were of course allied with the Turks. The United States was still officially neutral; thus U.S. missionaries, many of them, were staying on in Turkey. The official German view was quoted in the *Times*

when the German ambassador in Washington said on 28 September that
the reports were "pure inventions,"[10] and on the next day said that the
Armenians had brought the reprisals upon themselves by stirring up
rebellion.[11] All the same, the ambassador added, the reports about
extermination were "greatly exaggerated." However, a front-page article
a week later (4 October) reported that a committee of eminent Americans
had, after thoroughly checking out every eyewitness story, found that the
"Turkish Record" was "Outdone," that the atrocities had been "Unequaled
in a Thousand Years," and that "a Policy of Extermination" was "in
Effect Against a Helpless People." These phrases were headlined on page
1, as well as expanded in the piece. The text, in part, reads as follows:

> The Committee on Armenian Atrocities, a body of eminent Americans
> which for weeks has been investigating the situation in Turkish Armenia
> issued, yesterday, a detailed report of that investigation. . . . The report
> tells of children under 15 years of age thrown into the Euphrates to be
> drowned, of women forced to desert infants in arms and to leave them by
> the roadside to die, of young women and girls appropriated by the Turks,
> . . . of men murdered and tortured. Everything that an Armenian possesses,
> even to the clothes on his back, are stolen by his persecutors.

The signatories of this report—a compendium of church leaders,
businessmen, and financiers—included Oscar Straus, former secretary of
commerce and labor and former ambassador to Turkey; Cleveland Dodge;
Rabbi Stephen H. Wise; the Right Reverend David H. Greer, Protestant
Episcopal bishop of New York; George Plimpton; and several leaders of
the missionary movement, including the Reverend James Barton, secretary
of the American Board of Commissioners for Foreign Missions, and John
R. Mott of the International Committee of the YMCA. I mention these
names because, despite the many testimonies they collected and presented
confirming the Armenian genocide, those named except for Rabbi Wise
and the Episcopal bishop were among those who, after the war, lost little
time in seeking rapprochement with the Turks and thus, in effect,
repudiating their own earlier testimonies for reasons I shall presently
touch on.

First, let me document a little more of the news treatment:

- "Germany Says She Cannot Stop the Turks" (23 October);[12]
- "Americans' Deaths Laid to the Turks: Five Missionaries Succumb to
  Shock of Armenian Horrors," [Says Report of the Board of Commis-
  sioners for Foreign Missions] (3 November);[13]
- "Million Armenians Killed or in Exile: American Committee on Relief
  Says Victims of Turks Are Steadily Increasing. Policy of Extermination.

More Atrocities Detailed in Support of Charge That Turkey Is Acting Deliberately" (15 December);[14]
- "Saw Armenians Go Starving to Exile" (6 February);[15]
- "Tells of Great Plain Black with Refugees" (7 February).[16]

On 27 November 1915, Viscount Bryce, in London, had made public the details of atrocities that, he says in a letter accompanying his report, "surpass in horror, if that were possible, what has been published already."[17] He is quoted as saying, further, that

> these atrocities were not produced by imagination. Many of them are vouched for by several coincident testimonies. They are all in keeping and the evidence is most complete and some of it most terrible. At the present phase of events the civilized world is powerless to intervene but we must bear these unspeakable crimes in constant memory against the day of reckoning. . . .

Against that day Lord Bryce collected the evidence and published it in a Blue Book, engaging as the editor of this compilation a young professor of Byzantine history named Arnold Toynbee.[18] Unfortunately for history Lord Bryce died in 1922.

In the November 1916 issue of *Current History* magazine, in an article datelined Aleppo, there appears an impassioned letter of protest to the German authorities written by a group of German teachers:

> We feel it our duty to call the attention of the Foreign Office to the fact that our school work, the formation of a basis of civilization and the instilling of respect in the natives will be henceforth impossible if the German government is not in a position to put an end to the brutalities inflicted here on the exiled wives and children of murdered Armenians.
>
> How can we possibly read the stories of Snow White and the Seven Dwarfs with our Armenian children; how can we bring ourselves to decline and conjugate when in the courtyards opposite and next to our school buildings death is reaping a harvest among the starving compatriots of our pupils? Girls, boys and women, all practically naked, lie on the ground breathing their last sighs amid the dying and among the coffins put out ready for them.
>
> Forty to fifty people reduced to skeletons are all that is left of the 2,000 to 3,000 healthy peasant women driven down here from Upper Armenia. The good looking ones are decimated by the vice of their jailers while the ugly ones are victimized by beatings, hunger and thirst. Even those lying at the water's edge are not allowed to drink. Europeans are prohibited from distributing bread among them.
>
> Forty to fifty people reduced to skeletons are lying heaped up in a yard near our school. They are practically insane. They utter low groans and

await death. Ta-a-lim el Alman (the cult of the Germans) is responsible for this, the natives declare. It will always remain a terrible stain on Germany's honor among the generations to come.[19]

One of the signers of this letter, a Dr. Graetner, signed a separate letter as well, which *Current History* also published in the same article:

This time the question was not one of the traditional massacres but of nothing more nor less than the complete extermination of the Armenians in Turkey. This fact Talaat's officials cynically admitted with some embarrassment to the German consul. The government made out at first that they only wanted to clear the war zone and assign new dwellings to the emigrants. . . . Thereupon began expulsions everywhere. . . . Out of 18,000 people driven out of Kharput and Sivas only 350 reached Aleppo, only 11 out of 1,900 from Erzerum. Once at Aleppo . . . those who did not die here (the cemeteries are full) were driven by night to the Syrian steppes toward the Zor on the Euphrates. Here a very small percentage drag out their existence, threatened by starvation. I state this as an eyewitness.

Again in *Current History,* this in November 1917, a former German army officer and war correspondent in Turkey, who had left that country and gone to Switzerland when his Swiss wife pleaded that she could no longer live in Constantinople after witnessing the brutalities against the Armenians,[20] has written in part:

In spite of the pretty official speeches I often heard at the German Embassy, the diplomats at bottom had very little interest in saving this people. . . . I was often at the Embassy when the Armenian patriarch, after some particularly terrible attack on his people, came with tears in his eyes and begged for help. I could discern nothing in the excited hurryings hither and thither of our diplomats except anxiety to preserve German prestige and vanity—never a worry for the fate of Armenian people. . . . [On occasion] when no Turks were to be found to carry out orders and fire on women and children, German officers, without any orders, took up the matter to show their skill in artillery practice. When an instance of this criminal interference by military persons was officially brought to the attention of the [Ambassador] Count Wolff-Metternich [and] he reported the matter to Germany, this crime which he reported was made the pretext for his dismissal. . . .

Not every German will lightheartedly live down the shame of having history note that the refinedly cruel extermination of a civilized people coincided with the period of Germany's hegemony in Turkey.[21]

"Refinedly cruel" was an apt phrase, if one follows the testimony of U.S. Ambassador Morgenthau. In November 1918, precisely at the time of the armistice, he wrote, in an issue of *The World's Work,* a leading missionary publication:

> There is no phase of the Armenian question which has aroused more interest than this: had the Germans any part in it? Did [they] favor it, did they merely acquiesce or did they oppose the persecutions? . . .
>
> For centuries the Turks have ill treated their Armenians . . . with inconceivable barbarity. Yet their methods have always been crude, clumsy, and unscientific. They excelled in beating out an Armenian's brains with a club—and this unpleasant illustration is a perfect indication of the rough and primitive methods they applied. . . . They have understood the uses of murder, but not of murder as an art.
>
> But the Armenian proceedings of 1915 and 1916 evidenced an entirely new concept—the concept of deportation. . . .
>
> [In a conference held in Berlin some time ago] Paul Rohrbach "recommended that Armenia should be evacuated and the Armenians dispersed in the direction of Mesopotamia and their places taken by the Turks. . . ." Mesopotamia might be provided thus with farmers which it now lacked. . . . Germany was building the Baghdad railway across the Mesopotamian desert from Hamburg to the Persian Gulf. But this railroad could never succeed unless there should develop a thrifty and industrious population to feed it. . . . The Armenian was made of just the kind of stuff this enterprise needed. It was entirely in accordance with the German conception of statesmanship to seize those people in the lands where they had lived for ages and transport them violently to this hot, dreary desert. I found that Germany had been sowing these ideas for several years; I even found that German savants had been lecturing on this subject in the East.[22]

On July 13, 1919 the front page of the *New York Times* carried the news that the new government (of a new sultan) in Turkey had sentenced Enver, Talaat, and Jemal, the ruling triumvirate of the Young Turks, to death in absentia for their crimes against the Armenians. The article noted that "Henry Morgenthau, American Ambassador at Constantinople, and Sir Louis Mallet, the British Ambassador at the same place, have left no doubt in their dispatches, books, articles and interviews of the guilt of the Young Turk leaders which has just been proclaimed with sentences pronounced by a Turkish court-martial ordered by the new Grand Vizier. . . ."

Nobody, it seemed, knew, or admitted to knowing, where these former leaders were, however.

The Assassination of Talaat in Berlin
and the Acquittal of the Assassin

The assassination of Talaat in broad daylight on a Berlin street less than two years after the verdict referred to above, made only page 3 of the *New York Times,* interestingly enough. Much had happened in the interim to turn official U.S. policy, and its reflection in the U.S. press, toward Turkey. Public opinion, however, lagged behind.

The German press mourned Talaat as a friend, according to another *Times* story a few days later (the story added that Talaat had a 10-million-mark fortune in a Berlin bank and a wife who was "a champion of women's emancipation").[23] The assassin, a young student named Tehlirian, had witnessed his brother's head being split open with an axe, and his mother's and sisters' rapes and deaths by sword. He had been left for dead after being struck unconscious. Berlin's most famous criminal and international lawyers defended him. According to the *Times,* "The damning German angle to the Turkish war atrocities in Armenia was patent to all present."[24] Johannès Lepsius, the pastor who had gone into Turkey and secretly published his evidence, was among those who testified on the youth's behalf. The assassin was acquitted. Official Turkish documents produced at the trial and reproduced in the newspapers in the United States and London "proved beyond question," *Current History* magazine stated, that Talaat and other officials "had ordered the wholesale extermination of the Armenians including little orphan children."[25]

One of the documents published in *Current History* follows:

> We hear that certain orphanages which have been opened have received also the children of the Armenians. Whether this is done through ignorance of our real purpose or through contempt of it, the Government will regard the feeding of such children or any attempt to prolong their lives an act entirely opposed to its purpose since it considers the survival of these children as detrimental. Minister of the Interior Talaat.

Suddenly the Turkish Position Gains in the Press

One year later (in September 1922), *Current History* along with the *Literary Digest* and in fact any magazines still concerned enough to run articles on Armenians were giving equal time to the Turkish view. The following is from an article by a retired U.S. admiral, William Colby Chester. Chester declared that the Turks were falsely maligned during World War I, that their policy toward the minorities had been one of the utmost benevolence:

> The Armenians in 1915 were moved from the inhospitable regions where they were not welcome and could not actually prosper to the most delightful and fertile parts of Syria . . . where the climate is as benign as in Florida and California whither New York millionaires journey every year for health and recreation. All this was done at great expense of money and effort.[26]

What in the world happened to provoke such a shift? A shift, I need not add, that has remained to this day, granting that Chester's view is rather extreme—even the Turks have not dared go quite so far, as yet. He, and others like him, had powerful motives, however. Chester was on his way to Turkey to claim some rights that the German kaiser had promised him (*exclusive* rights, he mistakenly thought) to exploit the oil fields of Mosul, then belonging to Turkey and called "the greatest oil find in history." He was not alone in his longing to reach this treasure. The new technology that began to boom after the war demanded quantities of this liquid gold. Henri Berenger in a letter to French Premier Georges Clemenceau expressed the universal attitude in just nine words: "He who owns the oil shall rule the world."

For a more complete answer to "what happened," I researched for six years, looking into the United States archives of the Department of State and the Navy Department, the Library of Congress, the papers of the Board of Commissioners for Foreign Missions; read exhaustively in primary and secondary sources; and wrote a book that focuses on the burning of the city of Smyrna by the Turks in 1922 after their massacre of the Armenian and much of the Greek population.[27]

Those who underestimate the power of commerce in the history of the Middle East cannot have studied the postwar situation in Turkey between 1918 and 1923 when the peace treaty with Turkey was finally signed at Lausanne. There were, of course, other *political* factors that proved disastrous for the Armenians, the Russian Revolution high among them, but the systematic effort (chiefly by the Harding administration) to turn U.S. public opinion toward Turkey was purely and simply motivated by the desire to beat the Allied Powers to what were thought of as the vast, untapped resources of that country, and chiefly the oil. Needless to say, it was not possible to bring about the desired change in public opinion without denigrating what the Armenians had suffered. A close look at U.S. foreign policy toward Turkey in the years 1920-23 (and since) shows an unrelenting effort to maintain Turkey's friendship by maintaining a favorable image of that country in the U.S. press by every possible means.

During the war, the press, as has been pointed out, convinced the American public that the Turks had committed what was then considered the most barbarous and unforgivable act of extermination known to humankind. In setting out to change this opinion, the Harding administration had a cast of characters well suited to the task. Charles Evans Hughes, the secretary of state, had been an official of Standard Oil and was untroubled by conflict of interest. The official history of the Standard Oil Company of New Jersey covering those years boasts that the company flourished as never before when Hughes was in office.[28]

Allen Dulles, later to be head of the CIA, had been chief of staff to the U.S. high commissioner in Constantinople after the armistice, and under Hughes was put in charge of the State Department's Near East desk. And the high commissioner himself, Admiral Mark L. Bristol, was a positive gift to the Turks. A virulent anti-Semite, he equally abhorred Armenians and Greeks. ("If you shake them up in a bag you wouldn't know which one will come up first," he wrote in his diary and in letters to his friends, referring to Armenians, Syrians, Jews, Greeks, and Turks, "but the Turk is the best of the lot.") And, "The Armenians are a race like the Jews—they have little or no national spirit and poor moral character."[29]

Bristol was, in his own words, "a pitiless publicist." He set out to change the hearts and minds, first, of business and financial leaders and industrialists by a vast letter-writing campaign in which he pointed out the enormous opportunities that lay ahead for them in Turkey if they would just realize that "when it comes to violence all these people out here are all the same," and make friends with the Turks.

Bristol also cultivated the missionary leaders and leaders of the Near East Relief (originally the Armenian and Syrian Relief Committee), urging them to get together with the business community for the sake of their common interests.[30] In short, if they wanted to continue to work in Turkey, they had to forget the Armenians and get friendly with the Turks. It was obvious that Mustafa Kemal was going to be the new leader of Turkey, that he was going to secularize the state, dissolve the caliphate, and finally open the way for the missionaries to do what they wanted to do all along, i.e. convert Muslims.

The papers of the Board of Commissioners in the Houghton Library at Harvard University show that there was a good deal of breast-beating among the missionaries and that a good many left the movement in disgust. The leaders, however, went along with Bristol's suggestion, and thus the same people who had certified to the authenticity of the genocide— Cleveland Dodge, George Plimpton, and others—were now lending their names to articles insisting that the excesses of the Turks had been "greatly exaggerated."[31]

Bristol himself exercised strict censorship over the news coming out of Turkey, and when the Turks renewed their death marches in Cilicia, killing thousands upon thousands of Greeks and Armenians who had escaped the massacres and returned to their homes without the slightest doubt that they would henceforth be safe, he kept the news under wraps.[32]

It is instructive to note that in his reply to Bristol's pleas for stricter censorship in the United States, Allen Dulles wrote: "Confidentially the State Department is in a bind. Our task would be simple if the reports of the atrocities could be declared untrue or even exaggerated but the evidence, alas, is irrefutable and the Secretary of State wants to avoid giving the impression that while the United States is willing to intervene actively to protect its commercial interests, it is not willing to move on behalf of the Christian minorities." Dulles bemoaned the agitation on behalf of the Greeks, the Armenians, and the Palestine Jews, and added, "I've been kept busy trying to ward off congressional resolutions of sympathy for these groups."[33]

By now, the Near East Relief officials were cooperating to the extent of making their workers sign pledges of silence about anything witnessed (the excuse was that speaking out would be detrimental and create more victims).[34] In 1922, after two men named Ward and Yowell published the stories in London (the U.S. press would not touch them, having also been convinced that the Near East Relief was keeping quiet on behalf of the victims, or future victims), Bristol simply denied the stories publicly and called them "Yowell's yowl."[35]

During these years the press offered a very schizophrenic vision of the news from Turkey. Although many newspapers, including the *Times,* continued for several years to support the Armenians and the Armenian cause, articles giving "both sides" often ran side by side, each contradicting the other. This was particularly pronounced (and confusing) immediately after the burning of Smyrna in September 1922 when eyewitness accounts describing Turks in uniform pouring kerosene over buildings and setting them to the torch vied with articles implying that the Armenians and Greeks had set fire to their own homes, and that the Turks were doing everything possible to restore order.[36]

A year later Turkey carried the day at the peace conference at Lausanne. There was no reference in the treaty to Armenians or to past promises of a free Armenia. The conferees agreed that there should be an "exchange of populations" between Greece and Turkey; in all, over 1,300,000 Greeks were exchanged for about 400,000 Turks—this was deemed an admirable solution. One reads heartrending accounts in the British press, and in the *Toronto Star* by Ernest Hemingway, who was then its correspondent in Turkey, of the mass exodus of Greeks through the knee-deep mud of

Thrace, but little was made of this tragic drama in U.S. papers.[37] Americans were by now thoroughly confused and sick to death of violence and of Armenians, now referred to as "starving Armenians." Gradually such news petered out, and by 1927 even the new publisher of the once pro-Armenian *New York Times* was thoroughly sold on Turkey and the idea of bygones being bygones, especially when there were, after all, two sides to every story.

Are There Really Two Sides to Everything—Including Genocide?

At a well-reported four-day Institute of Politics at Williams College in the summer of 1928, Halidé Edib, Kemal's chief propagandist and the first emancipated woman out of Turkey (she had a degree from the American-run Constantinople women's college) led a round-table discussion on Turkey and "won the hearts and minds of 200 experts," according to the *Times* reporter.[38] There things pretty much remain. Before she had won them over, the fiction of the fifty-fifty theory of "two sides to everything, with the truth somewhere in between" had been superseded by the "plague on both your houses" school of history, as reflected in the press. After Edib won hearts and minds, the Turkish view that terrible things happened but the Armenians brought it on themselves prevailed. This of course was the identical justification the same media had repudiated, with documentation, during the genocide.

The Turks are now rewriting history, and our media are accepting the "new improved" version based on "new improved" census figures quite suddenly discovered in Turkish archives. In this version some 200,000 Armenians died in 1915–18 of the same causes—war, disease and hunger—that took the lives of over a million Turks.[39]

Some years ago, A. M. Rosenthal of the *New York Times* published an article titled "No News from Auschwitz." This powerful, understated piece unforgettably made the point that such horrors must not be forgotten, must continually be written about, lest they be repeated. Yet in a recent advertisement in the *Times,* a group of Turkish "associations" repeated this "new improved" version of 200,000 Armenians and 2 million Turks.

The treatment of the Armenian genocide in the press after World War I shows that when the media collaborate, *eventually* the public can be convinced (even within the same generation) that it had previously held the wrong view. This should be a lesson to those who believe that *their* case is different, that "it couldn't happen again." If it once did, the chances are all too certain that it *will* happen again. Indeed, to an extent it already did happen when, in the early forties, war crimes in Germany were reported almost apologetically, all too tentatively, in the back pages of the *New York Times* and other papers, as though, having been "fooled" by propaganda (as they now thought of it) in the previous war, they were not going to risk being "taken" again. One wonders how many lives might have been saved had the Armenian horrors and exterminations *not* been repudiated and forgotten by all but the perpetrators of the renewed horrors.

The help of a supposedly free press in exonerating and ultimately denying the crime of genocide is all it takes to bring about the Orwellian nightmare of laundered history, which of course can only encourage and indeed *insure* the repetition of genocide—as happened. It bears repeating that Germany was implicated in 1915-16, that the world not only forgot this soon enough but the Turkish deeds as well.

The day could come when—if the world survives—all but a handful of Jews will find the revision outside Israel complete: *Holocaust? What Holocaust?*

Notes

1. Johannès Lepsius, *Le Rapport secret sur les massacres d'Arménie* (Paris: Payot, 1918).
2. Joseph Grabill, *Protestant Diplomacy and the Near East* (Minneapolis: University of Minnesota Press, 1971), p. 27.
3. Julius Richter, *A History of Protestant Missions in the Near East* (Edinburgh: Oliphant, Anderson & Ferrier, 1910), p. 72.
4. *New York Times,* 22 March 1915, 4:3; 26 April 1915, 3:2; 1 May 1915, 1:7; 17 May 1915; 3:2; 18 May 1915; 3:4.
5. Ibid., 6 August 1915, 6:6.
6. Ibid., 18 August 1915, 5:7.
7. Ibid., 27 August 1915, 3:3.
8. Ibid., 5 September 1915, II 3:2.
9. Ibid., 3 September 1915, 1:2.
10. Ibid., 28 September 1915, 2:4.
11. Ibid., 29 September 1915, 1:2 ("Armenians' Own Fault Bernstorff Now Says").
12. Ibid., 23 October 1915, 3:2.
13. Ibid., 3 November 1915, 9:1.
14. Ibid., 15 December 1915, 3:5.
15. Ibid., 6 February 1916, II 9:3.
16. Ibid., 7 February 1916, 3:7.
17. Ibid., 27 November 1915, 4:4.
18. Having been overwhelmed by the evidence in the course of his work, Toynbee developed and advertised his dislike of Turks. Later, he would visit a Turkish hospital in the course of reporting for the *Manchester Guardian* on the Greco-Turkish War in 1921. Thus his first sight of Turks was as victims of Christian violence. This, according to his own admission in a published interview with his son Philip in *A Dialogue across a Generation,* made him remorseful enough to reverse his stand in such a way as to repudiate the testimony in

the Blue Book—even though he later protested that he stood by the truth of that testimony.

19. "Protest of German Teachers against Massacres of Armenians," *Current History Magazine* (November 1916):335–36.
20. Yet it was in Constantinople (and Smyrna) that the Armenians were relatively safe, simply because foreign eyewitnesses were so plentiful.
21. H. Sturmer, "Germany and the Armenian Atrocities," *Current History Magazine* (November 1917):336–39.
22. Henry Morgenthau, "Ambassador Morgenthau's Story," *World's Work* (November-December 1918, January 1919):92–116, 221–36, 294–304.
23. *New York Times*, 18 March 1921, 3:2.
24. Ibid., 3 June 1921, 1:4.
25. George R. Montgomery, "Why Talaat's Assassin Was Acquitted," *Current History Magazine* (July 1921):551–55.
26. Colby Chester, "Turkey Reinterpreted," *Current History Magazine* (September 1922):939–47.
27. *Smyrna, 1922, The Destruction of a City* (London: Faber & Faber, 1972). The American edition is titled *The Smyrna Affair* (New York: Harcourt Brace Jovanovich 1971). The book centers on the burning of Smyrna in 1922, but also deals with politics in Turkey after World War I.
28. George S. Gibb and Evelyn H. Knowlton, *History of the Standard Oil Company (New Jersey)*, vol. 2, *The Resurgent Years 1911–1927* (New York: Harper and Brothers, 1956), p. 277.
29. Letter to Admiral W. S. Sims, 18 May 1919, Bristol Papers, Library of Congress, Washington, D.C.; Diary, 25 May 1919, Bristol Papers; Letter to Admiral Benson, 12 July 1919, Naval Records; Letter to Admiral W. S. Sims, 5 May 1920, Naval Records; U.S. National Archives, Washington, D.C., Subject file WT, Record Group 45.
30. See, for example, Letter to Admiral W. S. Benson, 3 June 1919; Letter to Dr. C. F. Gates, President of Robert College, 13 December 1919; Letter to L. I. Thomas of the Standard Oil Company, N.J., 24 July 1922 (all in the Bristol Papers).
31. General Committee of American Institutions and Associations in Favor of Ratification of the Treaty with Turkey, *The Treaty with Turkey* (New York: General Committee, 1926).
32. See, for example, Bristol Diary, 12 May 1922, U.S. National Archives, RG 59, 867.00/1525.
33. Letter, Dulles to Bristol, 21 April 1922, Bristol Papers.
34. See Housepian, *Smyrna, 1922*, p. 96 and its notes (p. 255) for sources.
35. Ibid.
36. See, for example, dispatches about the fire of Smyrna, *New York Times*, 14–27 September 1922.
37. Hemingway's dispatches from Thrace have been compiled in *The Wild Years*, ed. Gene Z. Hanrahan (New York: Dell, 1967).
38. *New York Times*, 4 August 1928, 3:1.
39. Stanford Shaw and Ezel Kural Shaw, *History of the Ottoman Empire and Modern Turkey*, vol. 2 (Cambridge: Cambridge University Press, 1977), p. 316.

6

The Armenian Genocide and Patterns of Denial

Richard G. Hovannisian

The admission of genocidal operations by the perpetrator government or its immediate successor is rare in modern times, unlike the boastful inscriptions of ancient tyrants. The post-World War II admission and acceptance of guilt by the West German government stand out in stark contrast with all other cases in the twentieth century. But even in Germany, which made itself answerable for the guilt of the Nazi regime and engaged in various compensatory acts, thousands of implicated individuals claimed innocence or ignorance in the face of the incriminating evidence. Still, the postwar German governments, whether of free will, through coercion, or a combination of the two, extended reparations to the survivors, the families of the victims, and the state of Israel. Discussion of the moral and political implications of the Holocaust has now found a place in the educational curricula, literature, mass-media productions, and the scholarly forums of Germany.

No similarities exist in the Turkish response to the Armenian genocide. There has been neither candid admission nor willing investigation, neither reparation nor rehabilitation. On the contrary, state-sponsored attempts to suppress discussion of the Armenian genocide have reached unprecedented proportions. Presumably, the underlying cause for the Turkish attitude is political, for there still exists an aggrieved party, however disorganized and scattered, that demands some form of compensation. While many of the aggrieved would be satisfied with a simple Turkish admission of wrongdoing and the granting of dignity to the hundreds of thousands of victims by an end to efforts to erase the historical record, there are others who insist upon financial and even territorial restitution, thus adding to Turkish anxieties and attempts to obscure the past.

This political dimension at once raises the point that fundamental differences exist between the Armenian experience in World War I and the Jewish experience in World War II. Although comparative studies rightly draw parallels between the two tragedies, they cannot lose sight of the fact that the Armenians were still living in their historical homelands, had passed through cultural and political movements to the formulation of programs of social, economic, and administrative reforms in the Ottoman Empire, and were perceived as an obstacle to the realization of the designs espoused by some members of the ruling Turkish Union and Progress party. This observation in no way diminishes responsibility for the genocide or mitigates its effects. In fact, to question whether or not genocide occurred only serves to cloud the issue. Rather, a more appropriate direction of investigation lies in the study of the causes for the genocide, its implementation and dimensions, its consequences, and its relevance today.

At the time of the deportations and massacres beginning in 1915, there was virtually universal condemnation of the act and of its perpetrators. The accounts of eyewitnesses and officials of many nationalities as well as the testimony of the survivors themselves were too detailed and corroborative to doubt the systematic nature of the operation. Being born into the targeted group was in and of itself sufficient to mark an individual for elimination. United States Ambassador Henry Morgenthau testified that the deportations to the Syrian and Mesopotamian deserts were unquestionably meant to annihilate the Armenian population:

> The Central Government now announced its intention of gathering the two million or more Armenians living in the several sections of the empire and transporting them to this desolate and inhospitable region. Had they undertaken such a deportation in good faith it would have represented the height of cruelty and injustice. As a matter of fact, the Turks never had the slightest idea of reestablishing the Armenians in this new country. They knew that the great majority would never reach their destination and that those who did would either die of thirst and starvation, or be murdered by the wild Mohammedan desert tribes. The real purpose of the deportations was robbery and destruction; it really represented a new method of massacre. When the Turkish authorities gave the orders for these deportations, they were merely giving the death warrant to a whole race; they understood this well, and, in their conversations with me, they made no particular attempt to conceal the fact.[1]

The large corpus of evidence of genocide notwithstanding, the mechanism of denial and rationalization was put in motion as soon as the deportations began. Since then, that mechanism has moved through several major phases. During and immediately after World War I, with the evidence too fresh for total denial, the emphasis was placed on rationalization. Turkish publications and official declarations pointed to

Armenian disloyalty, exploitation, and imminent general rebellion at a time when the fatherland was struggling for survival in a war on several fronts. The next phase, beginning with the international abandonment of the Armenian Question and the founding of the Republic of Turkey in 1923, was characterized by downplaying of the unpleasant past and concentration on a new image, that of a new Turkey, in which minorities enjoyed cultural and religious freedom. Apparently convinced that the Armenian problem would evaporate in time, the Turkish government under Mustafa Kemal and his successors tried to deal with Armenian matters as quietly and expeditiously as possible through diplomatic channels with countries having active Armenian communities.

But in 1965 the worldwide Armenian commemorations of the fiftieth anniversary of the genocide and the increasingly demonstrative and militant stance taken by many second- and third-generation Armenians of the dispersion ushered in a new phase in Turkish strategy. While continuing to capitalize upon the geopolitical, military, and economic importance of their country in efforts to pressure foreign governments to disregard Armenian manifestations, Turkish leaders also authorized an active campaign of counterpropaganda. The resulting books and brochures were usually sent out from Ankara in the month of April, to detract from the annual Armenian commemorative programs marking the onset of the 1915 massacres, and were addressed primarily to policymakers and opinion makers abroad, to members of legislatures and state and local governments, and to libraries, scholars, and teachers.

Only in the most recent phase, brought on by intensified Armenian violence against Turkish officials, has the strategy been directed toward public opinion in general. In newspaper advertisements, brochures and newsletters, and other popular literature, the heavily financed campaign aims at linking Armenian activism with an international conspiracy associated with the Soviet Union and the Palestine Liberation Organization. Giving special attention to Jewish leaders and Jewish opinion, the strategy attempts to dissociate the Jewish experience from the Armenian one and to drive a broad wedge between the two peoples by expressing profound sympathy for the victims and survivors of the "true" Holocaust, while characterizing the Armenian "genocide" as a hoax and "the greatest lie of the century." Enlisting the services of Turkish academics and some non-Turkish writers, the architects of this strategy appeal to a Western sense of fair play in insisting that the "other side" of a grossly misrepresented situation be taken into consideration and that the Armenian movement be exposed historically as a treacherous but abortive national rebellion and currently as a scheme to subvert Turkey and alienate it from its allies. That the repeated denials and refutations have achieved a degree of success is evidenced by the recent use by some Western reporters and commentators of qualifiers such as "alleged" and "asserted" in reference to the genocide.

The transformation of a historic genocidal operation into a controversial issue causes anger and frustration among some, and leads others to ask if there might not be credibility in the Turkish assertions. This development may also serve as a warning of things to come. While several anti-Semitic groups have challenged the truth of the Holocaust, they have by and large been discredited, and the world remains strongly aware of the decimation of European Jewry. Yet, I would suggest that given conditions similar to those affecting the Armenians, the Holocaust, too, would be challenged, not only by prejudiced extremists and guilty governments but also by well-intentioned individuals who believe that in a relativist world there are always two sides to a story. To be more specific, let us ask how the Holocaust might be regarded under the following ten conditions, which approximate the Armenian situation. What if

1. the Jewish survivors of the Holocaust, left largely to their own devices, had scattered the world over as refugees;
2. the survivors, having no sovereign government to represent them, had to struggle for years merely to ensure the physical and economic survival of their families, with their limited community resources concentrated on the establishment of a new network of schools and temples to preserve the national-religious heritage as well as possible in diverse lands and circumstances;
3. no independent Jewish nation-state had been created, and the Allied victors, despairing of assisting the survivors, abandoned the Jewish question;
4. the Jewish communities were deprived of the leadership, inspiration, and impetus provided by a Jewish nation-state;
5. in the absence of such a state, few resources were allocated for the founding of research institutes and other bodies for the gathering and analyses of materials relating to the Holocaust;
6. Jewish survivors and expatriates were too few and lacked sufficient political and financial influence to affect their host governments or succeed in having the Holocaust dealt with in the media and in educational programs;
7. the survivors, nearly all with vivid memories and indelible details of the genocide, gradually passed from the scene, and their children and grandchildren found it increasingly difficult to recount with preciseness the experiences of the survivors or to challenge deniers with firsthand eyewitness accounts;
8. the German government, defying the harsh terms initially imposed by the Allies, succeeded in writing a new peace settlement that did

not necessitate some form of compensation to the survivors or even
a formal acknowledgment of the genocidal operation;

9. the strategic geopolitical, military, and economic value assigned to
Germany in international relations was sufficiently compelling to
incline foreign governments to disregard Jewish claims against Germany and even to participate in the cover-up;

10. a new generation of foreign students, scholars, and officials interested
in German affairs espoused the goal of showing Germany in a new
light as a progressive, democratic state and of revising its much
maligned image and unfair stereotypes, such as an oversimplified
picture of a victimizing Germany and a victimized Jewry.

It is likely that in these circumstances the Jewish people today would
be facing the same general indifference and even annoyance that surround
Armenians in their efforts to keep their case before world opinion, raising
for them the question whether truth and justice can ever prevail in the
absence of sheer political and military power.

With this broad overview of the problem, a look at the shifting
character of the denials may prove instructive. In the first phase, during
World War I, the Turkish authorities initially tried to hide the enactment
of the deportations and massacres, but once the operations had gotten
well under way, they shifted the blame for Armenian troubles to the
Armenians themselves. In response to the discomfort of Turkey's wartime
allies, the attempted intercession of neutral states, and the threatening
behavior of the Entente powers who gave notice that they would hold
all members of the Turkish government personally responsible, the Young
Turk rulers issued several publications incriminating the Armenians.
With a selective compilation of hostile editorials from Armenian newspapers abroad, copies of seditious correspondence between members of
Armenian revolutionary societies, and photographs of Armenian bands
and arms caches (many of them actually from the period of Sultan
Abdul-Hamid II), the Turkish leaders attempted to convince the world
of Armenian treachery.[2] Going even further, Ambassador to Washington
Ahmed Rustem Bey insisted that a government could not sacrifice its
preservation to sentiments of humanity, especially because the laws of
humanity were suspended in time of war.[3] After the Russian imperial
armies and Armenian volunteer units from Transcaucasia had occupied
most of the eastern provinces of Van, Bitlis, Erzerum, and Trebizond
in 1916, Turkish publications focused on the oppression of the Turkish
and Kurdish population in the region, in an effort to show that the
supposed Armenian lambs were quite capable of becoming merciless
wolves.[4]

The Turkish wartime publications were roundly refuted in the West, and it seemed that with the Ottoman defeat in late 1918 the Allied Powers would now fulfill their pledges to punish Turkey and its leaders and to rehabilitate the Armenian survivors. At this time various Turkish groups and political figures who had opposed the Young Turk dictatorship surfaced with the goal of deflecting blame away from the Turkish people and holding Turkish losses to a minimum. Acting under names such as the National Congress (Milli Congre) of Turkey, they reiterated the charge that many Armenians had been subverted by Russian and revolutionary propaganda and had turned against their government by assisting the armies of the Allies and creating grave security problems. The Armenian deportations, therefore, could be justified by the "exigencies of war," but the same did not hold true for the "policy of extermination and robbery" enacted by the Young Turk leaders, who ranked "among the greatest criminals of humanity." Justice demanded that the Turkish people not be punished for the "criminal aberration" of an "unnatural government," which caused as much torment to Muslims as to Armenians.[5] Similar arguments were made by Grand Vizier Damad Ferid Pasha as he pleaded the Turkish case before the Paris Peace Conference in mid-1919. Admitting that terrible crimes had been committed, he shifted the blame to the Germans and Young Turk dictators and reminded the Allies of Armenian excesses as well. Armenians and Turks had lived together peaceably for centuries, and there was no validity in the view that the Armenians were victims of innate Turkish racial or religious intolerance.[6]

Of the postwar Turkish writers, United States-educated journalist Ahmed Emin [Yalman] was perhaps the most candid in admitting that genocidal acts had occurred. Ascribing these to an unfortunate past, Emin's intent was to play upon the new, progressive image of Turkey in the 1930s.[7] Without discarding the standard rationalizations about the Armenian threat to state security in time of war, he nonetheless wrote, in a relativist manner, that the action against the Armenians "was not commensurate with military necessity" and added "a sad chapter to the horrible practices generally resorted to among Near Eastern peoples as a means of crushing revolts and securing unity." Noting that the deportees, whom he identified as being mostly women and children, were subjected to the harshness of climate and geography and to the primitiveness of facilities, he continued:

> In addition, as the event proved, the sufferings of the deported were by no means confined to those which were unavoidable in view of strict military necessity of the existing general conditions. In the first place, the time allowed for leaving a town or village and for selling out all movable

goods was extremely short, being limited in some cases to a day or two. Second, the deported were not only left unprotected from attacks which were sure to come from marauders, but the "special organization" created with the help of the two influential members of the Committee of Union and Progress was in some cases directly instrumental in bringing about attacks and massacres. Third, the area chosen as the home of the deported was in part a desert incapable of supporting the existence of a large mass of people who reached it from a cold mountain climate after endless hardships. The deportations taken as a whole, were meant to be only a temporary military measure. But for certain influential Turkish politicians they meant the extermination of the Armenian minority in Turkey with the idea of bringing about racial homogeneity in Asia Minor.[8]

Emin added that in 1917, because of the intensity of enemy propaganda and the pressure of those in government who opposed the greatly extended scope of the deportations, an official commission of inquiry looked into the reported violations, but "those favoring the deportations being very influential in the Government, the whole thing amounted more to a demonstration rather than a sincere attempt to fix complete responsibility." Those who pushed for "the policy of general extermination," Emin explained, knew that they would be universally condemned and believed that their personal sacrifice for the national cause might be recognized "only in a very distant future."[9] Ironically, the prediction gradually came to pass. The remains of Talaat Pasha have now been returned to a resting place of honor in Turkey, and there has been a general rehabilitation of persons widely regarded as the prime organizers of the genocide.

Not only did the opponents of the Young Turks attempt to lift the heavy onus of the massacres from the Turkish people in the postwar period but members of the Young Turk triumvirate themselves addressed the issue while they were fugitives under the sentence of death. Before his assassination in Berlin in 1921, former Minister of Interior and Grand Vizier Talaat Pasha joined his own Turkish detractors in combining denials, disclaimers, and rationalizations. Insisting that the Ottoman Empire had been forcibly drawn into the war, he repeated the charges against the Armenians, yet still made partial admissions that went further than subsequent Turkish governments and many revisionist historians have been willing to go. The Armenians, he said, were deported from the eastern provinces but not upon a premeditated plan of annihilation. The responsibility for their fate fell foremost upon the Armenians themselves, although it was true that the deportations were not carried out lawfully everywhere and that many innocent people suffered because some officials abused their authority. "I confess it. I confess, also, that the duty of the Government was to prevent these abuses and atrocities, or at least to hunt down and punish their perpetrators severely."[10]

Absolving himself of personal guilt, Talaat claimed that those involved were either common criminals and looters, or simple, uneducated, zealous but sincere Turks who believed that the Armenians should be punished and that they acted for the good of the country. Although it would have been relatively easy to deal with the first group, he explained, the second was strong and numerous and any punitive measures against it would have created great discontent among the masses "who favored their acts." It was not possible to divide the country and create anarchy in Anatolia when internal unity was essential for the war effort. Talaat concluded: "The preventive measures were taken in every country during the war, but, while the regrettable results were passed over in silence in the other countries, the echo of our acts was heard the world over, because everybody's eyes were upon us."[11]

Young Turk triumvirate member Ahmed Jemal Pasha was away from the capital during most of the war. He commanded the Ottoman army in Syria at the time of the deportations and remains the most controversial of the triumvirate as regards his attitude toward the Armenians. Deploring the breakdown of the traditional symbiotic relationship between Turks and Armenians and the subversion of the Armenians by alien influences, he indirectly admitted that the Armenian male population had been eliminated by claiming that he had managed to save as many as 150,000 widows and orphans, who made up the deportation caravans. He insisted that the decisions for the deportations had been made without his participation and that he had taken every possible measure to ensure that the type of violence reported in areas such as Kharput and Diarbekir would not occur in territories under his jurisdiction. Jemal stated that when orders for deportation had been extended to include the Armenians of Adana and Aleppo, he had opposed the decision not only on humanitarian grounds but because of the terrible consequences it would have upon the economic, especially agricultural, situation. The deportation operations, however, were in the hands of the civilian authorities, and Jemal, obliged to yield, managed to save thousands from certain death. "Just as I had nothing to do with the aforementioned negotiations about the deportations of the Armenians, I am equally innocent of ordering any massacres; I have even prevented them and caused all possible help to be given to all emigrants at the time of the deportations." He added that "the crimes perpetrated during the deportations of 1915 justly roused the deepest horror, but those committed by the Armenians during their rising against the Turks and Kurds do not in any way fall short of them in cruelty and treachery." Unfortunately, the government's response to the Armenian Question had opened the way to crimes committed by the

Kurdish and Turkish populations, and one could not but wonder whether some other solution to the Armenian problem might have been found.[12]

The postwar writings of both the Young Turks and their opponents, therefore, include partial admissions of wrongdoing and even oblique references to wholesale massacres and adherents of extermination. These are mixed with charges of Armenian treachery and disclaimers of personal and collective responsibility for the Armenian tragedy.

The triumphal conclusion of Mustafa Kemal's "War of Independence" and the establishment of the Republic of Turkey in 1923 began a new phase in the official Turkish attitude toward the Armenian problem. Having taken arms against the Armenians, destroying their hopes of a reconstituted homeland, annexing the Russian Armenian districts of Kars and Ardahan, and expelling thousands of survivors who had repatriated to Cilicia under French and English auspices, Mustafa Kemal nonetheless disassociated himself from the wartime massacres. His successful defiance of the Allies culminated in the treaties of Lausanne in which the former victors in war had to acknowledge the new frontiers of Turkey, which wiped away plans for an Armenian independent state or for even a small Armenian national home under Turkish sovereignty. The Lausanne treaties in 1923 marked the international abandonment of the Armenian cause. Although anti-Turkish sentiment was still too strong in the United States to allow for ratification of the treaty, diplomatic relations were resumed in 1927 and rapid strides were made in normalizing relations and developing economic and cultural bonds. United States educational and missionary groups that had previously called for the repatriation and protection of the Armenian survivors now joined economic interests in fostering the rapprochement through various friendship societies and investment schemes. Mustafa Kemal was viewed as a great reformer who moved forcefully to secularize and modernize his country, and American missionaries made their peace with the Turkish government in the hope of propagating an "unnamed Christianity" through educational and humanitarian endeavors.[13]

Efforts to surmount the stereotype of the "terrible Turk" were facilitated by Turkish reform programs and the general approval of these changes in the West. In the United States, the Department of State took steps to enhance the rapprochement and managed to push forward, despite the annoying but now waning pro-Armenian manifestations and reminders of unrequited wrongs. During this period the Turkish authorities tried to play down the unpleasant past. There was little discussion of Armenians in Turkish publications, and the rare references to Armenians in textbooks were found only in brief passages relating to sinister but unsuccessful Armenian and Greek imperialistic designs to encroach upon the integrity of the Turkish homeland. While writers such as Ahmed Emin and noted feminist Halidé Edib appealed for understanding from the Western world and spoke of the sad but not entirely one-sided excesses of the past world war, they essentially shared Halidé Hanum's sentiment that about such things: "It is best not to speak much—the sooner they are forgotten the better."[14]

In its approach to continued though weakened Armenian efforts to keep the Armenian case before world opinion, the Ankara government relied heavily on diplomatic channels in this period. An example of this tactic is the case involving the projected filming in Hollywood of Franz Werfel's celebrated novel, *The Forty Days of Musa Dagh,* the story of the desperate resistance of several Armenian settlements near Antioch during the deportations and the eventual rescue of some 4,000 of the defenders by Allied naval vessels. Plans by Metro-Goldwyn-Mayer studios to begin production in 1934 evoked strong Turkish protests. Requesting intervention by the Department of State, the Turkish ambassador complained that such a film would be "full of arbitrary calumnies and contempt against the Turkish people" and would give "an utterly false conception of Turkey," thereby hindering the course of friendly Turko-American relations. In response to the State Department's active involvement in the issue, the studio offered to alter the script to remove the most objectionable features and then agreed to allow the Turkish embassy to approve the revised script before filming began. The embassy, however, insisted that the story was so political and prejudicial that, regardless of what changes might be made, it could not be acceptable. At the same time, Turkish authorities let it be known that release of the film would lead to a Turkish ban on all U.S. films. To appease the Turks, the State Department wrote to the president of the Motion Pictures Producers and Distributors of America, asking for his assistance in a matter that had taken on "very large proportions in the minds of the officials at Ankara." After more than a year of exchanges, MGM announced that plans to produce the film were being dropped. Ambassador Münir Ertegun, in his letter of appreciation to the Department of State, concluded:

> I have already informed my government of the satisfactory result reached through the kind support of the State Department.
>
> In this connection it is an agreeable duty for me to extend to you my best thanks and hearty appreciation for the efforts you have been so kind to exert in this matter without which the happy conclusion which has created an excellent impression in my country could not possibly have been attained.[15]

An attempt in 1938 to revive the project met with a repetition of Turkish protests and State Department intercession, leaving the film in abeyance for more than four decades until its release in 1982 by a private group of Armenian businessmen. By the beginning of World War II, the Armenian massacres had faded from recent memory in the wake of new international crises, and the Turkish government, no longer acknowledging an Armenian Question, managed to keep the issue suppressed through diplomatic channels.

Turkey's wavering neutrality during World War II and the popular belief that some Turkish leaders admired and favored Adolf Hitler raised hopes among Armenians that the Soviet Union would apply enough pressure to restore the former Russian Armenian districts of Kars and Ardahan to Soviet Armenia. Armenian petitions were addressed to the United Nations in support of such a border rectification, but the Turkish government firmly rejected all bids and used the rapidly developing Cold War to gain strong U.S. support against the Soviet claims, which were soon withdrawn. Nonetheless, the occasional mention of Armenians in international forums brought renewed brief references to Armenians in Turkish publications. The passages were intended for foreign readers in Western nation-states that had recently passed through a world war. Writing about Turkey in the 1950s, the press attache of the Turkish embassy in Washington asserted that the Armenians had acted as willing agents of a foreign government and therefore had to be subjected to a limited deportation: "Turkish response to Armenian excesses was comparable, I believe, to what might have been the American response, had the German-Americans of Minnesota and Wisconsin revolted on behalf of Hitler during World War II." Fortunately, he continued, almost all the ill-feeling toward Turkey had disappeared and even the "poor starving Armenians" had largely been forgotten.[16]

Efforts to make the Armenian genocide a nonissue had registered impressive gains by 1965, the year marking the fiftieth anniversary of the deportations and massacres. The once influential and highly vocal Armenophile organizations around the world had virtually disappeared, and Armenian woes seemed to slip into an increasingly remote and nonrelevant past. But then the unexpected occurred. The relatively quiescent Armenian communities, though unable to sustain external interest in their cause, burst forth with unprecedented activity in the half-century year of the Armenian tragedy. The wave of demonstrative commemorations swept across international frontiers, driving the usually reserved Soviet Armenians and the diaspora Armenians alike into the streets. These manifestations received some media coverage, and a new, partially assimilated generation of Armenians in many countries began to express the pain and aspirations of the survivor generation and to place the Armenian question among other human rights issues. With increasing frequency municipal officials, legislators, governors, prime ministers, and presidents mentioned the Armenian tragedy when speaking about the obligation to remember the lessons of past instances of man's inhumanity to man. Armenian memorials were erected, studies and memoirs relating to the genocide appeared in various languages, and a rising generation took to the streets with placards and chants to remind the Turkish government and the world that the Armenian Question still existed. Then, in 1973, the words *Armenian* and *Turk* captured headlines for a moment when an aged Armenian survivor assassinated two Turkish consular officials in California. Armenian acts of political terrorism increased in subsequent years, focusing media attention not only on the violence but also on its background, the Armenian historical experience, and the Turkish denials of genocide.

The Armenian manifestations that began in 1965 drew the Turkish authorities reluctantly back into the arena. Initially, the Ankara government, together with many Armenians, believed that Armenians were incapable of such violent acts: the last political assassinations by Armenians had taken place in the 1920s and these had been directed against Young Turk fugitives who had been convicted of wartime crimes. Turkish political observers and newspapers now pointed the finger of guilt at the Greek Cypriots and suggested that the terrorists might well be Greeks hiding behind an Armenian mask. Yet, as Armenian demonstrations and sporadic political violence against Turkish diplomats continued, the veil of doubt lifted and the Turkish government found itself face to face with the stubborn Armenian annoyance. Nor were the Turkish government's attempts to rely on diplomatic channels to suppress Armenian endeavors as successful as in the past. Diplomatic pressure to prevent the erection of Armenian memorial monuments in Los Angeles and in Marseilles, for example, failed despite sympathy from some quarters within the United States and French governments.

By the 1970s the Turkish government came to the conclusion that it could no longer simply dismiss or ignore the Armenian problem and formulated a campaign to counteract Armenian propaganda. In this phase of the denial process, pamphlets and brochures sent out from Ankara to foreign countries were mostly reprints of the Turkish publications first issued between 1917 and 1919 and intended to cast blame for Armenian troubles on the Armenians themselves and, after the war, to minimize the Ottoman losses.[17] Evolving from this type of literature by the mid-seventies were new tracts prepared by several Turkish historians and contemporary writers. These materials, which were intended to prove the baselessness of Armenian claims, included nothing new and were riddled with contradiction, misquotation, and distortion. In his essay entitled *Armenian Question,* for example, Enver Zia Karal asserted that, despite their treacherous behavior, the Armenians were protected throughout Anatolia after the war. According to Karal, Major General James G. Harbord, head of an American military mission of inquiry to Asia Minor and Transcaucasia in 1919, admitted to this when he supposedly reported:

> Meanwhile, the Armenian, unarmed at the time of deportations, a brave soldier who served in thousands in the armies of Russia, France and America is still unarmed *and safe* [italics added] in a land where every man but himself need to carry a rifle.[18]

What Harbord actually wrote gives the opposite picture:

> Meanwhile, the Armenian, unarmed at the time of the deportations *and massacres* [italics added], a brave soldier by thousands in the armies of Russia, France, and America during the war, is still unarmed in a land where every man but himself carries a rifle.[19]

Typical of the distortions in this genre of political pamphleteering is the substitution by Karal of the words "and safe" for the words "and massacres." Harbord's real attitude about the genocide is public record:

> Massacres and deportations were organized in the spring of 1915 under definite system, the soldiers going from town to town. The official reports of the Turkish Government show 1,100,000 as having been deported. Young men were first summoned to the government building in each village and then marched out and killed. The women, the old men, and children were, after a few days, deported to what Talaat Pasha called "agricultural colonies," from the high, cool, breeze-swept plateau of Armenia to the malarial flats of the Euphrates and the burning sands of Syria and Arabia. . . . Mutilation, violation, torture, and death have left their haunting memories in a hundred beautiful Armenian valleys, and the traveler in that region is seldom free from the evidence of this most colossal crime of all the ages.[20]

Sometimes efforts to defame the Armenians entered the realm of the absurd. In a pamphlet sent out from Ankara entitled *Truth about Armenians,* Ahmet Vefa, aside from repeating the standard Turkish allegations, alerted the English-reading public to the existence of correspondence in the Hoover Institution archives at Stanford University making it known that "the Armenians were not and never could be desirable citizens, that they would always be unscrupulous merchants." Of greater interest is Vefa's contention that when Adolf Hitler asked rhetorically in 1939, "Who after all speaks today of the annihilation of the Armenians," he was making reference not to Turkish excesses against Armenians, but rather to the Armenian destruction of the pre-Armenian Urartuans in the seventh century before Christ.[21]

Unable to make significant headway with this type of literature, Turkish officials encouraged sympathetic foreign scholars to present the "Turkish side" in the West and even afforded limited access to a few relevant archival files. But long before the astounding writings of Stanford J. Shaw in the 1970s, the trend toward revisionism had already influenced a number of scholars involved in Turkish studies. Because the existence of the Republic of Turkey was seen as a good thing, there was a tendency to justify the events that had led up to it and its current boundaries. This disposition is reflected in the writings of Lewis V. Thomas, Richard Robinson, Norman Itzkowitz, and a significant number of younger scholars.

The tenor of the revisionist approach was already set in the 1950s in the works of Professor Thomas, who admitted that the Turks had overreacted to a perceived Armenian threat and who regretted the agony of the Armenians, but who nonetheless explained that the Turks had been driven to desperation. He put forth the following rationalization:

> By 1918, with the definitive excision of the total Armenian Christian population from Anatolia and the Straits area, except for a small and wholly insignificant enclave in Istanbul city, the hitherto largely peaceful process of Turkification and Moslemization had been advanced in one great surge by the use of force. How else can one assess the final blame except to say that this was a tragic consequence of the impact of western European nationalism upon Anatolia? Had Turkification and Moslemization not been accelerated there by the use of force, there certainly would not today exist a Turkish Republic, a Republic owing its strength and stability in no small measure to the homogeneity of its population, a state which is now a valued associate of the United States.[22]

In the 1970s revisionism reached levels that transcended all previous bounds in the writings of Professor Stanford J. Shaw. Under the guise of scholarly research he not only repeated but also enhanced the worn, unsubstantiated accusations against the Armenians. His treatment of the Armenian Question in *History of the Ottoman Empire and Modern Turkey* includes gross errors and surpasses even the excuses of the Young Turk perpetrators.[23] Setting a theme for subsequent Turkish propaganda, Shaw contests sources showing that there were between 2 and 3 million Armenians in the Ottoman Empire and maintains that there were actually no more than 1,300,000, thereby minimizing the number that could have been deported or killed. Characterizing the Armenians as the invariable aggressors, the victimizers rather than the victims, the privileged rather than the oppressed, and the fabricators of unfounded tales of massacre, he insists that the Young Turk government took all possible measures to ensure the safety of those people who had to be removed from the border districts and to provide them with food, water, and medical attention while en route to suitable new homes in prearranged relocation centers.

> Specific instructions were issued for the army to protect the Armenians against nomadic attacks and to provide them with sufficient food and other supplies to meet their needs during the march and after they were settled. Warnings were sent to the Ottoman military commanders to make certain that neither the Kurds nor any other Muslims used the situation to gain vengeance for the long years of Armenian terrorism. The Armenians were to be protected and cared for until they returned to their homes after the war. A supplementary law established a special commission to record the properties of some deportees and sell them at auction at fair prices, with the revenues being held in trust until their return. Muslims wishing to occupy abandoned buildings could do so only as renters, with the revenues paid to the trust funds, and with the understanding that they would have to leave when the original owners returned. The deportees and their possessions were to be guarded by the army while in transit as well as in Iraq and Syria, and the government would provide for their return once the crisis was over.[24]

In the face of the voluminous documentary evidence and eyewitness accounts to the contrary, Professor Shaw would have the reader believe that the Armenians were removed only from a few strategic regions, and this with the utmost concern for the safety of their persons and properties.

The counterpart of Stanford Shaw among Turkish writers who have learned the selective use of archival materials to support their denials is Cypriot-born Salahi R. Sonyel. Initiating his refutations early in the 1970s,[25] he subsequently authored several pamphlets with titles such as *Shocking New Documents Which Belie the Armenian Claim that the Ottoman Government Was Responsible for the Armenian Tragic Adventure 60 Years Ago* and *Greco-Armenian Conspiracy Against Turkey Revived.*[26] Denouncing Armenians who "stage demonstrations and publish propaganda material in certain European, American and Middle East capitals," Sonyel complained:

> These hysterical, illogical and sentimental fanatics seem to prefer sensationalism to scholarly research, and, being a party to the case, undoubtedly have an axe to grind, giving absolutely biased accounts of Armenian and Greek deportations and "massacres." . . . They prefer to write propaganda accounts, rather than to produce scholarly works based on *facts* and *figures,*

which would be more appreciated. But then they are typical vociferous Greek and Armenian propagandists, some of whom, recent documents prove beyond any doubt, were themselves directly responsible for the misfortune of the Greek and Armenian people.[27]

With the intent of showing that Talaat Pasha and other Young Turk officials, far from planning the elimination of the Armenian people, had taken measures to limit, localize, and ameliorate the deportations, Sonyel published in 1978 a batch of Turkish documents that had been deposited in the British archives.[28] It was established long ago that official correspondence relating to the safety of, and provisions for, the deportees was used to conceal what actually was happening to the Armenians, and this particular group of documents pertaining to the western Anatolian district of Hudavendigar was carefully selected and excerpted. Even so, there is evidence even in these papers that betrays Sonyel's objective, as seen in the following examples:

- 23 July 1915
  The Armenians within the province should be transported to the areas previously determined. The Catholics should be excluded from this displacement procedure.
- 25 July 1915
  It is decided that the Armenians should be moved to the interior of the country. In view of this, it is requested that necessary measures be taken to prevent the Armenian soldiers in the Workers Battalions within your area from violating the order and that a copy of this message be despatched to the Commanders of the Workers Battalions in your area.
- 29-30 July 1915
  The personal property belonging to the Armenian children who later became Moslem, got married or left under the care of reliable persons for training or educational purposes, will be left to the said children, if their legators are dead, their share of the property will be paid to them.
- [no date]
  The families of the military, the Protestants and Catholics who have not yet been displaced from their areas, the artists who are allowed to stay by the local authorities, the workers working in the factories producing the goods required by the people and those working in the railways and stations as well as their families will not be displaced.

  Boys older than 15 years and married women are not considered among the dependents of the head of a family.[29]

The boldness of contemporary writers such as Shaw and Sonyel has been facilitated by the death of most survivors of, and foreign eyewitnesses to, the massacres and is paralleled by renewed militancy within the Turkish government. Determined to prevent the Armenian Question from ever again becoming a topic of international diplomacy, the Ankara government has engaged in strong political lobbying to expunge even passing references to the Armenians. This policy is exemplified by the tactics used in relation to a United Nations subcommission draft report on the prevention and punishment of genocide. In 1973 the special rapporteur of the Subcommission on Prevention of Discrimination and Protection of Minorities wrote in paragraph 30 of the introductory historical section:

> Passing to the modern era, one may note the existence of relatively full documentation dealing with the massacres of Armenians, which have been described as "the first case of genocide in the twentieth century."[30]

The paragraph makes no mention of either the Ottoman Empire or of Turks, yet the Turkish mission to the United Nations and the Turkish government regarded the sentence as menacing and immediately applied pressure on governments and delegations represented on the full Human Rights Commission. Yielding to this pressure the commission adopted a recommendation that historic events preceding recent genocidal acts and the contemporary definition of genocide be omitted from the report. "It was pointed out that there was the dangerous pitfall of confusing the crime of genocide with the eventual consequences which might occur as a result of a given war and making such parallels without taking into account the historical and socio-economic background of the past events." Matters that had been subject "to controversial explanations and evaluations in different publications" should be avoided. Hence paragraph 30 should be deleted.[31]

When the issue was raised again in 1975, one delegate noted that the tragedy of 1915 was historical fact, "but in a civilized international community, consideration should also be given to the desire of a state not to be defamed on account of its past acts, which had been perpetrated by a previous generation and were probably regretted by the present generation." When the subcommission's rapporteur submitted the revised version of his report in 1978, the historical section began with the Nazi-perpetrated Holocaust. In the words of Leo Kuper, the Armenian genocide "had disappeared down the memory hole." When a few members of the subcommission questioned the deletion, it was now the rapporteur who explained:

> Concern had been expressed that the study of genocide might be diverted from its intended course and lose its essential purpose. Consequently, it had been decided to retain the massacre of the Jews under Nazism, because

that case was known to all and no objections had been raised; but other cases had been omitted, because it was impossible to compile an exhaustive list, because it was important to maintain unity in the international community in regard to genocide, and because in many cases to delve into the past might reopen old wounds which were now healing.[32]

When the Turkish measures to erase even the memory of the Armenian victims in a draft report of a United Nations subcommission became known, the story spread swiftly throughout the Armenian communities. Armenian groups around the world now mounted their own campaign, publicly invoking the human rights declarations of several member states of the UN Human Rights Commission. The subsequent lead of the United States in reversing its position during the Carter administration in 1979 was followed by several other countries, resulting in the request to the special rapporteur to take into account the various statements made in and to the commission about the Armenian tragedy. Now, after more than a decade, the matter of whether to mention the Armenians in the introductory historical section of the belabored report is still unresolved.

The most recent phase of denial, advanced in the 1980s by the Turkish military and civil governments, is characterized by efforts to reach the public at large. The decision to allocate substantial financial resources for newspaper advertisements, brochures intended for mass distribution, and various programs and productions enhancing Turkey's image abroad was taken in response to the more frequent acts of Armenian violence and, correspondingly, the more frequent attention given Armenians and Armenian history in newspapers and journals and on television.

One aim of the current phase is to create a broad breach between Jews and Armenians by emphasizing the true horror of the Holocaust and playing up Turkey's ties with Israel, while cautioning against an Armenian scheme to detract from the Holocaust and dishonor the memory of its victims by winning recognition for a mythical genocide fabricated solely for political purposes. This approach has been used in public announcements, in private meetings and written exchanges with Jewish leaders, and in international diplomatic correspondence. All these means have also been employed in repeated efforts to dissuade the United States Holocaust Council from including the Armenian genocide in any of its projected educational and commemorative activities. In this campaign to drive the wedge as deep as possible, Turkish sources link Armenian activism with the Palestine Liberation Organization and Soviet manipulation. "We recognize that Armenian terrorists have confirmed ties with international communist and terrorist organizations. As such they are tools in the hands of those who seek to destabilize the precarious peace of the Middle East and Europe."[33] When a Turkish terrorist attempted to assassinate Pope John Paul in 1981, Ambassador to the United States Şükrü Elekdağ and other Turkish officials tried in vain to establish an Armenian connection. Prominent Armenians in Turkey have also been pressed into service by having to sign statements attesting to their enjoyment of full human rights, condemning Armenian extremism past and present, and ascribing Armenian unrest abroad to the "Greek intrigue" to defame the Turkish republic and alienate it from its NATO allies.[34]

Although the Turkish rationalizations during and immediately after World War I were rejected by most foreign governments, they did include minor admissions that now seem to have paled before the unqualified contemporary denials. Speaking before the Los Angeles World Affairs Council in November 1981, for example, Ambassador Elekdağ declared: "The accusation that Ottoman Turks, sixty-five years ago, during World War I, perpetrated systematic massacres of the Armenian population in Turkey, to annihilate them and to seize their homeland, is totally baseless."[35]

This argument has been subsequently reiterated by Elekdağ, and elaborated in a booklet published in 1982 entitled *Setting the Record Straight on Armenian Propaganda Against Turkey*. The opening lines read: "In recent years claims have been made by some Armenians in Europe, America, and elsewhere that the Armenians suffered terrible misrule in the Ottoman Empire. Such claims are absurd."[36] Reflecting both the style and the methodology of the extreme revisionist historians, the brochure attempts to show that the Armenians, despite their many privileges, in the nineteenth century became Russian agents and initiated an indiscriminate reign of terror. "Muslims were brutalized as much as possible in order to stimulate reprisals and to bring about cycles of massacre and counter-massacre, which could only be ended by European intervention. Realizing the terrorist intentions, Abdulhamit II and his successors did all they could to prevent Muslim reprisals for the Armenian massacres, and they were largely successful."[37] In this manner the great Armenian pogroms in the 1890s are dismissed and Sultan Abdul-Hamid, previously discredited by many Turkish writers, is portrayed as a patient and tolerant ruler.

As for the events during World War I, there were, the brochure asserts, no generalized massacres, except by Armenians, and certainly no genocide. Perhaps as many as 100,000 Armenians may have died of various causes between 1915 and 1918, but that was not unusual compared with Turkish losses: "There was no genocide committed against the Armenians in the Ottoman Empire before or during World War I. No genocide was planned or ordered by the Ottoman government and no genocide was carried out. Recent scholarly research has discovered that the stories of massacres were in fact largely invented by Armenian nationalist leaders in Paris and London during World War I and spread throughout the world through the British intelligence." Moreover, "the Armenian nationalists have continued to spread their message of hate, relying on repetition of the 'big lie' to secure acceptance of their claims in a Christian world predisposed to accept the claims of Christians whenever they are in conflict with Muslims."[38]

The Turkish publication to "set the record straight" concludes with a denunciation of Armenian oral history programs: "Carefully coached by their Armenian nationalist interviewers, these aged Armenians relate tales of horror which supposedly took place some 66 years ago in such detail as to astonish the imagination, considering that most of them already are aged eighty or more. Subjected to years of Armenian nationalist propaganda as well as the coaching of their interviewers, there is little doubt that their statements are of no use whatever for historical research. . . ."[39]

The history of the denial of the Armenian genocide has passed through several phases, each somewhat different in emphasis but all characterized by efforts to avoid responsibility and the moral, material, and political consequences of admission. Only under the impact of the defeat of the Ottoman Empire and the flight of the Young Turk leaders were there partial admissions, but this trend was halted by the successful Kemalist defiance of the Allies and the subsequent international abandonment of the Armenian Question. In the absence of external force, neither the perpetrators nor successive Turkish governments have been willing to face the skeleton in their closet. Rather, they have resorted to various forms of avoidance, denial, repudiation, and vilification to keep the door shut. In the meantime, Turkish writers and scholars are still unable to deal honestly with their national past and continue to be drawn, wittingly or unwittingly, into the wheels of rationalization and falsification. Taking advantage of its strategic geopolitical and military importance, the Republic of Turkey has repeatedly impressed on other governments and international bodies that dwelling on a complex but no longer relevant past is unproductive, disruptive, and antagonistic. Yet the problem has persisted, and the tone and tenor of the denials are now more forceful than ever before. The Turkish position severely obstructs investigation of the genocide, its causes, effects, and implications, and the scholarly and humanitarian ends to which such studies should be directed.

As the number of persons who lived through World War I and who have direct knowledge of the events diminishes, the rationalizers and debasers of history become all the more audacious, to the extent of transforming the victims into the victimizers. At the time of the deportations and massacres, no reputable publication would have described the genocide as "alleged." The clouding of the past, however, and the years of Turkish denials, diplomatic and political pressures, and programs of image improvement have had their impact on some publishers, correspondents, scholars, and public officials. In an increasingly skeptical world, the survivors and descendants of the victims have been thrust into a defensive position from which they are required to prove time and again that they have indeed been wronged, individually and collectively. It is not surprising that they should look with envy upon Jewish Holocaust survivors, who do not have to face an unrepentant and uncompromising German government and a high-powered political campaign of denial that a state-organized plan of annihilation was in fact enacted. The Armenians search desperately for morality in politics and ask if there may be any just and practical alternative to the dictum "might makes right."

Notes

1. Henry Morgenthau, *Ambassador Morgenthau's Story* (Garden City, N.Y.: Doubleday, Page, 1918), p. 309.
2. See, for example, *Vérité sur le mouvement révolutionnaire arménien et les mésures gouvernementales* (Constantinople: n.p., 1916); and *Aspirations et agissements révolutionnaires des comités arméniens avant et après la proclamation de la constitution ottomane* (Constantinople: Ahmed Ingan, 1915).
3. Ahmed Rustem Bey, *La guerre mondiale et la question turco-arménienne* (Berne: Staempfli, 1918), p. 64.
4. See, for example, *Documents sur les atrocités arméno-russes* (Constantinople: n.p., 1917).
5. National Congress of turkey, *The Turco-Armenian Question: The Turkish Point of View* (Constantinople: Société papeteries, 1919), esp. pp. 74–92. See also *Memorandum of the Sublime Porte Communicated to the American, British, French, and Italian High Commissioners on the 12th February 1919* (Constantinople: Ahmed Ihsan, 1919).
6. U.S. Department of State, *Papers Relating to the Foreign Relations of the United States, 1919: The Paris Peace Conference,* vol. 4 (Washington, D.C.: G.P.O., 1943), 509–11; Great Britain, Foreign Office Archives, Public Record Office, Class 608, vol. 115, File 385/3/5.
7. Ahmed Emin [Yalman], *Turkey in the World War* (New Haven: Yale University Press, 1930).
8. Ibid., pp. 217, 219–20.
9. Ibid., p. 221.
10. [Talaat], "Posthumous Memoirs of Talaat Pasha," *Current History* 15 (November 1921):294–95.
11. Ibid., p. 295.

12. Jemal Pasha, *Memories of a Turkish Statesman, 1913-1919* (New York: George H. Doran, 1922), pp. 276–80.
13. See Roger R. Trask, *The United States Response to Turkish Nationalism and Reform, 1914–1939* (Minneapolis: University of Minnesota Press, 1971), esp. pp. 37–93, 147–51; Joseph L. Grabill, *Protestant Diplomacy and the Near East: Missionary Influence on American Policy, 1810–1927* (Minneapolis: University of Minnesota Press, 1971), pp. 269–85.
14. Marjorie Housepian, "The Unremembered Genocide," *Commentary* 42 (September 1966):59. See also Halidé Edib [Adivar], *Memoirs of Halidé Edib* (New York and London: Century, 1926).
15. U.S. National Archives, Record Group 59, General Records of the Department of State, Decimal File 811.4061 *Musa Dagh*. See also Department of State, *Papers Relating to the Foreign Relations of the United States: Diplomatic Papers, 1935,* vol. 1 (Washington, D.C.: G.P.O., 1953), 1053–55; Trask, *The United States Response to Turkish Nationalism and Reform,* pp. 90–91.
16. Altemur Kilic, *Turkey and the World* (Washington, D.C.: Public Affairs Press, 1959), pp. 18, 141.
17. See, for example, *Documents relatifs aux atrocités commises par les Arméniens sur la population musulmane* (Constantinople: Société Anonyme de Papeterie et d'Imprimérie, 1919); *Documents sur les atrocités arméno-russes* (Constantinople: Société Anonyme de Papeterie et d'Imprimerie, 1917); *The Turco-Armenian Question: The Turkish Point of View* (Constantinople: Société Anonyme de Papeterie et d'Imprimerie, 1919); *War Journal of the Second Russian Fortress Artillery Regiment of Erzeroum and Notes of Superior Russian Officer on the Atrocities at Erzeroum* (n.p., n.d.).
18. Enver Ziya Karal, *Armenian Question (1878–1923)* (n.p., n.d.), p. 22.
19. U.S. Congress, 66th Cong., 2d sess., S. Doc. 266, Major General James G. Harbord, *Conditions in the Near East: Report of the American Military Mission to Armenia* (Washington, D.C.: G.P.O., 1920), p. 11.
20. Ibid., p. 7.
21. Ahmet Vefa, *Truth about Armenians* (Ankara: n.p., 1975), pp. 7–8, 11.
22. Lewis V. Thomas and Richard N. Frye, *The United States and Turkey and Iran* (Cambridge: Harvard University Press, 1951), p. 61.
23. Stanford J. Shaw and Ezel Kural Shaw, *History of the Ottoman Empire and Modern Turkey,* vol. 2, *Reform, Revolution and Republic: The Rise of Modern Turkey, 1808–1975* (Cambridge: Cambridge University Press, 1977), esp. pp. 200–5, 240–41, 281, 287, 311–17, 322–24, 356–57.
24. Ibid., p. 315.
25. Salahi R. Sonyel, "Armenian Deportations: A Re-Appraisal in the Light of New Documents," *Belleten* 36 (January 1972):31–69. Also with Turkish text.
26. The two pamphlets were published in London in 1975 by the Cyprus Turkish Association.
27. Salahi R. Sonyel, *Greco-Armenian Conspiracy* (London: Cyprus Turkish Association, 1975), p. 2.
28. Salahi R. Sonyel, *Displacement of the Armenians: Documents* (Ankara: Baylan Matbaasi, 1978). Text also in French and in Turkish.
29. Ibid., pp. 1–2, 8.
30. Leo Kuper, *Genocide* (Middlesex: Penguin Books, 1981), p. 219.
31. Ibid., pp. 219–20.
32. Ibid., p. 220.

33. *New York Times,* 25 April 1982; *Los Angeles Times,* 25 April 1982, pt. I, p. 33.
34. See, for example, *Facts from the Turkish Armenians* (Istanbul: Jamanak, 1980). Text also in French and in Turkish.
35. Address to World Affairs Council of Los Angeles, 24 November 1981.
36. *Setting the Record Straight on Armenian Propaganda Against Turkey,* Publ. of Assembly of Turkish-American Associations (Washington, D.C.: n.p., 1982), p. 1.
37. Ibid., p. 4.
38. Ibid., pp. 4–8.
39. Ibid., p. 11.

7

Collective Responsibility and Official Excuse Making: The Case of the Turkish Genocide of the Armenians

Vigen Guroian

One evening, during a stopover in Istanbul on the return from their passage to Ararat, Michael Arlen and his wife meet for cocktails in a romantic hotel garden with two expatriate American professors of English. The Arlens and the professors chat politely for a spell until the conversation turns to the Arlens' visit to Soviet Armenia and their reasons for making the journey. The two professors are "perplexed as to why even an Armenian should wish to sojourn in Soviet Armenia." One remarks, "Of course, the Armenians were once a sizable population in Istanbul." Arlen's reply—"There doesn't seem to be much sign of them here anymore"— summons up the subject of the fateful years of 1914–1918. The same professor continues: "Yes, it's a pity. . . . But you must understand the Turkish point of view. The Armenians were a great nuisance to the Turks, and, after all, the country belonged to them. Those things are probably brutal, but they're life."[1]

Hearing such frivolous statements, for they were just that and not serious explanations for heinous acts committed against an entire people, stunned the Arlens. During their stay in Istanbul, the Arlens had listened to repeated Turkish denials that anything having to do with Armenians was of the least bit significant in Turkey's past or present. Such denials the Arlens had expected from Turks. But hearing them from the supposedly educated academics evoked from the Arlens the desire to utter the same shrill primal cry they had often heard in the voices of Armenians.

> Finally my wife said, "I think you're both fools for sitting here on your damned Bosporus and not knowing what really happened. . . ." Upstairs

in our room, my wife said, "No wonder so many Armenians sound so shrill."

"You mean, because 'nothing happened'?"

"Because the Turks don't admit to anything. And nobody else still gives a damn. There's no release."[2]

Since 1973 more than forty Turkish citizens, the majority in the Turkish diplomatic service, have been killed by members of Armenian radical groups. These radicals say that only such violent measures will make people and governments around the world give a damn about the Turkish genocide of the Armenians and publicly hold Turkey responsible for crimes committed some seventy years ago. That such acts of bloody vengeance have been directed against Turks by young men three generations removed from the Armenocide must surely strike some observers as not only bizarre but pathological. Yet the other related but no less bewildering fact usually overlooked by press reports of these killings is that since the immediate aftermath of World War I not one Turkish statesman, public figure, or scholar inside or outside Turkey in either an official or unofficial capacity has conceded that any genocidal acts were inflicted upon the Armenians of Ottoman Turkey during World War I.

Such systematic denials of a significant event of a nation's past has few if any parallels in modern history. Indeed, during the last several years Turkish governments and Turkish groups outside Turkey, particularly within the United States, have waged a costly campaign of denial. Those efforts have been directed especially at the United States Congress and the State Department.[3] Undoubtedly, the campaign has been inspired by a fear that the Armenian case might detract from Turkey's appeals for economic and military support from the United States and European nations. But the reasons for the campaign and its relentless pursuit go much deeper and in their depth present a highly instructive case study in the patterns of denial, justification, and excuse making that to one degree or another characterize the behavior of all national collectivities. Reflection on such diverse events as the Nazi extermination of European Jews, the systematic mass murders of whole populations within the Soviet Union, or the genocidal policies of the United States toward the American Indians raises questions about denial, collective guilt, and responsibility that could be assisted by study of the Armenocide. May this essay, written by a third-generation American-Armenian, serve to initiate such study; it emerges out of personal biographical recollection of the "old ones" whose words and gestures constantly reveal the traumatic effects of Turkey's denial of their suffering and the world's indifference.

My first objective is to explore the historical denials, justifications, and excuses used by Turkish persons and governments to dismiss charges that Turkey bears responsibility for genocidal acts committed against Armenians. These denials, justifications, and excuses raise the troublesome issue of collective responsibility, as well as the question of whether a national community remains, even after the lifetimes of the perpetrators, morally accountable, both collectively and distributively, for reprehensible acts committed in its name.[4] I do not propose, however, to examine with philosophical precision the meanings and uses of such terms as *denial, justification, excuse,* or *collective responsibility and guilt.* Rather, I wish to place in relief the moral significance of the kind of national behavior revealed by the Armenocide and its aftermath, and to suggest the kinds of challenges it presents to civil community and human relations.

Types of Turkish Justifications and Excuses

"In view of these new crimes of Turkey against humanity and civilization," declared the Entente nations on 24 May 1915, referring to the destruction already begun of the Turkish Armenians, "the Allied governments announce publicly to the Sublime Porte that they will hold personally responsible [for] these crimes all members of the Ottoman Government and those of their agents who are implicated in such massacres."[5] These charges elicited Turkish denials, justifications, and excuses that continue to this day. Nations, no less than individuals, regularly respond in this way when accused of morally blameworthy behavior. During World War I the Young Turk regime depicted its acts of genocide against the Armenians as the orderly deportation of Ottoman subjects and limited measures of reprisal against certain antagonistic elements of the Armenian population. Since that time Turkish governments, leaders, and historians, in their consistent denials that a genocide was planned or attempted, have admitted only that *some* Armenians met their deaths at the hands of the Turkish authorities and have persisted in offering "explanations" that deny that these deaths were the result of culpable acts.

For instance, during an interview held in June 1978, Professor Gündüz Ökçün, foreign minister of Turkey in the Ecevit government, gave this response to the question of genocide:

> What the Ottoman government did was to order the deportation of Armenians from one part of the Empire to another. This was done not in order to annihilate the Armenians who lived in Turkey, but to force their relocation—similar to what happened in previous periods of history. . . .

But in the process of executing these orders there was some overzealousness on the part of certain officials. And the Ottoman government didn't have complete control over these events.[6]

Ökçün's denial that the actions of the Young Turk regime were designed to exterminate the Armenians of Turkey runs in the face of massive evidence to the contrary. This includes hundreds of eyewitness accounts of organized mass killings, British, U.S., French, German, and Austrian diplomatic archival sources, statements by Turkish persons who were in one way or another acquainted with the inner workings of the Young Turk party and the Ottoman government, testimony from the special Inquiry Commission and court martial proceedings held after the war, and documents related to the rise of the Young Turk party and its relatively brief reign over the Ottoman Empire.[7] Conspicuously absent from these sources are the official Turkish records that, if they still exist, have been kept out of the hands of researchers.

Over the years, rationalizations of the deportations and deaths of Armenians within Turkey during World War I have followed a neat, if not entirely consistent formula and break down into three typical justifications and two typical excuses.[8]

Justifications Offered during and after the Atrocities

1. The Armenians had allowed themselves to become subversive instruments of foreign powers with designs on Ottoman possessions, and were scheming with these powers to gain for themselves complete political autonomy.
2. Armenians had joined the Russian army and were organizing themselves within the eastern Turkish provinces for armed insurrection. Unprovoked open rebellion had broken out by early 1915 in several provinces.
3. Exigencies of war made the deportations strategically necessary, but the deportations were limited to war zones.

Excuses Offered after the Atrocities

1. Certain irresponsible Young Turk leaders, government officials, and military people instigated sporadic massacres against the Armenians. The central government simply was not able to control the actions of every government official or military officer in every province. In any case, only a small number of Turks were guilty of this kind of activity and the killing was not part of a premeditated plan for genocide.

2. This was a period of Ottoman disintegration and world war. Many Armenians as well as Turks fell victim to the corruption and anarchy of the malaise.

Two matters were considered when setting up the above lists of justifications and excuses. First, I am persuaded that the "during" and "after" categories reflect the actual evolution of Turkish accounts of the events of 1915–18. Second, I believe a formal distinction between justificatory statements and excuses is helpful for making full sense of the testimony by Turkish spokesmen.

Sometimes persons or governments would have us judge an act as right that in other cases would be considered morally blameworthy on the grounds that, given the circumstances, this was the most, perhaps the only possible, responsible thing to do at the time. Such justificatory statements, at their purest, ask us to weigh freely all the facts of a case in light of relevant standards and render a favorable judgment of acts that otherwise would be considered objectively immoral or illegal. For example, the act of killing another person is one most people would say is immoral. Yet most people would say that there are certain mitigating circumstances in which that very same act is permissible, perhaps even praiseworthy, such as killing in self-defense or in order to protect the lives of innocents from assault by a pathological killer. Eric D'Arcy has pointed out that in such cases the "species description of the act" has not changed, but circumstances cause us to change "the predicate of its moral evaluation" and call the act "justifiable homicide."[9]

On the other hand, persons and governments sometimes appear to be offering not justifications but excuses for their actions. A paradigm of a perfect excuse would appear to be contained in the following situation.[10] I am standing at the edge of a cliff next to someone else. Suddenly without warning a third party pushes me with such force that I lose my footing and bump the person next to me off the cliff, as a result of which the person plummets down a mountainside to his or her death. What I did was neither intentional nor negligent. My *excuse* is that someone pushed me. The example suggests that an excusing circumstance is one in which it can be reasonably demonstrated that the harmful event of which someone was in some sense the agent was not something over which he or she had any control. The key factor is whether or not the act was *controllable*. In the example above, I was not in control of my bodily movement. Thus, by reason of circumstance an action that might otherwise have been considered a "wrongful act ... [is] placed outside the court of moral verdict."[11]

Veracity and Implications of the Turkish Justifications

The three types of Turkish justificatory statements about the Armen-ocide are congruent with certain historical facts and, therefore, achieve a measure of plausibility. The elevation of the Armenian Question to an international issue by the European powers during the latter part of the nineteenth century gave Armenians hope that the Ottoman government would feel compelled to make reforms improving, especially, the civil liberties of Armenians. Encouraged by the attention bestowed upon them by the great powers, Armenians began to press more actively for such reforms. Unfortunately, the motives of the powers were not disinterested. Inspired by European liberal, socialist, and nationalist movements, there arose among Armenians a new national consciousness that gave birth to several political parties. The most radical of these, the Hnchakian and Dashnaktsutiun parties, staged terrorist raids and incited riots. The Hnchakian party favored an independent state, whereas the Dashnak-tsutiun party, the larger of the two, sought "reforms within the framework of the Ottoman Empire."[12] But not even in 1915 did these radical parties have the means to pose a serious threat to the Ottoman state, as claimed by the first type of justificatory statement. In fact, the Dashnaktsutiun party had supported the Young Turks in the revolution of 1908, when it asked for less than full national autonomy. When the Russians entered the war, Armenians joined the Russian army. But, contrary to the claim of the second justificatory statement, almost all of these enlistees were Russian subjects. The Armenians of Van, Zeitun, and other cities did battle with the Turkish army and militia. But the large-scale slaughter of Armenians had already begun. The charge of unprovoked rebellion hardly applies. Lastly, the statement that the deportations were made necessary by the exigencies of the war and were restricted to vital war zones, though it has the ring of justifiability, ignores the fact that the deportations were not selective or limited. They, along with the rest of "the Porte's anti-Armenian program," were "sweeping in geographic scope . . . and indiscriminate" in application "to men, women and children."[13] The young men were conscripted into the military, later to be organized into "labor battalions" and eventually shot, or allowed to die from exposure or starvation. Women, the old, and the very young were force-marched, destined, if they survived the incredibly hard and long journey, for the desolate wastes of the Syrian desert.

My primary interest, however, is not to present historical argument against the Turkish justifications of the Ottoman policies toward the Armenians during World War I. This has been done by reputable scholars.[14]

In any final analysis, these justifications are not simply or even primarily historical but, rather, moral arguments. They have been offered to show that certain acts were *right*. They warrant evaluation as moral arguments. A good place to begin is with a document entitled *Vérité sur le mouvement révolutionnaire arménien et les mesures gouvernementales,* issued in 1916 by the Ottoman government responding to charges by persons and governments throughout the world that massive atrocities were being committed against the Armenians. This document became the model for all future Turkish denials of genocide and justifications and excuses for the measures that were taken against the Armenians. The document reads in part:

> In order to prevent the Armenians in the military zone from creating difficulties to the Army and the Government, in order to remove the possibility of Armenian riots against Moslem populations, in order to protect the communications of the Imperial Army and to prevent possible coups, it was decided to transfer the Armenians from military zones to other localities. . . . The primary necessity to assure internal order and external security of the country has made indispensable the removal of Armenians from places where their presence was considered to be dangerous. . . . During the application of these measures, regrettable acts of violence have sometimes been committed, but however regrettable these acts might have been, they were inevitable because of the profound indignation of the Moslem population.[15]

Of special interest in this text is the representation of the deportations as a "necessity," the removal of the Armenians as "indispensable," and the violence done to the deportees as "inevitable." Such "necessity statements" have the chameleon-like quality of appearing as excuses in one light and as justificatory appeals in another. In this case, some sort of inevitability is attributed to the deportations and the deaths of deportees. However, a responsible government decision also is indicated. The slippery question raised by necessity statements is to what degree can a decision be forced upon someone before we no longer want to say that it was freely made and conclude that there was no alternative but to do what was done.

Michael Walzer has suggested that in such necessity statements there are two levels of argumentation; these are (1) instrumental or strategic, and (2) moral.[16] On the instrumental-strategic level Turks have said that deportation of untrustworthy and rebellious elements was necessary in order to insure victory on the eastern war front. Yet, the removal from their homes of hundreds of thousands of persons and their relocation certainly were not the only possible means available to the government to prevent further alleged Armenian espionage, subversion, and insurrection. One could easily make the case that the enormous cost in financial and human resources of deportation damaged rather than assisted the war effort. The argument from necessity pales before reason and the facts. The compelling question raised by this argument is not even how the deportations might have been carried out in a less costly way, but rather what ends other than military-strategic lay behind the decision to deport the Armenians. On this level, the argument in the form of a justification looks in content more like a pretext for acts whose nature and purpose are other than those stated. Even if one were to accept as true all the Turkish claims about the internal threats posed by the Armenian population and as sincere the officially stated objectives of the deportation, what one has is a decision based on calculations of probability (i.e. that the odds of victory would be improved by the deportation) rather than one having to do with necessity.

The text cited above from *Vérité sur le mouvement révolutionnaire arménien et les mesures gouvernementales* argues that deportation of Armenians was necessary for "the order and external security of the country." Or as Talaat Pasha, the minister of the interior of the Young Turk regime during the war years and the man most responsible for the deportation policy, stated in his "Posthumous Memoirs":

> It was impossible to shut our eyes to the treacherous acts of the Armenians, at a time when we were engaged in a war which would determine the fate of our country. Even if these atrocities had occurred in a time of peace, our Government would have been obliged to quell such outbreaks. The Porte, . . . wishing to secure the safety of its army and its citizens took energetic measures to check these uprisings. The deportation of the Armenians was one of these preventive measures.[17]

In both texts it is proposed that the extraordinary measures taken with respect to the Armenians were justified because without them the military victories necessary to insure the very survival of the nation were not possible. As such, the statement clearly takes on the form of a moral argument. Presumably, the deportation of the Armenians and other measures taken to punish and prevent Armenian subversion and rebellion have their final *raison d'être* in the role they play in accomplishing the highest of political goods, the safety and well-being of citizens and the survival of the national community.

Of all Turkish justificatory arguments this one has the greatest semblance of plausibility. First at the hands of the British in Sinai during December of 1914 and again at the hands of the Russians in the Transcaucasus during January 1915, Turkey suffered major defeats in its offensive war. Although not faced with an imminent threat of invasion by Russia or Great Britain in early 1915, Turkey had been rendered incapable of presenting a sure defense should an attack come. Had the deportations initiated in early spring of 1915 been truly limited and selective, as claimed then and since by Turkish spokesmen, the argument might be credible. This, however, was manifestly not the case. As mentioned earlier, what amounted to a massive effort to move, if not destroy, the entire Armenian population of Anatolia was begun. Had the deportation involved only some unintended loss of life among the noncombatant Armenian population, the Turkish claim would have veracity as a moral argument. However, there was a massive loss of life. This throws into serious question all Turkish denials that innocent noncombatant members of the Armenian population were deliberately killed by state orders. Thus, while the form of this justification is correct, the actual case does not fit it.

In addition, Turkish spokesmen have muddied the waters on this matter by insisting that the Armenians were finally to blame for whatever loss of life and property they endured. Through treasonous acts and atrocities against their Muslim neighbors, Armenians brought upon themselves justifiable countermeasures by the government. In his "Posthumous Memoirs," Talaat Pasha gave what stands now as a paradigmatic statement of this argument.

> I admit that we deported many Armenians from our eastern provinces, but we never acted in this matter upon a previously prepared scheme. The responsibility of these acts falls upon the deported people themselves. Russia . . . had armed and equipped the Armenian inhabitants of this district [Van] . . . , and had organized strong Armenian bandit forces. . . . When we entered the great war, these bandits began their destructive activities in the rear of the Turkish army on the Caucasus front, blowing up the bridges, setting fire to the Turkish towns and villages and killing the innocent Mohammedan inhabitants regardless of age and sex. . . . All these Armenian bandits were helped by the native Armenians.[18]

The sense of Talaat's statement is not to argue *necessity* regarding deportation, although he moves to such a conclusion later in the text. Rather, the issue is the guilt of the Armenians and the argument for deportation is presented as just reprisal. Hence one returns to the question, was deportation a necessary action to insure victory on the eastern front and the security of the homeland? Or was it a collective act of retaliation against a people judged universally guilty? A 1916 interview in the *Berliner Tageblatt* offers a revealing statement by Talaat Pasha: "We have been reproached for making no distinction between the innocent

Armenians and the guilty; but that was utterly impossible, in view of the fact that those who were innocent today might be guilty tomorrow."[19] These words probably leave us at the threshold of the real reasons for the deportation of the Armenians.

Turkish Excuses and Excuse Making:
Traces of an Uneasy Conscience

A careful examination of the two types of Turkish excuses pertaining to the Armenocide leaves it fairly clear that neither measures up to the formal meaning of an excuse. Both fail to identify actual circumstances that place what might have been considered wrongful acts outside the court of moral verdict. In form the excuses ask the objective observer to conclude that whatever suffering Armenians in Turkey underwent during World War I was *out of the control* of the Ottoman government, even if some of that suffering can be attributed directly or indirectly to persons having governmental authority. The first "excuse" maintains that it was not within the power of the central government to protect Armenians from all harm at the hands of demented or evil persons. This excuse, of course, contradicts persuasive evidence that the death-dealing acts inflicted upon the Armenians were premeditated and freely executed by the leaders of the Young Turk party and the Ottoman government.

The second excuse raises a highly questionable ethical concept. We are asked to excuse normally blameworthy acts of people, some in positions of authority, on the premise that social, economic, and political forces used these people for destructive purposes. Such a deterministic interpretation of history is not readily proven. And our experience of common excuse making should leave us suspicious of such formulations.[20]

When we encounter someone in our common everyday life who persistently engages in excuse making, we are inclined to suspect that the person knows that something he or she has done is reprehensible but, consciously or unconsciously, by rationalization or self-deception, is avoiding acknowledgment of his or her genuine moral guilt. Thus such a person may not yet even feel guilty.[21] The habitual resort to excuse making through the years by Turkish persons and governments when asked about the Armenocide is good reason to suppose the same about them.

In separate 1978 interviews with the editor of the Armenian-American weekly newspaper, the *Armenian Reporter,* both the prime minister of Turkey at the time, Bülent Ecevit, and the foreign minister of the Ecevit government, Gündüz Ökçün, were questioned about the long-standing demands by Armenians that Turkey acknowledge the responsibility of the Young Turk Ottoman government for genocidal acts committed against its Armenian subjects. Both men offer the types of excuses I have identified. But of even greater interest are Ecevit's and Ökçün's resort to several arguments used in recent years by Turkish spokesmen to dismiss Armenian charges of genocide as both misguided and in bad faith. The arguments themselves are rather transparent, but what we see when we look through them is significant. They reveal the magnitude of Turkish rationalization and self-deception about the Armenocide and they expose an uneasy Turkish conscience.

During the interview Ecevit is asked to comment on the Armenian contention that the first prerequisite for reconciliation between Armenians and Turks is "acknowledgement of guilt on the part of the present [Turkish] government . . . for the acts of the rulers of the Ottoman Empire." Ecevit responds:

> I think that the disintegration of the Ottoman Empire should not in any way influence our relations because it was the disintegration of a multi-communal empire and during that period many of the elements making up the empire suffered a lot and fought among themselves. There were many provocations from outside as well. And Turks from Anatolia themselves suffered a great deal.[22]

Even beyond the several excuses raised by Ecevit is the reference to suffering of Turks during the same period. Ecevit's comment is not accidental. It comes in the context of a virtual war of numbers waged by Turkish spokesmen against the Armenian claims that nearly 1.5 million Armenians died between 1915 and 1918 as a result of Ottoman policies. They have maintained that *only* between 200,000 and 400,000 Armenians died in contrast to between 1 and 3 million Muslim subjects.[23]

The same line of argument appears in a letter sent to members of Congress in the spring of 1982 by the Turkish ambassador to the United States, Şükrü Elekdağ, advising them against making statements honoring the April 24 commemoration of the sixty-seventh anniversary of the Armenocide. It reads in part:

> Armenian extremists and their supporters justify their criminal actions on the pretext of avenging misrepresented events which took place during World War I. What took place was a complex tragedy which claimed Turkish as well as Armenian lives. Indeed, it was a civil war within a global war stemming from an armed uprising of the Armenian minority at a time when the Ottoman state was fighting for survival during World War I. Many more Turks than Armenians perished.[24]

The statement that "many more Turks than Armenians perished" is no answer to the charge that the Ottoman government perpetrated a genocide, except, perhaps, as it suggests that the Armenians who did die either received their just punishment for rebellion or fell victim to the same impersonal forces that took the lives of so many more Turks. Certainly, the case against Turkey does not depend upon a count of the dead. If a genocide was committed, the seriousness of the crime would not be less nor its reprehensibility reduced if *only* 200,000 Armenians died.

In fact, the Turkish reasoning on this matter is mystifying, unless one takes it as symptomatic of a psyche for which rationalization and self-deception take over when reminded of a particular part of its past. I suspect that, in the process of avoiding acknowledgment of guilt or responsibility for the Armenocide, Turks have persuaded themselves that the stain of the blood of not-so-innocent Armenians was washed clean, the sin expiated, by the blood of so many innocent Turks. When the excuses break down, there is always a way to erase the reprehensible act and forget it was ever committed.

Scattered throughout the Ecevit and Ökçün interviews are statements to the effect that it would be better for Armenians and Turks to forget about what happened between them in the waning years of the Ottoman Empire. For instance, Ecevit remarks:

> So, I think, it would be a good thing for all of us not to base our hopes for the future on the memories of the period of disintegration of the Ottoman Empire. Rather, we should base our hopes for the future on the memories of those other periods when all the elements that made up the Ottoman Empire coexisted in peace.[25]

To be sure, leaders of nations rarely have been disposed to recall for citizens the follies, sins, or criminal acts of the national past. The selective use of memory and deliberate forgetfulness about certain periods of the nation's history advocated by Ecevit may serve a narrow and morally circumscribed nationalism, but it does little to raise the moral sensitivities of citizens or to enhance the capacities of the national community to act rationally and responsibly.

In his interview Ökçün endorses the idea of encouraging international scholarly inquiry into the history of the period of the alleged Armenocide, but insists that any "attempt to uncover evidence of responsibility" would be counterproductive. In response to the query as to whether he is aware that Armenians insist that the present-day Turkish government acknowledge "guilt . . . on the part of the leaders of Ottoman Turkey" for the

Armenocide as "a prerequisite for establishing normal relations," he responds: "What purpose would such recognition serve?" The fact of such recalcitrance is not nearly as important to this paper as a reasonable explanation for its existence. Later in the interview, Ökçün states: "I think the Turks were mostly picked on. There are many other peoples of the world who could have been blamed for their attempt at committing genocides in the nineteenth as well as the twentieth century."[26] In these remarks we hear anger, frustration, and humiliation. They are also the most candid words spoken by Ökçün in the entire interview. They undoubtedly express the visceral feelings of many Turks about accusations and demands made upon them with regard to the Armenocide. The Turks have been unjustly treated, Ökçün is arguing. They have been asked incessantly not only to recall a period of national disgrace and humiliation, the very demise of an empire, but to make a public confession before the world for a crime that others have committed but have never been called upon to admit. There is no denial in this protest that the crime was committed, only the cry that Turkey does not deserve to be singled out.

Collective Guilt and Collective Responsibility

Philosophers and theologians often assert that in formal moral argument guilt can be attributed only to individuals. As Theodore R. Weber argued:

> Guilt, in the process of moral deliberation, always is individual guilt. Although as social beings our social interactions and cultural and institutional involvement may provide the occasions for guilty acts and attitudes, we do not thus become liable for all the guilt of all the occasions arising from this milieu and its processes. Although the consequences of actions which establish individual guilt may fall on others because of our social relatedness, they may not be brought justifiably on others deliberately on the assumption that social relatedness makes the others guilty.[27]

Yet Weber also allows for a legitimate use of the concept of collective guilt outside the realm of formal "moral argument in which claims are established and actions validated by reference to commonly accepted criteria of justification." He argues that in the context of self-awareness the concept of collective guilt has appropriate reference and applicability. In this context "there can be no authentic understanding of the defects and pain of personal and corporate existence, no adequate coping with limitations and possibilities of present and future, unless the self recognizes its solidarity in guilt as well as in honor."[28] Collective guilt that can be felt deeply by persons for injustices committed against others in the past, even the distant past, by their national community is of a different order from the objective guilt appealed to in formal moral and legal argument. (Weber's example is the guilt felt by members of an ascendent and ruling white majority in the United States for injustices done to black Americans in centuries past.) Such experience of guilt does not raise the usual objective questions of culpability or blameworthiness. Rather, it arises when the self gains an imaginative awareness that it not only participates in a common life with its contemporaries but also inherits as part of its own autobiography the past history, good and bad, of its fellows.[29] In addition to establishing within the self a deepened sense of social solidarity and interrelatedness, this experience of bringing into the open repressed or forgotten deeds of the self's social past can be freeing and can enable the self to act more rationally and responsibly in the future.

It is possible to extend Weber's discussion of collective guilt to a context of "representational group" self-awareness. By this I mean simply that individuals of a group acting in social roles can experience collective guilt for blameworthy acts committed by that group in the past as their own guilt and evoke in the group an awareness of the untoward nature of those acts. The positive results of this are similar to those for the context of individual self-awareness. It can deepen the group's under-standing of and sensibility toward certain social disorders and provide reasons of mind and heart for seeking their resolution. It also can establish the conditions for a regeneration and reconstitution of group identity. Such collective guilt has obvious negative potentialities. If it is made the object of accusatory moral arguments where questions of agency, causation, fault, or liability are raised,[30] it can become the source of any or all of the following: (1) sullen and morbid self-flagellation, (2) preoc-cupation with expiatory release, and (3) increased social discord.[31]

Guilt posits responsibility. Thus, the question of collective guilt inev-itably raises the question of collective responsibility. There is a sense in which even groups can be held collectively and distributively accountable for addressing both the good deeds and the misdeeds of their corporate past, since these deeds are carried into the present in the forms of persisting cultural values, dispositions, and character traits. Yet, as in the case of collective guilt, such collective responsibility is not readily subject to objective questions of agency, causation, fault, or liability. Such a sense of responsibility, however, does obtain in the common life. Joel Feinberg has called it " 'representational attributability.' "[32] Whatever we choose to name it, persons normally do hold other persons and groups responsible for their past and the values, dispositions, and character traits left imprinted on them by that past. Common sense tells us that if persons and groups refuse to take responsibility for their past, good and bad together, and the persisting values, dispositions, and traits in which that past is present, they are likely to be afflicted by inner disharmony and outwardly erratic and irrational behavior.

In light of these observations, Armenians certainly have had good ground upon which to hold Turkish persons and governments morally accountable for the Armenocide. The mistake in the Armenian argument has been to make such demands in a judgmental way, having conflated what Weber refers to as the context of self-awareness with the context of formal moral argument. This has left discussion between Armenians and Turks on an emotive level in which the accused persist in denying, justifying, and excusing themselves, and the accusers, in the face of such intractability, resort to revenge. Possibilities for truthful encounter and reconciliation are reduced as tribalistic and atavistic attitudes increase.

The appropriate role of the Armenian in the Turkish acknowledgment of national guilt and responsibility for the Armenocide is a prophetic one. In the same way that Blacks in the United States are in a unique position to sensitize white Americans to injustices in the national past that persist as negative values, dispositions, and traits of the national life, the Armenians are uniquely able to help the Turks remember the past that they have denied or chosen to forget, but which even denied or unremembered endures. That past must return to the Turks' consciousness as a revelation about themselves.

No Turkish leadership since the Armenocide has attained such a moral sensitivity and national self-awareness. When Ecevit says in the *Armenian Reporter* interview that "the present Turkish state is the result of an uprising against" the Ottoman state and then reasons from this that the Ottoman past is of no consequence to Turkey's present or future, we see the difficulty and the danger.[33] Such reasoning defies the commonsense perception that one national culture does not end and another begin as a result of a change in government or even a revolution in government. If there were Turkish national values, dispositions, and traits during the Ottoman era that made it possible for a genocide to be organized and executed against Armenians, there is no a priori reason to assume that they suddenly disappeared with the Nationalist revolution.[34] The irony that escapes Ecevit is that the capacity of a nation to transcend its past depends upon its willingness to remember it conscientiously, report it truthfully, and criticize it publicly. When a nation's leadership consistently refuses to do so, it risks burdening itself and its citizens with an uneasy conscience and inflicts upon the nation a deformation of character that will severely hinder its capacity to act rationally and responsibly.

Notes

1. Michael Arlen, *Passage to Ararat* (New York: Farrar, Straus & Giroux, 1975), pp. 278–79.
2. Ibid., pp. 279–80.
3. Surely influenced by this campaign, the following statement was made in the *Department of State Bulletin:* "Because the historical record of the 1915 events in Asia Minor is ambiguous, the Department of State does not endorse allegations that the Turkish government committed a genocide against the Armenian people." Andrew Corsun, "Armenian Terrorism: A Profile," *Department of State Bulletin* 82 (August 1982):35.
4. I leave aside in this paper the legal issue of liability raised by Armenians against Turkey for reparations due Armenians for expropriation of lands and property by the Ottoman state. So far as I understand such things, it is possible in principle and in light of precedent in international law to argue that the present Republic of Turkey is legally liable for certain wrongs committed by its predecessor state. The matter under discussion here is at once much simpler and more difficult to lay hold of. Is there any meaning or moral sense in the Armenian claim that the present Turkish state is responsible for acknowledging the guilt of the Ottoman state for a genocide attempted against the Armenians of Turkey? I am not suggesting that the moral issue explored in the paper is finally unrelated to the legal issue of reparations. Rather, in some deep sense the two issues are connected. I think both parties have understood this all along. There is good reason to believe that behind the long history of Turkish denials, justifications, and excuses is the recognition that once it is admitted that a genocide was attempted, the legal claims made against Turkey by Armenians will be difficult to ignore or deny.
5. U.S. Department of State, *Papers Relating to the Foreign Relations of the United States, 1915 Supplement* (Washington, D.C.: G.P.O., 1928), p. 981. According to Ulrich Trumpener, this "declaration originated in the Russian foreign office. . . . The French government saw to it that the originally proposed phrase, 'crime against Christianity and civilization,' was replaced by 'crime against humanity and civilization,' in order to spare the feelings of the Muslim population in the French colonies." *Germany and the Ottoman Empire, 1914–1918* (Princeton: Princeton University Press, 1968), p. 210 n. 26. In August of 1915 Germany, Turkey's ally, issued its own protest to the Sublime Porte regarding "the subject of the expatriation of the Armenian inhabitants of the Anatolian provinces and . . . to call attention on the fact that this measure had been accompanied in many places by acts of violence such as massacres and plunders which could not be justified by the aim that the Imperial Government was pursuing." These occurrences were referred to as "acts of horror" for which Germany "decline[s] all responsibility of all consequences which can result." The note verbale was in French and dated 9 August 1915. A copy was forwarded to the U.S. ambassador to Turkey, Henry Morgenthau. Another copy was delivered by the German ambassador to the United States, Count Johann Heinrich von Bernstorff, and to the State Department. Henry Morgenthau Senior Papers, Manuscript Division, Library

of Congress, Container 4; also Washington, D.C., National Archives, Department of State, 867.4016/173 and 174.

6. "Transcript of the Armenian Reporter Interview with Professor Gündüz Ökçün, Foreign Minister of Turkey," *The Armenian Reporter* (New York), 6 July 1978, p. 2.

7. Before the premature termination of the special Inquiry Commission and the courts martial, several important Young Turk leaders were sentenced to prison or death for their complicity in the massacres. Included among these were the persons who made up the ruling triumvirate during the war years. Talaat Pasha, minister of the interior, Enver Pasha, minister of war, and Jemal Bey, minister of marine, fled Turkey after the war but were sentenced to death in absentia.

8. The text that follows under this section of the paper on types of Turkish justifications and excuses is a revised and expanded version of a discussion in my article, "A Comparison of the Armenian and Jewish Genocides: Some Common Features," *Thought* 58 (June 1983):207-23. See also Vahakn N. Dadrian, "The Methodological Components of the Study of Genocide as a Sociological Problem—The Armenian Case," in *Recent Studies in Modern Armenian History* (Cambridge: Armenian Heritage Press, 1972), esp. pp. 88–90.

9. Eric D'Arcy, *Human Acts* (London: Oxford University Press, 1963), p. 84.

10. This example is one that was suggested to me in conversation by my colleague Professor David Little of the University of Virginia.

11. D'Arcy, *Human Acts,* p. 81.

12. Louise Nalbandian, *The Armenian Revolutionary Movement* (Berkeley and Los Angeles: University of California Press, 1963), p. 182.

13. Trumpener, *Germany and the Ottoman Empire,* p. 268.

14. The "classic" texts in any list of scholarly refutations of the Turkish claims were penned by Arnold J. Toynbee, *Armenian Atrocities: The Murder of a Nation* (London: Hodder & Stoughton, 1915); and *The Treatment of Armenians in the Ottoman Empire, 1915-1916* (London: H.M.S.O., 1916), pp. 593–693. Also included in this category is Johannes Lepsius, *Deutschland und Armenien, 1914-1918: Sammlung diplomatischer Aktenstücke* (Potsdam: Tempelverlag, 1919). Recent important studies include Richard G. Hovannisian, *Armenia on the Road to Independence* (Berkeley and Los Angeles: University of California Press, 1967), esp. ch. 4; Leo Kuper, *Genocide* (New Haven: Yale University Press, 1982), ch. 6; Howard M. Sachar, *The Emergence of the Middle East: 1914-1924* (New York: Alfred A. Knopf, 1969), ch. 4; Trumpener, *Germany and the Ottoman Empire,* ch. 7.

15. *Vérité sur le mouvement révolutionnaire arménien et les mesures gouvernementales* (Constantinople: n.p., 1916), pp. 13–15; quoted in Joseph Guttman, "The Beginnings of Genocide," *Turkish Armenocide,* Documentary Series, vol. 2 (Philadelphia: Armenian Historical Research Association, 1965), p. 11.

16. Michael Walzer, *Just and Unjust Wars* (New York: Basic Books, 1977), pp. 240–42.

17. "Posthumous Memoirs of Talaat Pasha," *Current History* 15 (November 1921):294–95.

18. Ibid., p. 294.

19. Quoted in Henry Morgenthau, *Ambassador Morgenthau's Story* (Garden City, N.Y.: Doubleday, Page, 1918) p. 336.

20. Such "deterministic interpretation" has crept into historical studies of the period. Lewis V. Thomas writes: "How else can one assess the final blame [for what Thomas calls "the unrelieved tragedy which the Armenian Christian population of Turkey suffered"] except to say that this was a tragic consequence of the final impact of western nationalism upon Anatolia?" Lewis V. Thomas and Richard N. Frye, *The United States and Turkey and Iran* (Cambridge: Harvard University Press, 1951), p. 61.

21. David H. Jones, "Freud's Theory of Moral Conscience," in *Conscience*, ed. John Donnelly and Leonard Lyons (Staten Island, N.Y.: Alba House, 1973), p. 113.

22. "Transcript of the Armenian Reporter Interview with Mr. Bulent Ecevit, Prime Minister of Turkey," *The Armenian Reporter* (New York), 29 June 1978, p. 2.

23. See, for example, the booklet *Setting the Record Straight on Armenian Propaganda Against Turkey* (Washington, D.C.: Assembly of Turkish American Associations, 1982). A portion of the text reads: "The losses [of Armenian] population . . . during World War I could not have exceeded 300,000 at most. Due to a variety of reasons, far more Turks than Armenians—about 3 million—died in the same war. Very few of these fell dead on the battlefront. Consequently, one cannot conclude that the Armenians suffered more terribly or that the Ottoman government attempted to exterminate them."

24. U.S. Congress, House, 97th Cong., 2d sess., 4 May 1982, *Congressional Record* 128:E 1993–94. The letter was placed into the *Congressional Record* by the Hon. Robert H. Michel. The same text was addressed and sent to other members of Congress.

25. "Interview with Mr. Bulent Ecevit," p. 2.

26. "Interview with Professor G. Ökçün," p. 2.

27. Theodore R. Weber, "Guilt: Yours, Ours, and Theirs," *Worldview* 18 (February 1975):20.

28. Ibid., p. 17.

29. H. Richard Niebuhr, *The Meaning of Revelation* (New York: Macmillan, 1941), pp. 114–15.

30. Joel Feinberg, *Doing and Deserving* (Princeton: Princeton University Press, 1970), p. 251.

31. Weber, "Guilt," pp. 13–14.

32. Feinberg, *Doing*, pp. 250–51.

33. "Interview with Mr. Bulent Ecevit," p. 2.

34. Despite consistent denials by Turkish governments past and present, the roughly 70,000 Armenians of Turkey continue to endure gross violations of human rights. See David M. Lang and Christopher J. Walker, *The Armenians, Minority Rights Group*, Report 32 (London, 1977); *Christian Minorities of Turkey* (Brussels: Churches Committee on Migrant Workers in Europe, 1979).

8

The Armenian Genocide and the Literary Imagination

Leo Hamalian

We live in a society with a guilty conscience about
suppressed truths . . . and there will always be much that
we don't want to hear but need to know.
—Ronald Sukenick

In this paper, I propose to examine and assess if possible the impact of the Armenian massacres on narrative writing and fiction in Europe and the United States during the years between 1920 and 1980. How did the imagination of writers respond to those catastrophic events, when the leaders of the Ottoman government and their successors sought to wipe out the Armenian population confined within the borders of Turkey? Although the poets are no longer the unacknowledged legislators of the world, literature has always been one of the forces that forges the morality and sensibility of a civilization—so that the question may be seen as a way of testing the fundamental attitudes and convictions of that civilization. That premise is not so debatable as one might at first assume. Limitations of space do not permit me to discuss the implications of this assertion, but I want the reader to understand that I feel that my statements in this paper have application beyond the scope of the literature under discussion.

To begin, let us see how Armenian writers themselves responded to the attempted genocide. We all know that the Armenians who managed to survive the atrocities fled to such havens as the Balkans, the Arab-speaking countries, the Far East, Latin America, Ethiopia, and Soviet Russia; many of them were offered refuge in France, Greece, and Italy, and somewhat later, in England and the United States. Few of these immigrants had the time or chance to achieve a writer's fluency in the language of their adopted countries. Hence, during the 1920s and 1930s by necessity Armenian writers had to address themselves to a very small, special audience made up of the readers of Armenian-language publications or English-language (and French) publications aimed at Armenians (where William Saroyan got his start). In the young state of Soviet Armenia, there was a brilliant but short-lived renaissance in Armenian literature created by such writers as Zabel Yesayan, Marietta Shahinian, Yeghishe Charents, Vahan Totovents, Axel Bakounts, Avedik Isahakian, and Gurgen Mahari. The Stalinist purges of the thirties rudely arrested this promising movement and any writing about the genocide that was regarded as "nationalistic" was thereafter forbidden until after World War II.

In the diaspora, Gostan Zarian, a multilingual autodidact who had barely escaped with his skin, was slowly gaining a reputation as an original voice in literature (and later as a guru much admired by younger artists such as Lawrence Durrell, whose Armenian barber/philosopher in *The Alexandria Quartet* may owe its inspiration to the figure of Zarian). One of his best books, *The Traveller and His Road,* was published serially in the now-defunct monthly *Hairenik* of Boston. We meet the central figure, Zarian himself, in Constantinople in the summer of 1922, just before Mustafa Kemal was about to enter and incinerate Smyrna. Haunted by memories of happier times and disturbed by the turmoil of political events in Constantinople, Zarian departed for the new state of Soviet Armenia, where he endured three years of material hardship intensified by political harassment. He finally decided to take up once more the bitter road of exile. While residing in Rome, he lectured frequently on the Armenian cause and once remarked, "The people of Italy displayed great sympathy and compassion for the victims of the massacres." The same cannot be said about her writers in print: they were probably too preoccupied with the suffering of their own people to take up the Armenian cause as a theme in their fiction.

In France, another refugee, Shahan Shahnur, wrote a novel called *Retreat without Song,* which some Armenian critics regarded as the most poignant novel in the language despite its denunciation of the clergy. An exile at the age of twelve, Shahnur dramatized the aftereffects of the massacres rather than the massacres themselves. The novel concerns six young men from Constantinople stranded in Paris, growing away from their roots, living in almost total despair because they are convinced that they belong nowhere. The tone is bitter and angry, frequently reflecting the frustration of the victim powerless to redress his wrongs. Under the pseudonym of Armen Lubin, Shahnur published in the literary magazine *Nouvelle Revue Française* several stories based on life in a hospital, later included in his only volume of French prose, *Transfert Nocturne.* He also produced several volumes of poetry in French that won a certain recognition among his new countrymen. His themes dealt with abandonment and loss (much like the paintings of Carzou), with the helpless sorrows of the lonely and the alienated, in a mood that would later be known as "existentialist."

As the Armenians began to acquire the language of their new neighbors in the diaspora, several new voices in addition to Shahnur's began to make themselves heard. In the wreckage that followed the great war of 1914-18, it was predictable rather than paradoxical that the three best-known writers of Armenian blood would write in a language other than their own native tongue.

In England, the son of a Bulgarian Armenian merchant changed his name from Dickran Kouyoumdjian to Michael Arlen (though his friends like D. H. Lawrence continued to address him as "Dickran") and became the author of the world's most popular novel up to that time, *The Green Hat*. Unfortunately for the Armenians, who needed someone with Arlen's skills to bring their case to the attention of a world which was already beginning to forget the horrors of 1915, Arlen was too committed to adapting to his new identity as an English writer. Later, with his reputation secure, Arlen did write about the Armenian atrocities, but only in the less widely read short stories and articles in *New Age* and *The Tatler*. Perhaps his strongest statement on the subject is to be found in an essay called "I Knew Dr. Goebbels," in the January 17, 1940, issue of *The Tatler*. He describes a curious encounter with Hitler's chief of propaganda. Arlen had been standing on the verandah of his hotel in Athens when he saw Goebbels below, "an arrogant and intolerable little monster in whom was concentrated all the venom and corruption of this unhappy world." He continued thus:

> It made me mad. It always makes me mad when people get away with murder and grin happily ever after. I wanted to throw a brick down at him. . . . I wanted to knock his hat off. I wanted to forget that I was a naturalized Englishman and become an Armenian again. I wanted to be a Jew and revenge all Jews. . . . The Young Turks slew us, but we slew them also. And to teach us our lesson as slaves and dogs, they slew us in our thousands and they raped our sisters and whipped our mothers. So we lay hidden, and murdered them one by one. . . . To hell with suffering patiently. . . . To hell with resignation. Were I a Jew in Germany, were I a million Jews, I had rather one day be killed, as my people and their children were no longer than twenty years ago, than be made to lick a beastly German's spittle . . . and so I spat on the Reichmaster Dr. Goebbel's superb silk hat as he passed below me.

Similar emotions are expressed fictionally in what may be Arlen's best short story, "The Man with the Broken Nose," about an Armenian from

Zeitun who wishes to avenge the massacres and in that cause enlists the assistance of two prominent aristocrats. However, both Arlen and his dwindling audience were distracted from the case of the Armenian victims by rumors of an equally ruthless operation under way in Europe under the direction of a German leader who could afford to boast, "Who remembers what happened to the Armenians?"

Another Armenian writer of the pre-World War II period is William Saroyan, whose family fled from the Lake Van area of Turkey to a small dusty village in the San Joaquin Valley, a place called Fresno, which he would soon put on the map. The young Saroyan wrote about the Armenian massacres perhaps too obliquely in "70,000 Assyrians," a story about a decimated race of people, published in his first successful collection, *The Daring Young Man on the Flying Trapeze* (1934). In his next volume of stories, *Inhale and Exhale* (1936), there are two selections that reveal Saroyan's feelings about the massacres, "Antranik of Armenia" and "The Armenian and the Armenian." With great pride he eulogizes the power of survival and continuity, which for him were the characteristic qualities of his people whenever they were faced in history with the threat of extinction. This book was not well received by the critics and had limited circulation. As his fame increased, Saroyan turned in other directions for his subject matter, though he continued to maintain his interest in Armenian affairs. Furthermore, World War II was about to begin, and most Americans, like the English, did not wish to hear about events that had taken place two decades earlier in towns and regions whose names they could not even pronounce. By the middle of the century, reality had overtaken history with fresh and unthinkable horrors invented by the Nazis if inspired by the Young Turks, long birds of a feather. It must be said, in addition, that the events of 1915 proved to be so traumatizing, so destructive to simple self-esteem, that they may have induced in the survivors a kind of racial amnesia—after all, who among them wanted to remember that the decent world had watched in a near-paralysis of will while the cruel Turks worked to liquidate their vassals? When memory did operate, often the tongue was stunned into silence on the subject.

Michael Arlen did not go totally unread or unheard by his circle of friends in England. D. H. Lawrence wrote a powerful story (1929) called "Mother and Daughter," in which the protagonist is an elderly Armenian suitor for the hand of an English woman. Lawrence writes:

> The Turkish Delight was sixty, grey-haired and fat. . . . His manner was humble, but in his bearing was a certain dogged conceit. . . . He was tired, but he was not defeated. He had fought and won, and lost, and was fighting

again, always at a disadvantage. He belonged to a defeated race which accepts defeat but gets its own back by cunning. He was the father of sons, the head of a family, one of the heads of a defeated but indestructible tribe. His whole consciousness was patriarchal and tribal. And somehow he was humble, he was indestructible.

Arnault, the Bulgarian Armenian, stands for life and endurance; he is one of Lawrence's earth-figures who knows the secret of survival, closely linked to the Italian peasants whom Lawrence admired so much for their intuitive powers and their "blood-knowledge." Any sense of Arnault's previous life is absent, but Lawrence, who was deeply interested in history, seldom reveals the past of his fictional characters.

Virginia Woolf, in *Mrs. Dalloway,* her most famous novel, is even more incurious about the Armenian past than Lawrence, though she refers to it in passing. As she walks down a London street, Mrs. Dalloway muses to herself:

> She cared much more for her roses than for Armenians. Hunted out of existence, maimed, frozen, the victims of cruelty and injustice (she had heard Richard say over and over again)—no, she could feel nothing for the Albanians, or was it the Armenians? But she loved her roses (didn't that help the Armenians?).

A little later, she confesses that she always "muddled Armenians and Turks." Since the novel perhaps suggests the tyranny of accepted modes of thought over the individual, much of this passage may be ironic. One cannot help regretting that the facts of the Armenian holocaust left such a light impression on two of the most influential writers of the age.

Another English novelist of note, Evelyn Waugh, mentions two extraordinary Armenians whom he met while attending the coronation of Ras Tafari in Addis Ababa, and comments about the Armenians living in the Ethiopian diaspora: "A race of rare competence and the most delicate sensibility, they seem to me the only genuine 'men of the world.' " In two of Waugh's novels, *Scoop* and *Black Mischief,* Armenians appear as comic characters, but he has little to say about the events that brought them to that pass. Lawrence Durrell also includes Armenians in his *Quartet,* Mnemjian and possibly Balthazar. Mnemjian may be based on Gostan Zarian, whom Durrell speaks about in several of his other books. But once more there is almost no reference at all to the massacres—as though the person were separated from his past.

English travel writers and historians (Toynbee in particular) of this period tried to inform their readers about the attempted genocide, but often one is struck by their failure to understand the true magnitude of the events or to recognize what it would mean to their own lives if the Turks were permitted to go unpunished. Furthermore, the audience for travel literature and history, in the 1920s and 1930s, appears to have been relatively modest compared to the readers of fiction. Again the message got buried.

Among the writers of the United States, there were two budding authors who were sent by their American employers to interpret the events taking place in the Near East during the early twenties. They wrote about the survivors with great sympathy but with little comprehension of the scope or significance of what they were reporting.

Ernest Hemingway was working as a foreign correspondent for the *Toronto Star* in Turkey when Mustafa Kemal burned the city of Smyrna to the ground. He sent back several dispatches about the exchange of populations in Thrace and the occupation of Constantinople by Kemalist troops. His craft in these dispatches is not the craft of factual reporting, although the reporting appears to be factual, but the craft of fiction. The language is cool, clear, and resonant, and his strategy is to probe beneath the surface for what was happening. It is not clear whether he ever got to Smyrna itself or whether he pieced together an account of the events from reports that he read or heard, but one of his most moving pieces in *In Our Time* is the story called "On the Quai at Smyrna." Hemingway describes the dying city and its victims with the precision of an eyewitness:

> You remember the harbor at Smyrna. There were plenty of nice things floating around in it. That was the only time in my life I got so I dreamed about things. You didn't mind the women who were having babies as you did those with the dead ones. They had them all right. Surprising how few died. . . . It was all a pleasant business. My word yes a most pleasant business.

Hemingway's famous technique of understatement for counterpoint, though it has a devastating aesthetic effect, perhaps suffers from its very virtues. Such drama needs direct statement rather than satire if the truth is not to be obscured. Yet it is no exaggeration to say that the spectacle of misery and suffering among the refugees left a permanent mark on Hemingway and put him on the side of the underdogs of the world. He told Malcolm Cowley that he "really learned about war" in the Near East. "I remember," he wrote thirty years later, "coming home from the Near East absolutely heartbroken at what was going on and in Paris trying to decide whether I would put my whole life into trying to do something about it or to be a writer." He decided "as cold as a snake, to be a writer and to write as truly as I could all my life." Hemingway never forgot what he saw and even when he had gained the adulation of the world, he always responded quickly and generously to grief and injustice. In his writing, at the heart of his hatred of fascism and tyranny smoldered the memory of those innocent victims of Mustafa Kemal and perhaps his predecessors. What went into his vision of such fictional figures as Lieutenant Henry, Harry Morgan, and Robert Jordan can be better appreciated against the background of the harsh and bitter reality that helped to create the conscience of a great writer and a compassionate human being, his so-called male chauvinism notwithstanding.

Another remarkable American novelist, Henry Miller, was also shocked by the Turkish brutality at Smyrna. In *The Colossus of Maroussi* (1941), an account of his visit to Greece, he writes:

> Every time I hear of the Smyrna catastrophe, of the stultification of manhood worked on the members of the armed forces of the great powers, who stood idly by . . . while thousands of innocent men, women, and children were driven into the water like cattle, shot at, mutilated, burned alive, their hands chopped off when they tried to climb aboard a foreign vessel, I think of that preliminary warning which I saw always in French cities . . . whenever a newsreel was shown of a bombing of a Chinese city.

In *The Rosy Crucifixion,* Miller depicts the squalorous and impoverished lives of the Armenian refugees in Athens, who despite their misfortune seem to move with a fierce and relentless energy. Deeply moved by the "holy glow" of their impoverished dwellings, Miller concludes: "Only in sorrow and suffering does man draw close to his fellow man." It is likely that an Armenian "soothsayer" whom Miller met there, one Aram Hourabedian, may have told Miller about the Smyrna catastrophe. In the "Plexus" volume of *The Rosy Crucifixion,* Miller draws upon his persona for the character of the mysterious guru Claude (and also on another Armenian, George Gurdjieff). Had Miller in those days enjoyed the widespread notoriety that he was to win later, his views might have stirred many of his readers, and he might have been remembered for his sympathy toward the Armenians rather than as a gifted pornographer.

A third young writer who would achieve fame later, John Dos Passos, gives us a grim picture of the murderous starvation that afflicted Turkish and Russian Armenia after the war, in a book first called *Orient Express* (1922), then republished under the ironic title of *The Best Times* in 1966. Dos Passos is traveling with an Armenian "whose mother, father, and three sisters were cut up into little pieces before his eyes by the Turks in Trebizond." A Turkish doctor in Ankara says to him:

> When Turkish soldiers get out of hand and kill a few Armenians who are
> spies and traitors, you roll your eyes and cry massacre, but when the
> Greeks burn defenseless villages and murder poor fishermen, it's making
> the world safe for democracy.

Dos Passos answers him in these words:

> The last Turkish attack, in 1920, on the villages near Alexandropol, had
> wiped the country clear; not a house intact in the villages, no crops, even
> the station buildings systematically destroyed, and everything moveable
> carried away. Even Genghis Khan and his Tartars couldn't have laid waste
> more thoroughly.

Unfortunately for the Armenian cause, all three writers had not
commanded the wide audiences who would later idolize them. Their
brief if powerful accounts did not raise a public outcry for justice or for
a tribunal to try the criminals. Oddly enough, not one of these percipient
writers realized that they were describing the birth of military operations
in which civilians and noncombatants were the chief targets.

A large number of missionaries had gone to Turkey to help the
survivors of the tragedy. One of them, Elgin Groseclose, upon his return
to the United States put down his impressions in a novel called *Ararat*
(1939). This book was the fullest treatment of the genocide in English
up to that time, but it was buried by the news that Europe was going
up in flames—World War II had started and Groseclose had to wait
more than twenty years to get a fair reading. When the book was
republished in the sixties, it received a National Book Award. Even in
paperback the novel about a Russian officer converted to the Armenian
cause attracted only a modest number of readers.

Nikos Kazantzakis, who earned the Nobel Prize for Literature, wrote
about the Armenian atrocities in *Toda Raba,* one of his early novels
(1939). As we might expect from a Greek writer, the Turks are villainous
and the Armenians heroic, in particular Azad, the Chekist gunman:
"What suffering he had endured! What suffering he had inflicted! . . .
Everywhere around him he created around him the tumultuous atmosphere
he required in order to breathe. Now he had returned to his own vast
land." The book is full of authentic details, even to the lines quoted
from Tumanian and the techniques of torture the Turks used on the
Armenians (shoeing them like horses, then setting them loose). Some
years later, Kazantzakis clothed Azad as a sheepherder and converted
him into his most famous creation, Zorba the Greek. Only the readers
of this novel know that Azad is brother to Zorba.

As every Armenian is aware, the most memorable novel about the genocide is Franz Werfel's *The Forty Days of Musa Dagh* (1933), now long a classic. During a trip to the Orient, Werfel, a Jewish writer born in Prague, visited Damascus, where the sight of the refugee children working in a carpet factory gave him "the final impulse to snatch from the Hades of all that was, the incomprehensible destiny of the Armenian nation" (preface). By the time he had completed the book three years later, the threat of a fascist state (which stalked the background of Werfel's previous work) had now emerged and was gaining power in Italy and Germany. The tragedy of the Armenians as imagined in *The Forty Days* would soon become reality for the Jews of Europe.

The novel concerns an assimilated Armenian living in Paris, who decides to go to Turkey and fight for his people near the site of the present-day Iskenderun. A small band of Armenians fend off superior Turkish forces and equipment until they are taken off the mountain of Moses by a French battleship. The book is based on fact—Werfel carefully studied the source material and was a friend of the French attaché, one Count Chauzel, who made available to the author documents dealing with the genocide, taken from the archives of the Ministry of War in Paris. Also, the account of Johannès Lepsius, the spokesman for the Armenian cause in the novel, served as material for two chapters and several episodes ("Mein Besuch in Constantinople," *Orient,* July-August 1919).

The actual siege lasted fifty-three days, according to reliable German sources. By changing the number to forty, Werfel made it clear that he was writing about the passion of the Armenian people: Moses fasted for forty days before climbing Sinai; for forty days the tribes of Israel wandered in the desert; Christ spent forty days in the wilderness before returning to his people. Thus Gabriel, the young Armenian from France, is cast both as a modern Moses leading his countrymen to safety and as a modern Christ prepared to lay down his life for others. Werfel's novel, for all its dramatic power, is not a large enough canvas to catch the tragic sweep of history. To many people, in spite of Werfel's efforts, Musa Dagh was an isolated episode rather than the tip of the iceberg.

A second holocaust, twenty five years after the first one in 1915, inspired a large number of novels in the following years, from *Exiles* to *The White Hotel.* Millions of people read them. Fiction may have been exploiting history, but the process was educational. It is hard to find a literate person who does not know that the Nazis slew up to 6 million Jews in concentration camps and in pitched battle. And it is possible that the attention these books received may have awakened some writers to the theme of the earlier and almost forgotten genocide. At any rate, during the postwar years, novelists began to incorporate into their works accounts of the Armenian massacres, sometimes brief, sometimes fairly lengthy, but almost always sympathetic (the fact that Russian Armenians fought on the side of the Allies and that Turkey remained a neutral friendly to the Axis may have helped some writers to choose sides).

Among the post-World War II generation of Armenian writers who are fluent in English, Leon Surmelian, Peter Sourian, Richard Hagopian, and Peter Najarian have written about the suffering of their people during the massacres and the aftermath. The anger of the previous generation of writers has been muted, but the sorrow and the sense of grief are unabated.

In France, Vahé Katcha is making thousands of readers of a later generation aware of the genocide. In England, Rose Macaulay in her witty novel *The Towers of Trebizond* writes: "The Turks had long since pronounced *delenda est* Armenia over this so unfortunately fragmented people, and did not care to hear them referred to." She travels to Armenia and is so impressed by the rebuilt country that she hates to leave when the time comes. Edward Whittemore's *Trilogy* gives considerable space to Armenian history and appears to be enchanted by Armenians of all classes and kinds. Alec Waugh seems fond of his reckless hero, Alex Belorian in *The Mule in the Minaret* (1965). Belorian puts his talent as a spy up for sale to the highest bidder, with one condition, which he explains to a Turkish student working for the Allies during World War II: "I don't care who wins or loses as long as it doesn't involve another Armenian massacre." Alec Waugh (who enjoyed *The Green Hat* immensely) apparently shared his brother Evelyn's admiration of the Christian survivors who withstood the Muslim whirlwind.

Among American writers of the postwar period, Elia Kazan devotes the early chapters of *America, America* to the cold-blooded murder of the Armenians of Anatolia—especially searing is a scene in which Armenians are herded into a church that is then set on fire. The novel is about a Greek family that emigrates to the New World, but Kazan seems equally concerned about the fate of the Armenians, who are indistinguishable from the Greeks—in fact, the protagonist takes the name of a dying Armenian as their boat approaches the Ellis Island immigrant station. Saul Bellow, in *The Adventures of Augie March,* gives the last chapters over to an Armenian lawyer who becomes Augie's guru. The lawyer tells Augie the sad history of his people and their fate at the hands of their Ottoman overlords. Clearly, Bellow saw the parallel between the genocide of the Armenians and the genocide of the Jews and generously chose to have Augie learn empathy for the victims of pathological authority from the almost-forgotten history of the Armenian genocide.

Sol Stein has written three novels centering on an Armenian lawyer named Thomassy. In *Other People,* he explains why he is taking on a case of rape:

> There'll be a lawyer at the accuser's side who is of Armenian extraction. Perhaps that lawyer has a strong feeling about rape because the Armenians, the first Christian community in modern times, were early in this century subjected to rape as well as murder by the Turks on a scale that, in your reflections, can only be described as genocide.

Among other writers of a popular vein who work anywhere from a paragraph to a page on the massacres into their novels are Joseph Wambaugh (*Onion Fields*), Irving Wallace, Ivan Gold (*Sick Friends*), Sandra Hochman (*Walking Papers*), Ivan Morris (*Liberty Street*—a fine novel that never got the attention it deserved because it was published in 1944), Herman Wouk (*Youngblood Hawke*), and Cyrus Sulzberger (*The Tooth Merchant*—not a terribly good novel whose hero, an Armenian survivor, talks at the drop of a hat about his people's sad history). Now with increasing frequency, accounts of the massacres are woven into novels of intrigue that deal with the Cold War or with the Middle East—there is an Armenian presence in both—but usually these accounts are incidental to the main action and the reader may feel that they have been inserted rather than integrated into the plot. Ironically, the best-known book in recent years on the genocide is by the former television commentator Michael Arlen, Jr., the son of the novelist. In almost every instance cited above, the author seems to have freshly stumbled on the facts of the Armenian genocide and seems eager to convey them to the reader regardless of whether they fit into the design of the book.

A writer of international background, the late Arthur Koestler gave prominence to the tragic fate of the Armenians in *The Age of Longing* and *The Invisible Writing.* More than any writer with the exception of Franz Werfel, he took the trouble to acquaint himself intimately with the facts and showed the sympathy and insight of a man who has spiritually relived the Armenian experience. The dominant character in *The Age of Longing* is an extraordinary Armenian cobbler called "Grandfather Arin," who is an active member of the Hnchakist, "the secret society which aimed at the resurrection of a free, independent Armenia." Koestler described his tragic past: "On Christmas Day, anno domini 1895, twelve hundred Armenians, men, women, and children, were burnt alive in the Cathedral of Urfa. Grandfather Arin escaped by a miracle, but his wife and his six children died in the flames." It seems likely that Koestler's more immediate inspiration was the incineration of the Jews by the Nazis and the similar fate that befell many Armenians in 1915 and 1922. Koestler's strength as a writer was his ability to make fresh connections, to recognize how one event could be the harbinger of another like it.

Elias Canetti, who also won a Nobel Prize, entitled one volume of his autobiography *The Tongue Set Free.* Canetti, a Jew born in Constantinople, describes the rage of an Armenian survivor awaiting the judgment of justice on his persecutors. The ax-wielding Armenian is the first refugee that he has met and his love for him becomes the affection for all displaced persons in his future life. Canetti writes: "When I asked my mother why he was so sad, she said that bad people had wanted to kill all the Armenians in Istanbul, and he had lost his entire family. He had watched from a hiding place when they had killed his sister." Most recently, D. M. Thomas has followed *The White Hotel,* a novel about a survivor of the Jewish holocaust, with a novel-within-a-novel called *Ararat.* One reviewer described it as "a maelstrom of nightmares with Armenia at its center." A character named Finn compulsively recounts his role at Babi Yar, the Nazi concentration camps, at Erzerum, and Trebizond. "I've never really retired," the shadowy traveler remarks. "One becomes indispensable." Thomas has written letters to the London *Times* objecting to the Turkish revisionist views of the genocide.

Barry Unsworth's splendid novel *The Rage of the Vulture* is set in the declining years of the Ottoman Empire and describes the Armenian massacres that ravaged Constantinople in 1896. Unsworth's deep feeling for the fate of the Armenians raises this book to the level of genuine tragedy. The scene in which the Turks gang-rape his Armenian fiancée before his eyes while he watches passively becomes a symbol of all the atrocities committed by the Turks.

The heroine of James Clavell's bestseller, *Noble House,* is Casey Tcholok, a young, beautiful, cultured financial wizard who comes to Hong Kong with her business partner with the intention of taking over the giant corporations of that city. It turns out that Tcholok is a short version of her real name, Tcholakian, and that her maiden name was Kamalian Ciranoush. She tells her uninformed associates the story of her people:

> "My people were spread all over the Ottoman Empire, about two million, but the massacres, particularly in 1915 and 16." Casey shivered. "It was genocide really. . . . There were nearly 50,000 Armenians in the Turkish Army before they were disarmed, outcast and shot by Turks during World

War I—generals, officers, and soldiers. They were an elite minority and had been for centuries."

"Is that why the Turks hated them?" de Ville asked.

"They were hardworking and clannish and very good traders and businessmen for sure. . . . But perhaps the main reason is that the Armenians are Christians—they were the first Christian state in history under the Romans—and of course the Turks are Mohammedan."

To summarize: between the wars, the massacres barely registered on the literary imagination. *Ararat* by Elgin Groseclose went unread until the sixties. Hemingway, Miller, and Dos Passos, and several other writers advert to the events but show no deep curiosity about the history behind them. There is almost a total absence of rational analysis even in the minds of the characters or in the dialogue. Franz Werfel was the one writer who explored the meaning of these tragic circumstances, though he confined himself to a relatively minor action in western Turkey (the real business took place chiefly in central and eastern Turkey). The Armenian writers of this period, with the exception of William Saroyan, had not yet had their tongues set free (to borrow a phrase from Canetti).

After World War II, once the concept of genocide was argued and defined at the United Nations, it became obvious to any intelligent observer that the Armenians had undergone a golgotha twenty years earlier than the Jews of Europe. A number of writers used the tragic events of 1915 as "set pieces" in their novels. Among the most responsive to the Armenian holocaust were the Jewish writers, who seemed to understand the importance of remembering these events better than any other ethnic group except the Armenians themselves.

9

The Impact of the Genocide on
West Armenian Letters

Vahé Oshagan

From 1750 to 1915, the West Armenians used a colossal amount of idealism and energy to awaken from four centuries of slumber. And they did wake up under the combined effect of European contacts and ethnic traditions. Within a short time, from 1840 to 1875, they had forged an adequate literary language, set up a network of schools, newspapers, journals, charitable and cultural organizations, public libraries, and museums.[1] Most important of all, an intelligentsia of sorts had come into existence, many of them European-trained professionals, and had taken in hand the affairs of the communities in the Ottoman Empire. Also, some intellectual ties had been established with the Young Ottomans, with French political and literary circles, as well as with the East Armenians in tsarist Russia.[2] A secular literature had begun to flourish around 1840, decades before that of the Ottoman Turks or the Arabs. Poetry, lyrical and epic, classical and romantic drama, novels, short stories—all the genres had taken a start, gathering momentum during the century as the educated public grew in number, the translation of European best-sellers increased and flooded the market, and the twin Mekhitarist Congregations in Venice and Vienna brought their passion for scholarship and the life of letters into closer contact with the Armenian intelligentsia.[3] Then, around 1885, a decline of some twenty years set in, under the effect of repression and state censorship.

The widespread massacres of 1894-96, which claimed some 200,000 lives, were the first real contact most Armenian writers had with Turkish brutality. These massacres were like a dress rehearsal for the real genocide of 1915, and the writers did not fail to respond to the shock. The literature at the turn of the century is in the main one of idealism and of violence, a poetry of fire and passion, short stories and novels of a

167

political nature, all expressing the horror and the revolt but making no effort to draw any meaning or message from the national experience. Then in 1909 another massacre occurred in Adana that took around 30,000 victims, but the literary reaction was again an outpouring of pathos and woe. By now, these killings and disillusionment with Europe to solve the Armenian Question moved the literati to readjust their values respecting Western models and the world of the present. There was a general mood to return to the glorious past and to seek fresh inspiration as well as self-respect in the pagan, heroic history of the ancestors of the race.[4] This step into refusal of a "brutal world," into isolation seems to have given the writers the necessary spiritual incentive for artistic maturation, for, in those ten years preceding the 1915 massacres, all five major West Armenian poets made their appearance—Taniel Varoujan, Siamanto, Misak Medsarents, Diran Tchirakian, and Vahan Tekeyan. Only one, Tekeyan, was destined to survive the genocide.

So, by 1915, the West Armenians had some reason for pride. The century of toil, sacrifice, and dedication had borne fruit and an intelligentsia of around a thousand souls made up of writers, poets, actors, musicians, painters, journalists, teachers, educated professionals, and intellectuals graced the coarse fabric of Armenian life. In the seven years following the overthrow of Sultan Abdul-Hamid II, from 1908 to 1915, no fewer than 135 books were published by the Armenians in the Ottoman Empire, as many as in the preceding twenty-five years. Armenians, middle class and professional, occupied key posts in the economic life of the empire while many others reached positions of power in the Ottoman civil service. All in all, Armenians saw themselves at a higher cultural and social level than most peoples of the empire, although their contacts with them were rather superficial. The apparent end of the tyranny increased the general optimism.

Despite this state of euphoria, the mood of the people was conservative and traditionalist. In day-to-day life, the average Armenian felt crushed by the Turk and yet nowhere in Armenian literature is this Turk present. This kind of inhibition at work in the literary consciousness is also at the root of the deep-seated mistrust Armenians have always had for artistic experimentation, avant-garde tendencies, dissent in any form whatsoever, a mood that surfaces at this time. Finally, the period is characterized by the great extension taken by satirical literature as well as the popularity of political journalism.[5] Such is the general picture in the spring of 1915, on the eve of the massacres, with the Armenians oblivious of the doom hanging over their heads.

On the night of 24 April 1915, Turkish police quietly and very politely rounded up almost to a man this entire intelligentsia in Constantinople and other major cities and proceeded to deport and destroy 250 that night; the figure rose to 600 in a few days. Almost all the great names in Armenian letters—Krikor Zohrab, Varoujan, Roupen Zartarian, Tlgadintzi, Siamanto, Roupen Sevag, and others—disappeared in the carnage. Parallel to this, the genocide of the population killed off about 1.5 million out of a total of some 2.5 million.

Besides the loss of life, the genocide cost the Armenians their entire cultural infrastructure—countless libraries and artifacts, priceless manuscripts, more than 1,100 churches and monasteries totally demolished and 691 partially destroyed, 1,717 convents and churches ransacked, property looted and occupied.[6] And, of course, the loss of their historic fatherland, perhaps the one irreplaceable, nonnegotiable component of the Armenian reality.

The Armenian nation had been crushed but not destroyed, not defeated, although the overall picture was very grim and hopeless indeed. Almost overnight, a huge, sprawling diaspora had come into shaky existence with hundreds of thousands of ungainly, undernourished orphans housed in bleak orphanages, shaken by nightmares, crying out for affection, while other masses, dazed, traumatized remnants of the slaughter, tried to get a foothold in the world, mainly in the Middle East. The one and overriding imperative of the first decades, until the 1930s, was *survival*. The Armenians had no options left in life, no choices. Everything had to be sacrificed to win the fight against starvation, despair, and assimilation. The only reason for optimism was the innate stamina and intelligence of the race that showed themselves very quickly in the economic revival and the communal reorganization of the survivors in the host countries.

It is during those morbid and desperate years that postgenocide literature was born. The decade saw the emergence in the media of mainly young poets calling for the basic satisfactions of life, for love, dignity, and above all for a home. From Helsinki to Djibouti, passing through Berlin, Paris, Athens, Beirut, and Rio de Janeiro, the same pitiful yearning fills the writings of these orphans, mostly devoid of talent. The prose is also very crude, while drama is almost nonexistent. This first decade is the most sterile period in modern Armenian literature. The reasons are many; perhaps some of them could be found in the general mood of the people and its leaders. In the past, Armenian psychology had shown clear signs of isolationism from the "hostile" world, something approaching paranoia, and the massacres, the gloom following the dispersion had had the effect of intensifying this collective feeling. As a result, intolerance, xenophobia, authoritarianism, sexism, and purism became more and more widespread in Armenian life, while the fear and the hatred of the Turk turned into almost obsessive feelings. People became more narrow-minded, averse to change, and submissive to authority, represented at that time by the church and the political parties, which decided every issue in national life. Thus, caught up by these feelings, the Armenian masses turned their backs to the world, and clinging to slogans such as *Haiabahbanum* (preservation of Armenianness), *Hai hoki* (the Armenian spirit), *jermag chart* (white massacre or the need for resistance to assimilation), *gensabaikar* (fight for survival), soon isolated themselves within the host cultures, trying vainly to recreate, or at least to preserve, the ideals of the heroic, good old days, the memory of the pregenocide national life.

It is not difficult to weigh the devastating effect of such a state of mind on the arts and letters. For close to fifteen years, literature was stifled until, around the 1930s, a sudden break appeared in Paris. In a wild reaction against their elders, whom they blamed for their misfortunes and humiliation, a group of talented young orphans founded a journal called *Menk* (We) and proceeded to attack the sacred taboos in Armenian life, the establishment of their times, such as it was, and the artistic values of the West Armenians. A decade of acrimonious debates and bitter infighting between the young rebels and the old generation of writers who had managed to escape the massacres, produced one major book—*Nahanche Arants Yerki* (Retreat without song). This novel by the young writer Shahan Shahnur had one dominant theme, despair at the prospects of Armenian survival, and is a direct product of the negativism and pessimism engendered by the massacres. The book's appeal was immense and immediate, which reflects the dispositions of the demoralized masses, but needless to add, fifty years after its publication, the book's basic premises appear unfounded, even though it itself had been a powerful factor working against survival.

By and large, however, the other writers of the group shunned this theme, content to grapple with their private tragedies, although their writings all draw a certain anxiety and a feeling of insecurity from their common Armenian experience and their ambiguous attitude toward French culture, which they rejected all the while being attracted by it.[7] The verse of the most gifted poet Nigoghos Sarafian highlights the disarray of the inner forces and of the sense of destiny of the nation. During the following decades, the center of cultural gravity of the Armenians shifted to the Middle East communities, which by then had become well established. The anguish and the yearning for affection had disappeared but not the feeling of spiritual insecurity and self-pity, nor the complex of being a persecuted and victimized nation. These were the reasons that the literature of that period remained ethnocentric and highly emotional, repetitive of the pregenocide themes and style, refusing to accept the new values in letters, rejecting all efforts of stylistic innovation, and closed to the direct experience of the massacres.

This total adherence of the writers of the Middle East to the imperatives of survival has been repeated in various ways in the other communities as well, mainly because after the end of the war, these communities assumed the role of leaders in national life. Apart from some young writers of today, almost all poets and novelists have paid tribute to the virtues of the race, have extolled the purely moral and emotional aspects of Armenian culture, have glorified the church as the main bastion of survival, have praised the reality and the ideal of the fatherland, indulging in highly sentimental yearning for Armenia, and in one way or another adhered to the traditions and ideology of the ruling classes. This ideology can be stated in the following manner. We Armenians are virtuous and innocent people, the first Christian nation on earth, victims of Turkish barbarity. The Turk is the anti-Christ and the rest of the world is hardly better. This world is a hostile place for us and a good Armenian will associate only with other Armenians. Our artists should rally round the struggle for survival and serve the higher interests of the nation.

Such has been the national ideology. The genocide did not create it but made it an absolute, which for fifty years set the criteria in letters from the Far East to the Far West. No writer dared face the reality of the massacres let alone draw from it any message, neither for the Armenians nor for the rest of mankind. That was the main reason that almost all literature in the United States from 1920 on aimed at recreating a pregenocide, rural, and idyllic world, as if the massacres had never taken place and the writers were living in the villages of their childhood.[8] The overall picture of diaspora literature is one of a nation living under a spell, mesmerized by the moral pain and the humiliation of the atrocious event, the catastrophe where everything ends and nothing begins, even after half a century. Almost hypnotized by their suffering, Armenians could not fully use their creative powers, could not think about or describe the experience but only repeat that something beyond words had happened to them, something unnamable, almost magical. Through the years, countless eyewitness accounts, ritualistic commemorations and ceremonies, annual speeches, lamentations, and church services maintained alive the feeling of some mysterious calamity that had molded the individuals together. There was hardly an Armenian family in the diaspora that did not have its tale of Turkish hell and its horrors. This suffering held the Armenians together, gave them strength, and assured their survival.

Yet all is not impotence. Some of the elder writers who survived the genocide have at least faced the challenges. Two are noteworthy, though both have failed. First was Vahan Tekeyan, a major West Armenian poet. He was not an eyewitness of the massacres but much of what he wrote after 1915 bears the stamp of an exile suffering in solitude, haunted by the past and unable to accept the present. His writing carries the effect of the event that, itself, is absent. A poet of love, Tekeyan was perhaps the least suited of all to express Armenian suffering, but he did it, pity, compassion, and frustrated rage choking him all the while as he tried to express the national emotion and the enormity of the inhuman experience. Yet his poems show no hatred for the Turk, nor does he make an effort to understand the catastrophe. He has some timid lines of revolt against God and mankind, but his powerful works are poems of hope for the future, poems of grief for the dead, and pleas for justice for his people. Hardly ever does he transcend the Armenian ethos to feel the event as a larger, purely human experience, set in the context of world history. Perhaps the pain is too fresh or the poet is too close to the events—in any case, his suffering is so intense that it closes him even further within himself, making him a kind of prototype of the reaction of the entire nation. In a sense, Tekeyan becomes the conscience of the Armenian people and this identification is nowhere so apparent as in the short poem entitled "We Shall Say to God" (1917):

> Should it happen we do not endure
> this uneven fight and drained
> of strength and agonized
> we fall on death's ground, not to rise
> and the great crime ends
> with the last Armenian eyes
> closing without seeing a victorious day,
> let us swear that when we find
> God in his paradise offering comfort
> to make amends for our pain,
> let us swear that we will refuse
> saying No, send us to hell again.
> We choose hell. You made us know it well.
> Keep your paradise for the Turk.[9]

What is remarkable about this poem is the total absence of hatred for the Turk. This spirit, and the hope and need for a new start, characterize not only the poetry of Tekeyan but also that of some of the best writers of the diaspora, such as Nigoghos Sarafian, Leon Surmelian, and Gostan Zarian. This fact appears to be the best sign so far that the creative slump of the last fifty years may be coming to an end.

The second important survivor is Hagop Oshagan, the prose writer, the only major writer who knew the Turk well enough to write about the massacres, having lived among the Turks in his native rural region and also in Constantinople, where he was hounded by the police for three years before escaping to Bulgaria in 1918. The genocide turned Oshagan the short-story writer into a novelist, and he produced eleven dense volumes of novels anchored in the Armenian experience in Turkey from 1894 to 1915. This oeuvre is the most ambitious fictional enterprise in Armenian letters to date and recreates in Balzacian fashion the gradual transformation of the Armenian rural society into an urban society, the whole process set against the background of Turkish repression, Armenian revolutionary activity in the Ottoman Empire, and the racial antagonism between Turks and Armenians.[10] This pregenocide canvas, which captures all the complex atavistic and Freudian drives at work in the Turkish psyche as well as the mythological structures of the cultural life of the Armenian rural populations, was in fact meant to serve as an introduction to his major opus, *Hell,* which is about the great massacres of 1915-18. In February 1948 as he was about to set off to explore the sites of the slaughter at Deir el Zor in Syria, a heart attack put an end to his life.

For Oshagan, peoples and literatures live through myths that often change or die in time. In the case of the Armenians, old myths of the pre-1915 society have reached the end of their life span but continue to live on and so no new urban myths can be born. The 1915 Turkish genocide ended the old world by giving rise to the diaspora, but the prolongation of the mythic cycles of the old world into modern times has prevented the birth of the real diaspora. Oshagan wants to end the old world and this can be done only through a work of art that conquers the irrational event called the catastrophe that haunts the consciousness and the literary imagination of the Armenians.[11] Until that happens, the "murder" will continue unabated, no new myths will come to life to structure the life of the Armenians and hence no solid literary work will be born. In a word, Oshagan places the Armenian tragedy within the vaster human experience in which Turks and Armenians enact age-old myths of death and birth, murder and punishment, passion and tradition. But he never lived to carry out his plan. "One day," he has written, "the Turks will have to read my books to understand who they are."

The theme of the most horrid experience a people can go through awaits its master and masterpiece. To date, there have been several eyewitness accounts of the deportations and massacres, but being devoid of literary value, they do not interest us. Writers of the first diaspora generation have published scores of books describing their childhood experiences prior to the massacres, usually in an idealized and lyrical style. Many have written also about the suffering endured in the orphanages and in early youth in the aftermath of the deportations and the killings. These are valuable contributions to Armenian letters and some (the childhood memories of Leon Surmelian and Vahan Totovents, among others) have been published in English.[12] But about the actual genocide, the trip to hell and back, there is no artistic work. It is true that few writers have survived to tell the tale, but then, in literature, actual experience is hardly a prerequisite for creation. The fact is that the magnitude of the suffering, both physical and moral, seems to stagger the imagination and the sheer bestiality appears to crush the creative powers of most writers. Franz Werfel's *The Forty Days of Musa Dagh* is but a pale echo of the atrocious reality. The recent novel by Vahé Katcha, *Un Poignard dans ce jardin,* is anything but a work of literature.

In conclusion, we can say that almost seventy years after the catastrophe, the Armenian literary imagination has still not been able to grapple with the reality of the pain and of death and has not formulated the human message. In a sense, the genocide is a privileged experience that puts an added duty on a people to share its central truth, not to say its message, with the rest of mankind. So far, the Armenians have not been in a position to rise to that challenge, often letting political imperatives and passions, the thirst for vengeance, absorb all their energies. Perhaps some consolation can be drawn from the fact that the Turks have been punished after all because the abject coverup and refusal to admit their guilt has, for seventy years, poisoned the Turkish elites. Another fact is the cultural value of a diaspora (a direct result of the genocide), which, for small nations choked by powerful neighbors, offers a possibility to participate, through its colonies, in spiritual life of all advanced nations.

But that is a double-edged sword, for in a reflex of self-defense, the literary intelligentsia has turned its back to the world and, as a consequence, has largely failed to mature. Most diaspora writing today is a modernized version of the pregenocide aesthetics. But there are signs of change, and young writers of today with no psychological blocks, independent-minded and open to the world of influences, have begun to heed their own literary conscience rather than that of the public.

The Armenians have weathered the genocide but the cost has been enormous in artistic and human terms. A great deal has yet to be done to stop the continuing effects that inhibit the complete flowering of artistic talent. A fresh start in life and letters is becoming more and more urgent; otherwise the genocide will pursue its terrible course, and bitterness and anger will continue to restrict the creative powers. What choices do Armenians have? Now that the battle for survival has largely been won, a viable course between anger on one hand and forgetting on the other will have to be found.

Much depends on the native vitality and the basic moral traditions of the Armenians, as well as on the course of historic events in decades to come. We can say with some assurance that once they have recovered their ancestral homelands, the Armenians will be able to heal the wounds and gradually dilute the poison. Then, and only then, will their creative energies be set free to function to the full.

Notes

1. By 1876, there were fifty-three Armenian schools in Constantinople alone (the Armenian population of the capital was around 100,000) with 5,620 students. All schools were free, mixed, and public or church supported (the minorities in the Ottoman Empire were allowed to open schools only after 1789—see Arshag Alboyadjian, "Fifty Years of Education," *Puzantion*, no. 2229, 1903). There were also more than a hundred charitable and educational societies for financing the schools. By 1863, fifteen public and neighborhood libraries had been set up in Constantinople. By the same date, twenty-five newspapers had been put into circulation; by 1884, this number had risen to eighty-eight. In 1900, there were six dailies and eight monthlies in Constantinople alone.

2. Sharif Mardin, *The Young Ottomans* (Princeton: Princeton University Press, 1962), gives details of Krikor Odian's relations with the Young Ottomans in Paris.

3. Some of the best-sellers were *René* and *Atala* (F.-R. de Chateaubriand); *Les Aventures de Télémaque* (F. Fénelon); *Le Comte de Monte-Cristo* and *Les Trois Mousquetaires* (Alexandre Dumas): *Les Mystères de Paris and Le Juif errant* (Eugène Sue); *Notre-Dame de Paris, Lucrèce Borgia,* and *Les Misérables* (Victor Hugo); *L'Avare* (Molière); *Raphaël* (A. de Lamartine); *Micromégas* (Voltaire); *Le Tour du monde en quatre-vingt jours* and *L'Isle mystérieuse* (Jules Verne); *Werther* (Goethe); *Gulliver's Travels* (Jonathan Swift); and *Ivanhoe* (Walter Scott).

4. Some of the publications with pagan associations were the journals *Navasart* (the name of the first month of the Armenian calendar), *Mehian* (Pagan temple), *Pakin* (Pagan altar); the books *Hetanos Yerker* (Pagan songs) and *Tseghin Sirde* (The heart of the race) by Taniel Varoujan, *Khorhurtneru Mehian* (Temple of mysteries) by Hagop Oshagan; and a play *Hin Asdvadsner* (Antique gods) by Levon Shant.

5. Satire, the weapon of the underdog, has always been popular with the Armenians. At this time, the popularity of Yervant Odian, the prolific satirical writer, is at its zenith.

6. Le Centre d'information Arménien, *Les Arméniens se souviennent* (Beirut: Centre, 1965), p. 47.

7. The following were some of the most outspoken: Shahan Shahnur, Vazken Shushanian, Nigoghos Sarafian, Shavarsh Nartuni, Nshan Beshigtashlian, Hrach Sarkisian, Zareh Vorpuni.

8. Such is the literature of the most gifted writers—Hamasdegh, Aram Haigaz, Peniamin Nurigian, Vahé Haig.

9. See *Anthology of Armenian Poetry*, trans. and ed. Diana Der Hovanessian and Marzbed Margossian (New York: Columbia University Press, 1978), p.

172. Vahan Tekeyan died in 1945, but a great number of young poets have carried the influence of his art into our times.

10. The most celebrated is the saga-novel *Mnatsortats* (To those remaining). A short, dramatic passage has been translated by A. Sevag and published in *Ararat* 34, no. 1 (1983).

11. See M. Nishanian, "From Myth to the Novel," ibid.

12. The most celebrated of these books are Leon Z. Surmelian's *I Ask You, Ladies and Gentlemen* (New York: Dutton, 1945) and Vahan Totovents's *Scenes from an Armenian Childhood,* trans. M. Kudian (London: Oxford University Press, 1962).

10

Psychosocial Sequelae of the Armenian Genocide

Levon Boyajian and *Haigaz Grigorian*

Although there is a substantial literature on survivors of the Jewish Holocaust, we know of only two formal efforts to deal with the psychological impact of the Armenian genocide on survivors and their offspring. We are not aware of any other than English literature on this subject. Alen Salerian's material was obtained through interviews with ten Armenian genocide survivors and their offspring from the Washington, D.C., area and taped interviews of Armenian-American survivors recorded as part of an oral history project on the Armenian genocide.[1] Salerian, in addition, includes observations of Armenian survivors whom he has known personally. Aside from their personal observations and Grigorian's in-depth interviews with a survivor who sought him out for treatment, the authors were involved in a two-day conference that focused on the sequelae of the Armenian genocide. The conference consisted of testimony by two survivors followed by several formal historical and sociopolitical presentations regarding the Armenian genocide and genocide in general. Subsequently, roundtable discussions and interviews were conducted by a psychologist and several psychiatrists with a survivor who had recently published a book about his childhood experiences during the genocide and with children of survivors, mature adults at this time. The open discussions continued to include several authors as well as other persons of the generation of Armenians who are children of survivors and two grandchildren.

In a series of articles beginning in 1961, Niederland and others have reported their findings and described "the survivor syndrome."[2] We have learned much from our colleagues who have studied the Jewish Holocaust, and these studies have helped us in our understanding of the survivors of the Armenian genocide. It is clear, both from our own observations and from those of Salerian, that many of the characteristic features of the survivor syndrome as described by Niederland are present in the survivors of the Armenian genocide. Despite the similarities, however, there seem to be more important differences in the survivors of these massive traumatizations.

Three major manifestations of the survivor syndrome are (1) survivor guilt, (2) anxiety symptoms, and (3) reactive depression. Anhedonia, hypermnesia, and persistent nightmares have also been described as common.

Survivor guilt manifests itself in different forms with each stage of the life cycle. Bedros Norehad related his experience as follows: "I stand before you with apologies. I live because I was fortunate enough to be the student of an American school"—apologies for surviving! The guilt feelings of survivors do not clear up completely even with therapeutic intervention. Kerop Bedoukian, who was the author of the book *Some of Us Survived,* stated: "There are a lot of scars, and I haven't been able to resolve them."[3] Niederland, in referring to symptoms of survivors states, "The psychological and physical traumas of persons brutally persecuted, incarcerated, and tortured rarely heal."

In the family of one of the authors, there was a very strong belief that the good ones had died during the genocide, and this left them with the feeling that they were not worthy of having survived.

Sometimes survivor guilt becomes manifest in depressed survivors years later when a fellow survivor dies or moves away. The loss of a fellow survivor reactivates the early losses and precipitates survivor guilt. This phenomenon has been observed among several survivors, who after leaving their adopted countries, have migrated to the United States in the past twenty years. In spite of the good fortune that came their way, these survivors showed extreme discomfort at enjoying their good fortune and freedom, as if enjoyment would bring punishment, misfortune, and disaster.

Salerian makes a point of the inability of Armenian survivors to enjoy the fruits of their labor and their good fortune in having emigrated to the United States. "Feelings of disappointment and generalized anhedonia, not enjoying life, persisted, and it seemed that this was a result of complex psychological mechanisms, including guilt, depression, and unresolved anger that clearly interfered with the survivors' ability to enjoy what they had accomplished."

Survivors have reported alterations in their sense of identity, which also has been described by Niederland in survivors of the Holocaust. Norehad indicated, "Although we survived, we had been robbed of our Armenian identity and our Christian faith. Therefore, every moment we lived in that totally Turkish environment was nothing but a sham and a lie." This was a reaction to being put in a Turkish orphanage and being trained, along with other Armenian children, to accept the Muslim faith. Bedoukian described it as a form of despair. Upon arriving in Canada as a young man, he went to live on a farm, and began to believe and feel that there were no more Armenians left in the world, and therefore, his own identity was in serious danger.

Anxiety is part of the posttraumatic stress disorder precipitated by the genocide. In 1966, Chodoff reported that survivors aged twenty to thirty chiefly manifested chronic anxiety states, and that in those aged thirty to forty, chronic depression had been most prominent.[4] His explanation was that in the first group, the survivors had to deal with the loss of parents, grandparents, and siblings; in the older age group, loss of children and spouses. The survivors of the Armenian genocide, who have been studied in these recent years, primarily fall into the earlier category but seem to manifest a mixture of the two sets of symptoms described by Chodoff. Hypermnesia is very easily discernible in the survivors of 1915, as well as the frequent sense of detachment from the horrifying events occurring around them. The two seem to go together. The events are witnessed with an absence of affect, and simultaneously, they are indelibly imprinted, never to be forgotten, frequently to be recalled, and often accompanied by persistent nightmares.

At the time of the massacres, Kerop Bedoukian was a nine-year-old boy, and he describes his feelings of security as, "I had a strong-willed mother and just as strong-willed older sister. As long as they were within my sight, I had no fear." However, he experienced feelings of insecurity and anxiety whenever his mother or sister began to show despair. He also describes the ability sometimes to have been an observer rather than a person subjected to pain during the massacres, which was clearly a psychological defense against anxiety and pain.

The psychic vulnerability of survivors was described by Bedoukian in the form of pictures coming to his mind whenever a particular event took place that had its tragic counterpart during the massacres. One such event was the handing over of a baby to a soldier, which ended with the brutal death of the infant. He has never forgotten this horror and experiences the image and pain every time he witnesses the common passing of a baby from one person to another. He has described other such events that he constantly recalls.

A very frequently reported phenomenon has also been the need of survivors as they approach the end of their lives to make testimony of what they experienced and witnessed, in a sense, to come to terms with themselves. Bedoukian emphasizes the writing of his book with the quote, "Thank goodness I have paid my debt."

One of the authors saw a man clinically who was seventy-nine years old and had sought out an Armenian-speaking psychiatrist because he had the urgent feeling that he should talk about his life. He had been fourteen years old during the genocide, and all those years he had kept his story to himself. He was having frequent nightmares and wanted to unburden himself. After three hours of relating his experiences in detail, he left the office, and reported in the following session that for the first time in a year he had been able to sleep through the night without an anxiety attack.

Another major form of symptomatology described among survivors is reactive depression and depressive life-styles. Among Armenian survivors seen clinically for the treatment of depression, there is a frequent concomitant reactivation of some components of the trauma experienced during the massacres. For example, if a loved one had been killed during the massacres, the depressed survivor will ruminate about that person and mourn that loss over and over again.

So far we have concentrated on the similarities of individual adjustment of the survivor. However, the culture into which the survivor immigrates is just as important in the understanding of his or her adjustment. The survivor who ended up in Persia versus the survivor who ended up in the United States—how isolated each was from the church and compatriotic communities and organizations was an important factor in adjustment. A survivor family that ended up in Kansas where there were no other Armenian families became isolated and very reluctant to talk about its experiences during the massacres. However, the survivors who settled in large Armenian communities had the opportunity to mourn together and have commemorations annually on April 24 through religious and cultural events.

From his studies in the kibbutz, Klein points out that collective mourning integrates the generations and the community, and provides feedback through which the individual can affirm his or her own feelings.[5] This affirmation, a vital aspect of sharing, is continuously reexperienced by Holocaust survivor families.

The knowledge acquired from the Jewish Holocaust helps us to understand the psychosocial implications of the Armenian genocide. However, Stanley L. Rustin points out that no generalization regarding the survivors is a safe generalization.[6] The background, coping mechanisms, and any therapeutic work being done with the survivor must start with setting aside stereotyping and prejudging of the survivor. The authors nonetheless believe that sensitivity and knowledge of common characteristics might be useful in enhancing a feeling of well-being.

Several themes emerge regarding the children of survivors, some of which are similar or identical to those experienced by the children of the Jewish Holocaust.[7] In the opening pages of her book regarding the children of the Holocaust, Helen Epstein writes about the feeling of dark secrets within her about the experiences of her parents, and of her need at least to explore these hidden recesses.[8] For Armenian children of survivors of the genocide, a dominant theme that emerges is the feeling of being "special"; special in the sense that there is an obligation that was placed upon them directly or indirectly, to be the bearers of the hopes and aspirations, not only of a given family but of a whole people. A striking similarity to the Jewish experience expressed by one Armenian man was the feeling that his bodily integrity had to be maintained at all cost; that he was such a precious item to his parents that he could not take the ordinary risks other children did at play, and had to make sure he stayed whole and healthy. This was carried through to the point that there was a sense of relief and freedom when his parents died. This observation of overprotectiveness is common to the children of survivors.[9]

Furthermore, many of the children bear the names of dead relatives, that is grandparents, aunts, uncles, and in some cases even lost or killed siblings. Along with the names some carried a sense of shame and guilt for having survived while those less fortunate perished in unspeakable ways.

The children also grew up in many instances with a sense that life was a serious business; that because of this past and the sufferings of their parents, they were required to be serious and in some sense, almost sad; that they did not have the right to be happy and cheerful. Of course, they have all experienced directly the sadness and the tears of their own parents. It should be further made clear that the sadness of the survivors themselves goes beyond the simple loss of family and friends to include and encompass the total loss and wiping out of one's home and homeland, transportation to an alien land, and no foreseeable hope for a return to one's roots. This sense of total loss of one's origins plays a significant role in the psychological experiences of the surviving generations of Armenians, and will be touched upon below.

Another theme that emerges is the issue of martyrdom and victimization. Whatever else might be said about the experience of survivors, there is no doubt that "martyrdom" plays a major role in that identification with the past. Bedoukian described the survivors as heroes and those who did not survive as martyrs. The reason he characterized the latter as martyrs was that they may have saved themselves by becoming Muslims but did not. His intent was to elevate the victims to what he considered the proper spiritual recognition. Michael Arlen expressed the view that perhaps this dwelling upon martyrdom may be less than desirable for two reasons: (1) that it may not truly be martyrdom, and (2) that the martyr willingly or unwillingly places a burden upon those who survive.[10] Furthermore, was it really martyrdom, or was it simply victimization and being the recipients of much hatred? The idea of martyrdom also may promote the notion of persons going to their death without resistance. To the extent that the choice was present and was made by many to die rather than give up their faith, the designation of martyrdom must be given. Whether it can be universally applied seems to be irrelevant.

Connected with these ideas clearly is the shame associated with being a persecuted and despised people, that is, within the Ottoman Empire. Even more complicated for the survivors, in the diaspora and particularly in the Western world, is the total lack of general knowledge of what transpired. Thus, a peculiar burden is placed upon the children and, to a lesser extent, the grandchildren of survivors, who may feel a familial obligation to maintain their ethnic identity. This in its diluted and uninformed aspect becomes a people who were slaughtered and expelled from their homeland for no "apparent reason" and who subsequently were known as "starving Armenians." What an identity to maintain!

One of the questions raised is, does the pendulum swing the other way? Do some of the children say, "Forget it all. I don't want to have anything to do with that background. I want to deny my identity as an Armenian. I will become totally involved with my adopted land, and have nothing to do with the past." That, too, is a solution that has been used by some. For obvious reasons, an evaluation and study of those individuals would be extremely valuable but very difficult to secure.

Because of the historical differences between the public recognition of the events of the Jewish Holocaust and the denial of the Armenian genocide by the Turks, the impact upon the subsequent generations is very different. The issue of Armenian identity and insistence upon the recognition of that event by the world plays a central role in the identity formation of subsequent generations of Armenians. How do you explain who you are to others as well as to yourself when no one acknowledges the reality and validity of your past?

This point was eloquently made by Peter Sourian, who found that now as his own children, the grandchildren of a survivor, were growing up, he felt compelled in some way to let his children know what an Armenian is, and what the truth is because of the lack of recognition and acceptance in the historical sense of what had transpired.[11] This bit of truth, which touches upon him so personally, was much less of an issue when he had no children. He knew who he was, and it mattered less to him, but how does this sense get imparted to another generation? The distortion of the truth impacts directly upon his own identity, and therefore the identity of his children, because their identity formation is so closely tied to his own perceptions and feelings about himself, his past, and his worth.

Conclusions

In the genocide, the Turks attempted to wipe out the Armenians not only physically but psychologically as well, by forcing them, as a possible means of physical survival, to deny their religion and identity. The examples given above clearly indicate how the genocide is still operative today. In the United States, where these events are not well known, it becomes particularly relevant, and as a consequence gets mixed up with the issue of assimilation, which is a problem for all immigrant peoples, but in this context takes on a totally different dimension.

One of the questions raised often is "Why has this Armenian genocide impacted so heavily on the identity of Armenians of whatever generation?" The general response is that it is not something that one can put aside and say that it has happened in the past and should be forgotten, because one cannot do that when it has never been accepted as a fact. One must clear one's name and set the record straight. It is not that Armenians wish to take on an identity of martyrs and victims; it is simply that those ghosts won't go away.

Another difference between the Jewish and Armenian experiences is that with rare exception the entire Armenian community of the world is composed of survivors or their progeny. All were touched by the massacres. Before that the number of Armenians in the diaspora was infinitesimal. The genocide is not the experience of only a portion of the Armenian people; it is the experience of *all*. There is no forming of small communities as with some Jewish survivors. All Armenians consider themselves survivors and all consider the events their own background because all either were victims or had close relatives who perished, and all have lost their ancestral homeland.

Finally, by a continued denial by the Turks of the genocide and by the general lack of knowledge and acceptance of the truth about the massacres, the psychological genocide continues. The legacy it leaves for the identity formation of subsequent generations is that those who perished deserved to be brutally exterminated and forgotten or that our parents and grandparents and we, in turn, are all liars and again unworthy of consideration and dignity as honest human beings. Is it any wonder then that generations of Armenians are unwilling and unable to put aside the events of 1915 as past history and "let bygones be bygones"? The first genocide of this century is still reaping its virulent results.

Of particular importance is the recent emergence of Armenian terrorist groups with varying claims and demands who seek redress through violence. They are young adults, grandchildren of survivors, most of whom have recently been uprooted once again from their adopted homes in the Middle East. They find themselves deprived of their ancestral homelands and their recent national history denied. In light of these developments it is especially important to consider future investigations regarding the continued impact of the genocide and the Turkish position regarding it on Armenians and the world in general. Will they spawn increasing anger, resentment, and violence, or will time diminish the magnitude of the response?

The nonrecognition of the Armenian genocide generates an identity formation problem in the life cycle of Armenians. This identity devaluation may continue for generations to come unless and until it is resolved by proper recognition of the genocide by the world at large.

Notes

1. Alen J. Salerian, "A Psychological Report: Armenian Genocide Survivors—67 Years Later" (Paper presented at the International Conference on the Holocaust and Genocide, June 1982, Tel Aviv); personal communications.
2. William Niederland, "The Problem of the Survivor," *Journal of the Hillside Hospital* 10 (1961):237, and "The Survivor Syndrome: Further Observations and Dimensions," *Journal of the American Psychoanalytic Association* 29, no. 2 (1981).
3. Kerop Bedoukian, *The Urchin: An Armenian's Escape* (London: John Murray, 1978).
4. Paul Chodoff, *American Handbook of Psychiatry,* vol. 3 (New York: Basic Books, 1966).
5. H. Klein, *The Child in His Family,* vol. 2, ed. E. J. Anthony and C. Koupernick (New York: Wiley, 1973).
6. Stanley Rustin, *Journal of Contemporary Psychotherapy* 2, no. 1 (1980).
7. Shamai Davidson, "Transgenerational Transmission in the Families of Holocaust Survivors," *International Journal of Family Psychiatry* 1, no. 1 (1980); "Holocaust Aftermath: Continuing Impact on the Generations," *Journal of Psychology and Judaism* 6 (Fall 1981); *Generations of the Holocaust* (New York: Basic Books, 1982); Milton E. Jucovy, "The Effects of the Holocaust on the Second Generation: Psychoanalytic Studies," *American Journal of Social Psychiatry* 3 (Winter 1983); Martin S. Bergman, "Therapeutic Issues in the Treatment of Holocaust Survivors and Their Children," ibid.; Judith S. Kestenberg, "History's Role in the Psycho-Analyses of Survivors and Their Children," ibid.

8. Helen Epstein, *Children of the Holocaust* (New York: G. P. Putnam's Sons, 1979).
9. Karl J. Kalfaian, "Point, Counterpoint: A Legacy of Horror," *New York Times,* 13 May 1979, sec. 11, p. 27.
10. Michael J. Arlen, *Passage to Ararat* (New York: Farrar, Straus & Giroux, 1975).
11. Peter Sourian, *The Gate* (New York: Harcourt Brace Jovanovich, 1965).

11

An Oral History Perspective on Responses to the Armenian Genocide

Donald E. Miller and *Lorna Touryan Miller*

Considerable media attention has been given in recent years to terrorism as a response by the Armenian community to the 1915 genocide. The purpose of this chapter is to demonstrate that responses to the massacre are far from uniform and, indeed, are exceedingly variegated and complex. While *revenge* constitutes one response of survivors (and of the Armenian community as a whole), terrorism, we believe, must be seen within the context of five other equally distinct responses: *repression, rationalization, resignation, reconciliation,* and *rage.*[1]

Methodology

Our research is based on ninety-two in-depth interviews with survivors of the genocide. The majority of these survivors live in Pasadena, although some interviews were done in Los Angeles and San Francisco. All of those interviewed are in their seventies, eighties, and nineties, many of them being in poor health; in fact, several have died since the time of the original interview. Most interviews lasted a minimum of two hours, and quite a few spanned two interview sessions.[2] Almost all interviews were conducted in Armenian and took place in the homes of interviewees. Questions were asked from a schedule of open-ended queries that focused on survivors "telling their story," but also included were specific questions dealing with memories of home life and customs prior to the deportations, as well as some interpretational questions asking why they believe the deportations occurred, how the events of these fateful years have affected their lives, and so on.[3]

Initially our goal was simply to tape record the stories of survivors as a contribution to the growing body of oral history documentation of the massacres.[4] It soon became apparent, however, that nearly as interesting as the stories being told was the *response* of survivors to the fateful years of their childhood. Particularly poignant were the frequent occasions when survivors wept as they told about the deaths of their mothers, fathers, and siblings. Although a few survivors were stoical during the interviews, many more were angry and bitter over what they had experienced. And for some, sorrow, grief, and melancholy overpowered any hostile reactions. In short, we started to see that depiction of events surrounding the deportations was only one element of what was being communicated in these interviews.[5]

Response and the Life Cycle

One of the important findings of our research is that survivors' feelings about the massacre tend to change over the course of the life cycle.[6] Most of those whom we have interviewed were between six and fifteen years of age at the time of the deportations. They did not have a political consciousness in most instances, although they were sometimes aware of the existence of revolutionary groups within their town or community. During the deportations and thereafter, these children, by their own reports, were consumed with one thing: survival. Secondarily, they sought to remake connections with parents and siblings (if they had survived), relatives, and/or other people that they knew from their home town.[7] These children certainly talked about their experiences and feelings in the orphanages—even sang about the fate of the Armenians. But the wonderful resilience of youth seemed to propel them into the future with at least a modest sense of hope and anticipation.

Many of these children continued or started their education in orphanages.[8] They vividly recall their admission: the delousing baths, the clothing, the feeling of protection and security. They remember their entire orphanage population being moved out of Turkey to Beirut or Greece. After leaving Turkey, they started to learn trades, married, and for many the problems of survival with spouse and growing children were preeminent in their minds, many of them moving repeatedly from place to place and country to country in search of a better life. All of the above is by way of saying that after the deportations ended, survivors we have interviewed report by and large that they lived in the present and for the future and did not dwell on their past. Instead, *it is as they became older,* as they established their own families and careers, that they began to look back and try to make sense out of what had happened to them. Many reported that it was in their later years that the bitterness and anger began to fester. On the other hand, a few grew more reconciled as the years passed. Almost all of them said, however, that the more they have advanced in age the more preoccupied they have become with thoughts of the massacre. The important generalization is that responses change with time. Hence, responses are neither uniform from individual to individual, nor are they uniform over an individual's lifetime.

Factors Affecting Responses

In a very preliminary way, we are prepared to identify some of the important variables impacting the responses of survivors. We resist, however, formulating axioms relating to each of these variables for three reasons: (1) the size of our sample precludes such generalizations, (2) the interaction of factors would make prediction unbelievably complex, and most important, (3) we reject a narrowly deterministic view that would discount the important role played by an individual's own inter-pretation of events and how he or she chooses to respond to them. Nevertheless, even given our open and phenomenological view, it is possible to identify several factors that survivors frequently reported as milestones in their own response to the massacre.

First, there is little question that the *degree of suffering* experienced by survivors, and/or witnessed by survivors, plays a key role in their response. Those who were not deported, or did not suffer extreme deprivation during the deportations, tend to be more reconciled to the massacre and less resentful toward the Turks.

Second, those survivors for whom *one or both parents survived* seem also to be more reconciled. The feeling of absolute abandonment and aloneness profoundly affected those who lost both parents and siblings in the deportations. Indeed, it is truly remarkable that so many children of seven and eight years of age survived totally alone, without any parental resources.

Third, *religion* played a major role in the lives of many of those whom we interviewed.[9] Many of the orphanages were run by Protestants, and not a few of those whom we interviewed had religious conversion experiences while living in the orphanage. These experiences tended to have a profound impact on their feelings toward the Turks, as did later religious experiences and interpretations of adulthood.

Fourth, for those who lived in orphanages, the *quality of their orphanage experience* had significant implications. For some children, orphanages functioned very successfully as surrogate families. Most of the orphanages provided excellent educational opportunities and in this way helped to mitigate the disruption occasioned by the deportations. In most cases, those who did not attend orphanage schools did not receive a formal education.

Fifth, the *sex of the survivor* may play an important role—we are not certain. Women in our sample tended to be both more reconciled and repressed than men, while men tended to be more outspoken and more expressive of strong feelings. It is possible, indeed one might expect in Armenian culture, that males would feel more internal pressure to respond overtly to the injustice of the massacre. This is not to say, however, that there were not women in our sample who expressed many angry feelings.

Sixth, we found that those survivors currently *affiliated with an Armenian political party* tend to be more militant in spirit. We do not draw a cause-and-effect conclusion from this observation; it is very likely that individuals with more militant feelings have chosen to affiliate with one of the Armenian political groups. On the other hand, it is probably also accurate to state that attending political functions nurtures specific attitudes.

Seventh, the positive or negative *experience of living with a Turkish family,* either as a son/daughter or as a servant, influenced the perceptions of survivors. Some interviewees were well kept and treated like one of the family. Other survivors were abused and treated as slaves. Those who were treated well tend to make a distinction between *policies* of the Turkish government and Turkish character in general.[10]

What is common to all those whom we interviewed, regardless of their current response to the massacre, is a profound sense of grief, sorrow, and sadness.[11] Even those who appear reconciled remember the past with considerable emotional pain. Hence, when analyzing responses to the massacre one must begin with the base assumption that there is no question but that an enormous tragedy occurred; the present still reverberates with the effects.

Conflicting Feelings

Initially it was our goal to classify each interviewee according to one of our types, realizing that there would be, of course, some overlapping or mixed types.[12] However, the more carefully we listened to our respondents, the more we realized that many survivors have extremely ambivalent and conflicting feelings. Repeatedly we found individuals saying, "*As a Christian* I feel I must forgive the Turks, *but as a human being* I find that I have deep resentments." Alternatively, some people might be very militant in their expression about Turkish reparations and establishment of an Armenian homeland, but when asked if they would return to Turkey, or if they thought Armenians would repeat the pattern of Jewish Zionism, the answer was no. Or, we had tentatively classified someone under "repression" or "rationalization" and then heard through secondary sources that when they first heard of the assassination of the Turkish consul general in Los Angeles, Kemal Arikan, they uttered a celebratory "Good!" Also, within a given interview we often found that the same individual would give conflicting indications of his or her feelings depending upon the context of the questions asked: Whether, for example, the question had a religious or political implication.

The conclusion must surely be that survivors (and Armenians in general) have many unresolved feelings. The present period is particularly volatile for several reasons: (1) the fact that the last generation of survivors is dying without any retribution or justice having occurred, (2) Armenians have been forced to leave Lebanon by the thousands, losing a fragile sense of a displaced homeland, (3) Armenians have witnessed the success (and yet often ultimate failure) of terrorism by other oppressed peoples, (4) Armenians are facing the same problems of assimilation common to every exiled ethnic group living in a foreign homeland, (5) Armenian scholarship is functioning to create an increasingly better informed populace, and (6) the sporadic news of assassinations, and the corresponding press coverage of these events, serve to agitate unresolved feelings. So these are difficult times, with young and elderly alike seeking what it means to be Armenian in this latter part of the twentieth century.

The Typology

Repression, rationalization, resignation, reconciliation, rage, and *revenge* would appear to be both logically possible responses to unjust traumatic events as well as responses that emerged from the lived experience of those whom we interviewed. In the spirit of Max Weber, we are aware that ideal types are artificial constructs of the investigator and are to be valued only insofar as they have explanatory value.[13] Also, we are aware that no individual will perfectly fit any given type and, as has been mentioned, may be best characterized under two or more conflicting types, depending upon the circumstances or context at hand. What follows is a description of each type and some illustrative quotations drawn from our interviews.

Repression

Repression, as we are using the term, refers to unconscious forgetting, conscious attempts to deny feelings, and active avoidance of occasions that invite recall of the violence and suffering experienced as a result of the deportations. Repression is a way of coping with events that are too painful to deal with in everyday conscious life. Figuratively speaking, repression is a way of "putting a lid on" painful memories—which does not make these experiences disappear but does protect the individual from the pain of constantly reflecting on them. Blocking from consciousness attention to extremely unpleasant memories is a natural and perhaps even healthy response, although it is a well-known psychological insight that repressed memories often are expressed in a variety of disguised ways ranging from depression to displaced anger.

Repression was expressed in several different ways by those we interviewed—or attempted to interview—for on occasion our request for an interview was rejected with such statements as, "Whenever I talk about my past, I become upset and lose sleep." Other survivors reported to us that telling their story actually makes them physically ill. Several times a survivor has agreed to be interviewed and then called to cancel, saying that just *anticipating* recalling the past was making him or her nervous and upset. And to our considerable surprise, a number of survivors stated that they have never told their story, even to their children (or if they have, they have told only parts of it).

The pattern of repression just noted began early in the life cycle for some individuals. One survivor, who upon returning to Kharput as an eleven-year-old child, said that she was frequently asked about her experiences. "Once I started talking, I couldn't stop and would inevitably end up in tears. So since then I have tried not to talk about it, even to my own children. My story is too sad."

The pain of remembering events from the deportations was obvious in many interviews. Men, otherwise strong and assertive, would stop and weep as they told how their mothers had died during the ordeal of the deportations, or how their fathers had been taken to be butchered. Other times, survivors read from poetry they had written as a way of expressing their deepest feelings. One woman visibly shook during the interview, describing her condition as a result of "weak nerves" stemming from her deportation experience. She, for example, had never told her story to her children, but said that she still dreams at night about being chased by Turks. Another survivor who told her story punctuated by many tears, whenever asked about her feelings replied, "I have my Bible and my God; I occupy myself with these things."

One reason events are repressed is surely that they are too horrible to contemplate. But we also suspect that in some cases survivors' life histories are tinged with guilt and shame: memories of rape, forced nudity, humiliation of parents, the abandonment of siblings, coerced conversion to Islam, and so on. Since this generalization regarding guilt and humiliation is based upon events that were told to us, one wonders about experiences *not* recounted.

Although repression definitely exists among survivors, it is not a dominant category in our research. As children, many survivors seemingly told their stories to each other, there being something of a "community of sorrow" that united them. Currently the massacre is a frequent topic of social conversations among survivors, this discussion being aided by the fact that survivors often live in Armenian neighborhoods and continue an active "old-world" tradition of visitation and socializing.

Rationalization

A second response involves constructing explanations that justify why the massacre occurred, or more commonly, arguing how *ultimately* a positive benefit may perhaps have accrued to the Armenians as a result of the massacre. *The impulse to rationalize events stems from the human desire to give meaning to one's life.*[14] At one level, nothing is psychologically more unsettling than the inability to place unexplained events within a meaningful frame of reference. In our sample, rationalization took three forms: political, pragmatic, and religious.

The political explanations for why the massacre occurred varied from simple, monocausal explanations to elaborate, highly complex, and historically detailed assessments. The more simplistic explanations, when taken singly, attributed the massacre to Turkish jealousy of Armenian prosperity, the brutality of Turkish character, and German influence over the Turks. To understand the reasons offered by survivors, it is important to realize that they were children when the events of 1915 took place and consequently some survivors' understanding of the massacre is not very sophisticated. There were other survivors whom we interviewed, however, who had a complex and historically sophisticated understanding of the political dynamics of the times, often talking extensively about pan-Turkism, the role of the European powers in Turkish affairs, and so on. Of those offering political explanations of the massacres, many stated that due to the minority status of the Armenians within the Ottoman Empire, they were powerless to have effected an alternative outcome to what occurred. In over ninety interviews, only one individual justified the deportations on political grounds, stating that the Armenian revolutionary parties were to blame for what happened.[15]

A pragmatic and somewhat different type of rationalization was offered by some survivors who said that it took a massacre of this proportion for the Armenians to finally flee Turkey; otherwise, they said, in the long term there would have been the same eventual toll of human life (if, for example, the 1895 and 1909 massacres were repeated on a systematic basis). Said one survivor: "If it had not been for the genocide, we would have still been there with a massacre to face every fifteen years or so. This way we all got out and are doing well in all different parts of the world." Numerous survivors (including those not fitting the "rationalization" identification) have noted with some satisfaction that when the Armenians left Turkey, so did the "blessings" ("Ermeni getti, bereket getti").

Some of our Protestant sample, but certainly not all, attributed the massacre to God's punishment of the Armenians. Stated one survivor: "We should have preached the Gospel to them [the Turks]. We should have not repeated their wrong. We should have been examples to them. If you associate with them, they too accept Christ." Another survivor said, "God used the Turks as a club for us. We had the light but did not give it to the Turks. As a Christian nation we lived as atheists."

A complicating factor for some of those whom we interviewed was that it was in orphanages that they became, in their view, "true" Christians (i.e. "born again"). Hence, they interpreted their own salvation as having been a direct result of the massacre. Reflecting a similar fundamentalist viewpoint were those who quoted such biblical injunctions as "God punishes those whom he loves." Having stated these various theological explanations for why the massacre occurred, we hasten to add that in no instance were such interpretations offered as *justifications* for Turkish political intentions; rather, they were after-the-fact rationalizations in which individuals seemed to be searching for some explanation for the fate of the Armenians.

It is noteworthy that justifications of the above sort were not offered without considerable probing. Also, those offering religious explanations were aware of the tension existing between what happened to the Armenians and the Christian view of an omnipotent, loving, and just God. Frequently we heard the comment, "It's not understandable on human terms. God's ways are not our ways. It's all a very great mystery now, but in heaven we will find the answers to our many 'whys.' " Hence, religious justifications would seem to emerge from a worldview that says God is in control of the universe and therefore there must be some meaning to the Armenian genocide. It is noteworthy that we did not find Protestants less nationalistic than other survivors we interviewed even though they were somewhat more likely to explain events as being a result of God's will, as well as to affirm that God's justice will eventually prevail.

Resignation

Resignation is born of the feeling of impotence, that nothing different could have been done *then* to avoid the massacre, and nothing can be done *now* to seek restitution. Resignation is rooted in a feeling of helplessness. Resignation is linked to the failure of hope and a loss of belief in the world as a moral universe. For the resigned survivor, feelings of sadness, grief, and despair frequently prevail over the more active feelings of anger, revenge, or even rationalization. In the case of survivors we have interviewed, resignation was almost always matched with deep sorrow and, on occasion, melancholy, although in at least one instance resignation was expressed in a profound stoicism with almost no affective response being evident as this survivor told of the most horrible atrocities.

Many survivors described how prior to the deportations many young men were drafted into the army and therefore no longer lived in their town or village. They told how the leaders of their area, and then their own fathers, were led away to prison, never to return. They described how in many instances it was primarily the women who were left to pack a few belongings, prepare some food, and then set off on a journey of unspecified destination and duration. Stated one survivor:

> If the Armenians knew that they were going to be massacred, starve in the deserts, and suffer so much, they would have never left the cities. They could have fought, even though they knew that they would lose. But they would have died there! I am convinced that the poor women really did not know that the purpose of their deportation was a slow death.

Hence, one source of the feeling of resignation is rooted in the deportation experience itself, namely, that the Armenians were incapable of having done anything to avoid the disaster that befell them.

The other feeling of resignation relates to the difficulty of doing anything in the *present* about the injustices that have occurred. The ongoing denial by the Republic of Turkey, and until recently the wide-scale lack of awareness by the non-Armenian population regarding the fact of the genocide, have contributed greatly to a feeling of resignation. Survivors suffer from the lack of a "public catharsis" (i.e. widespread public acknowledgment) such as occurred for the Jews following the Holocaust of World War II. Short of terrorist acts that draw media attention, those with a less militant spirit despair that their burden is a private testimony to the human potential for evil, but it is a witness borne only by their own community. Without a homeland or political power base, and in the face of a United States foreign policy that courts Turkish sympathy, survivors have felt keenly the hopelessness of seeking any form of reparation, even if it be the minimal acknowledgment that the former regime perpetrated a policy with genocidal consequences.

The dynamics of the present feelings of resignation are rooted in the experience of the deportation itself. Stated one survivor: "We had become like animals, without much feeling. We had reconciled to crying, being hungry, walking. We knew this was our fate. After a while I was no longer afraid because no feelings remained in me. We were concerned only about where we were walking and where we could get food and water."

Also, when we asked some of the men we interviewed (teenagers during the time of the massacre) why they did not resist the few gendarmes that were herding their caravans, they responded that they thought of the possibility many times but resisted, asking themselves, "Being in the deserts of Syria, to where would we escape, and how would we survive?"

The dehumanization, degradation, and humiliation that occurred during the deportations—expressed especially when deportees were forced to walk naked, when caravans were marched by water sources and not allowed to drink, when parents were forced to abandon children, to say nothing of the acts of plunder, rape, torture, separation from parents—established the experiential basepoint from which some survivors have never recovered. Militancy takes a certain amount of strength; indeed, this may be one reason that it is the second and third generation, not the first, that have been most revengeful.

Reconciliation

The reconciled response is very different from the response of repression. Although outwardly neither the repressed nor reconciled survivor may demonstrably appear to be reacting to the past; the repressed individual has dealt with his or her past by attempting to block childhood memories from consciousness, whereas the reconciled person acknowledges the pain and sorrow of the past and turns to the future with a spirit of forgiveness and understanding as well as a sense of hope and purpose. Reconciliation is analogous to a "healed wound," where the scars remain but the injury no longer debilitates.

The likelihood of reconciliation is dependent upon many factors, not the least of which is survival of a nurturing parent.[16] It is indisputable that nothing comforts like the emotional support of a mother or father, although many of the orphanage personnel performed heroically as surrogate parents. Reconciliation also may correlate with how debilitating one perceives the massacre to have been in one's personal life, especially as related to its detrimental impact on one's education, career, and family life. Compensations related to current professional success, wealth, well-being of children, and so forth may definitely help mitigate, although not erase, the burdens of childhood suffering.

In our sample, religion and life philosophy played an important role in enabling people to reconcile to their past. Many survivors said that on human grounds alone they could not forgive the Turks for what had happened to them, their parents, and siblings, but the Christian ethic of "forgiving your enemies" and "doing good to those who persecute you" had helped them to deal with their own bitterness and hostility. One survivor told of her experience of reconciliation after an April 24 commemoration of the genocide:

> That night I found myself in tears, agonizing with God as to how and why do you allow the Turks to go on when they wiped out our people. I actually felt God standing next to me and talking with me saying, "If I have not revenged the death of my own son, then you need to be patient."

This individual stated that from that day forward she felt a new peace in her heart. For other survivors, however, reconciliation is a daily struggle.

> I am glad I am a Christian. If not, with these feelings I would have delighted to kill as many Turks as I could; especially, for example, when I think of my grandchildren. How could the Turks have killed children before their mother's very eyes? Believe me, it is unbearable.

For a number of survivors a spirit of reconciliation and revenge coexist, distinguished only by the framework or context from which, at a particular moment, they are viewing their past.

Other survivors seem to be reconciled on rather pragmatic grounds. One survivor concluded: "I don't get upset and cry over spilled milk. Worrying and crying over something doesn't help you in any way." Another survivor stated that she has learned to view every experience "as a stepping stone for a better life." Disasters, she said, are part of life (such as the recent death of her husband), but there is always tomorrow. Similarly, another interviewee said, "It's something God allowed us to go through. I'm now alive. It did come to an end."

In our interviews we encountered some survivors who stated that they owed their very lives to Turks who had been kind and helpful to them. On occasion, Turks hid Armenians in their basements and cellars; Turks provided Armenians with food and clothing; they adopted children and cared for them as their own. For Armenians with these experiences, it is impossible to engage in unqualified statements about Turkish character. We sometimes heard, "It is what some Turks *did* that I hate, not individual Turks themselves." Or survivors may make a distinction between government policy and individual Turks who were honorable and helpful.

One inverviewee described her experience of living next door to a Turk after the massacre: "When living in Egypt one of our neighbors was a Turk and when I first met her I felt no hostility. Instead, I felt like she was one of my homeland people. My heart truly went to her and I was friendly to her."

It is apparent from our interviews that although survivors may accept that individual Turks are human beings like themselves (and therefore not to be blamed or hated), a qualitatively different order of reconciliation is involved in dealing with the injustice of the massacre itself, it being something that is nearly irreconcilable within the context of the canons of modern civility.

Echoing through most of our interviews were statements about Turkish denial of the genocide as being the principal impediment to reconciliation. For some survivors, however, it would take more than public acknowledgment by the current Turkish government to effect reconciliation; reparations would also need to be paid and an Armenian homeland reestablished. Whatever the position of survivors, it is indisputable that Turkey's current propaganda campaign simply fuels feelings of resentment and hostility. If reconciliation is analogous to a "healed wound," it would be quite appropriate to say that Turkish denial simply continues to "rub salt" in the wound, thus precluding it from healing.

Rage

Rage is an emotion of extreme anger, often born of intense frustration. In the case of Armenian survivors, rage is a response to a perception that the *moral order* was violated, with no recompense having followed this disruption. Death and suffering quite naturally produce feelings of sorrow and sadness; but if the victim perceives that such events were unjustifiable, then anger and rage are nearly automatic responses that team with sorrow and grief. Rage is closely related to revenge, but it differs in that revenge results in approval of physically "acting out" hostile feelings, whereas rage is a much more internalized emotion. Both rage and revenge may stem from a sense of being wronged, mistreated, or dealt with unjustly, and indeed the revengeful person may feel considerable rage.

Rage is something that all of our interviewees appear to have felt *at some time.* Rage is oftentimes expressed in the characterological qualities assigned to Turks: "They are liars, two-faced, wild beasts, lazy, destructive. . . ." The very word *Turk* clearly elicits very visceral reactions from many Armenians. One survivor said, "Even if I hear the word I get nervous." Another survivor stated, "I hate the Turks. The kind of things they have done cannot be forgiven."

The anger felt by some survivors leads, on occasion, to extreme statements, such as that by one woman who said that she would prefer her nieces or nephews *dead* than living in Turkey as Muslims, thoroughly Turkicized. Another woman, a devout Protestant, said she once confronted a missionary from Turkey saying, "Why don't you try to save some other nation?" Such hostility is fueled by the fact that some survivors are unable psychologically to distance themselves from the traumas experienced in their childhood years. Many survivors said that they still dream at night that they are being pursued and are running for their lives. One survivor, not too many years ago, struck with his fist the wall of his bedroom during a fitful dream in which he was fighting with a Turk.

Many of those survivors who are characterized by rage, rather than revenge, fit the former categorization because on religious or philosophical grounds they reject retaliatory violence. That is not to say, however, that they do not vicariously experience some satisfaction from the actions of those who are more militant. What, asked one survivor, are a few innocent Turks to the hundreds of thousands of Armenians whose bones lie scattered across Turkey in unmarked graves.

Revenge

Revenge may be defined as retaliation for acts perceived to be wrong or unjust. Revenge may take a direct physical form (as in violence against persons or property) or a more symbolic form (as in character assaults or affirmation that God will avenge). In order to give some background to the current campaign of political assassinations by militant Armenians, it is important to examine very briefly the actions that immediately followed the conclusion of World War I.

The key members of the Committee of Union and Progress were systematically hunted down by Armenians and killed. Talaat Pasha, the former Ottoman minister of the interior and later, in 1916, grand vizier, was killed by Soghomon Tehlirian in a Berlin street. Tehlirian was acquitted after testimony was given by, among others, Johannes Lepsius and Liman von Sanders (both intimately aware of conditions in the

Ottoman Empire). The former Ottoman foreign minister, Said Halim, was assassinated by Arshavir Shiragian, who also gunned down two other collaborators who had organized and inspired the deportations.[17] Jemal Pasha, military governor of Constantinople and subsequently minister of the marine, was killed next; while Enver Pasha, minister of war, died in an ambush (rumored also to have been killed by an Armenian).[18]

One survivor, interviewed in his one-room apartment, pointed to a cluttered bulletin board. There in the center was a picture of Soghomon Tehlirian. This survivor said not once but several times: "I would have done it myself, believe me. . . . I look at this picture each day for inspiration." Another survivor stated: "I remember that when Enver Pasha was killed, I said 'good.' After all, it was the three of them—Talaat, Enver, and Jemal—that took the life of a nation in their hands."

On January 28, 1973, Gourgen M. Yanikian, a survivor who had lost most of his family in the massacre and then seventy-eight years of age, killed two Turkish consular officials in Santa Barbara, California. Since then, a variety of acts of political violence have occurred in a number of countries. Most of these activities have been credited to two groups, the Justice Commandos of the Armenian Genocide and the Armenian Secret Army for the Liberation of Armenia.[19]

In asking survivors about these assassinations we encountered a variety of responses. Typical of those characterizing the revenge response was a seventy-three-year-old man who vigorously said that he was willing to go and fight *now* in order to liberate his homeland. He enthusiastically stated concerning the assassinations: "Let the Turks feel it," adding parenthetically, "but they don't have feelings!" Another survivor said of the assassins:

> If the boys are doing it [i.e. militant Armenian youth] they do well! We've given thousands of sacrifices—died in deportations, in hangings, in prisons—let a few more go to jail, it doesn't make a bit of difference [i.e. if justice can be served].

The response of other survivors to the assassinations was somewhat more qualified. A woman said, "I don't get happy, but they are reaping their punishment." Another survivor ambivalently noted:

> What would I accomplish by revenging? If today I saw a Turk fallen, I'd go and help him and bring him in . . . [but] the killings as revenge are necessary to let the youth and world know what did happen; to wake up the brains [the intellectuals]. What Yanikian did in Santa Barbara was a great act.

A similar sentiment regarding the necessity for the assassinations was echoed by a survivor who commented:

> All Armenians have the "blood call"—the blood [i.e. of slain Armenians] calls them. But in order to listen to the blood call, a storm [i.e. continued assassinations] is essential for us. We need movement, action, to stay awake; otherwise we are lost.

In our sample of survivors, a considerable number said that God, rather than humans, should be the avenger. Earthquakes, political unrest in Turkey, and poverty are all seen as signs of God's wrath against the Turks for what happened to the Armenians. Said one survivor pointedly: "Our revenge is done poorly, but God will do it marvelously, overwhelmingly." Another survivor used the analogy of God being the miller who grinds slowly but finely. Another, when asked whether natural tragedies in Turkey were the handwork of God, said: "Yes, and I'll say, 'God the Father, you did a little, do a bit more!' "

Not every survivor, however, acknowledges a theory of divine retribution. "I don't think," averred one survivor, "that God will punish the Turks. His punishment should have been then so they would have known that they were wrong and would have stopped then. Even if God does punish them now, it does me no good."

Certainly not every survivor favors either divine retribution or political revenge. One survivor spoke aphoristically: "If a bird is too far away to reach, why throw the stone?" In her view, revenge does not bring the dead back from the grave; furthermore, the present Turkish government seems unwilling to admit the guilt of a previous regime, so why waste energy on a futile effort? Other survivors believed that in addition to assassinations being morally wrong, terrorism has given a bad name to the Armenians and therefore is counterproductive (especially in light of their hard-won status and economic gains).

Conclusion

In conclusion, it is important to state how very unique each survivor whom we interviewed is. In order to gain some clarity regarding the range of responses survivors have made to the genocide, it is justifiable to create the ideal types that have formed the basis for our discussion. But at the same time, it must be recognized that whatever typification we may have applied to a survivor's response, individual persons are always more complex than sociological instruments or analytical labels.

What we felt above all in interviewing these individuals is their profound humanness: their courage, their dignity, their struggle to maintain themselves in a hostile world. Many times in pondering the transcripts of our taped interviews we were reminded of the enormous distance these people have traveled from their days of disaster, loneliness, and abandonment. For most of them, their residence in the United States is the culmination of having moved from place to place and country to country, not once but three, four, five, a half-dozen times.

These people are "survivors" in more than one sense. One wonders at their stamina and will to live. Yet they have not emerged from their experiences unmarked. Just as there are those who are heroic, their lives being a testimony to the tenacity and grace of the human spirit, there are those who, because of their experience of a failed moral order, bear many a mental and spiritual wound. The current preoccupation of many survivors with the past is not in our view a sign of weakness or senility; rather, it is an indication of a healthy attempt to integrate morally unresolved events into an acceptable framework of meaning.[20]

Notes

1. For related but somewhat different discussion of issues presented in this chapter, see Donald E. Miller and Lorna Touryan Miller, "Armenian Survivors: A Typological Analysis of Victim Response," *Oral History Review* 10 (1982):47–72.

2. The interviews were done principally by the second author. A number of them were arranged by her father, the Reverend V. S. Touryan, himself a survivor and currently the pastor of the Armenian Brethren Evangelical Church in Pasadena, California.

3. Copies of the questionnaire may be obtained by writing to the authors, School of Religion, University of Southern California, University Park, Los Angeles, CA 90089-0355.

4. It is estimated that there are approximately 1,500 interviews extant in the United States. Some of these have been done by students enrolled in Armenian Studies courses (at the University of California, Los Angeles, for example, under the direction of Professor Richard Hovannisian); others have been undertaken by concerned Armenian Americans in response to oral history workshops (i.e. urging those in attendance to tape record the stories of relatives and friends before it is too late). In 1977 the Armenian Assembly of America, the national coalition office of the Armenian American community, was awarded a matching-funds grant from the National Endowment for the Humanities to record the oral histories of four hundred survivors. Correspondence regarding this project should be directed to the Armenian Assembly, 122 C Street, N.W., Suite 350, Washington DC 20005. Currently the Zoryan Research Institute is conducting a project of videotaping the stories of survivors (85 Fayerweather Street, Cambridge, MA 02138).

5. More than one interviewee who began the session reluctantly, looking sickly and tired, ended the several hours in a spirited, energetic, if not crusading frame of mind. The transformations were remarkable and, we suspect, emotionally healthy. We nevertheless attempted to be sensitive to the trauma of remembering such painful events and often lingered for coffee, cakes, and small talk.

6. See the extensive research being done on generational and life-cycle issues related to survivors of the Jewish Holocaust in Martin S. Bergmann and Milton E. Jucovy, eds., *Generations of the Holocaust* (New York: Basic Books, 1982).

7. Some of the stories told to us of the incredible efforts made by survivors (as children seven and eight years of age) to regain contact with their next of kin are nothing short of remarkable.

8. For an excellent account of orphanage life, see Ida Alamuddin, *Papa Kuenzler and the Armenians* (London: Heineman, 1970).

9. Our sample contained a disproportionate number of Protestants, which may account for some of the more conservative religious statements cited in the pages that follow.

10. In at least one instance, a survivor reported that he was treated extremely well as a grandson by his wealthy Turkish grandfather, and yet it is ironic that this same Turk ordered the death of several Armenian children who were his servants.

11. The Armenian word commonly used by survivors to express this constellation of feelings is *huzum*.

12. For a discussion from a phenomenological perspective of the possible co-existence of conflicting attitudes and perspectives, see Alfred Schutz, "On Multiple Realities," in *Collected Papers,* edited and with an introduction by Maurice Natanson, vol. 1: *The Problem of Social Reality* (The Hague: Martinus Nijhoff, 1973), pp. 207–59.

13. Max Weber, *The Methodology of the Social Sciences* (New York: Free Press, 1949), pp. 90ff.; see also, Schutz, "On Multiple Realities," pp. 40–47.

14. See Peter L. Berger, *The Sacred Canopy: Elements of a Sociological Theory of Religion* (Garden City, N.Y.: Doubleday, 1967), ch. 3.

15. See Louise Nalbandian, *The Armenian Revolutionary Movement: The Development of Armenian Political Parties through the Nineteenth Century* (Berkeley and Los Angeles: University of California Press, 1963).

16. Several women who had suffered greatly from the feeling of abandonment as children said that it was only after they had their own children, and the feeling of aloneness had vanished, that they were able to experience some sense of reconciliation.

17. See Arshavir Shiragian, *The Legacy: Memoir of an Armenian Patriot* (Boston: Hairenik Press, 1976).

18. See Christopher J. Walker, *Armenia: The Survival of a Nation* (London: Croom Helm, 1980), p. 344.

19. See Michael M. Gunter, "The Armenian Terrorist Campaign Against Turkey," *Orbis: A Journal of World Affairs* (Summer 1983):447–77.

20. R. N. Butler, "The Life Review: An Interpretation of Reminiscence in the Aged," *Psychiatry* 26 (February 1963):65–76.

About the Contributors

Levon Boyajian, M.D., has been active in community psychiatry and psychiatric administration for more than twenty years. He is Clinical Associate Professor of Psychiatry at the New Jersey Medical School, Newark, and previously was Chairman, Department of Psychiatry, St. Joseph's Hospital and Medical Center, Paterson, New Jersey. In recent years he and Dr. Haigaz Grigorian have been involved in the study of children of survivors of the Armenian genocide.

Israel W. Charny is Executive Director of the Institute of the International Conference on the Holocaust and Genocide in Jerusalem and Associate Professor of Psychology at the Bob Shapell School of Social Work at Tel Aviv University. He is the author of *How Can We Commit the Unthinkable? Genocide, The Human Cancer,* and the editor of *Toward the Understanding and Prevention of Genocide: Proceedings of the International Conference on the Holocaust and Genocide.* He edits the newsletter *Internet on the Holocaust and Genocide.*

R. Hrair Dekmejian is Professor of Political Science at the State University of New York, Binghamton. His publications include *Egypt under Nasser, Patterns of Political Leadership,* and *Islam in Revolution.*

Terrence Des Pres is Professor of English at Colgate University and author of *The Survivor: An Anatomy of Life in the Death Camps.* He is a member of the United States Holocaust Council.

Marjorie Housepian Dobkin is Associate Dean of Studies and teaches English at Barnard College, Columbia University. Her publications include *A Houseful of Love, The Smyrna Affair,* published in Great Britain as *Smyrna, 1922: The Destruction of a City,* and "The Unremembered Genocide," in *Commentary.* She has been awarded the Anania Shirakatsi prize of the Academy of Sciences of Soviet Armenia.

Haigaz M. Grigorian, M.D., is Assistant Professor of Psychiatry at the University of Medicine and Dentistry of New Jersey and Director of the Department of Psychiatry at Bergen Pines County Hospital in Paramus, New Jersey. He has written on aging and depression and was a delegate to the White House Conference on Aging in 1981.

Vigen Guroian is Associate Professor of Theology and Ethics at Loyola College in Maryland. His recent articles have appeared in the *Journal of Ecumenical Studies, Thought, The Journal of Religious Ethics,* and *Greek Orthodox Theological Review.* He is completing a book on Eastern Orthodox ethics.

Leo Hamalian is Professor of English at the City College unit of the City University of New York and has taught as a Fulbright scholar in the Middle East and in Germany. He is the editor of *Ararat,* a quarterly of arts and letters, and is the author of *William Saroyan: A Celebration, D.H. Lawrence in Italy, Ladies on the Loose, As Others See Us, Burn After Reading, The Shape of Fiction,* and *The Existential Imagination.*

Richard G. Hovannisian is Professor of Armenian and Near Eastern History and Associate Director of the Near Eastern Center at the University of California, Los Angeles. His major publications include *Armenia on the Road to Independence, The Republic of Armenia,* Volumes I–II, and *The Armenian Holocaust: A Bibliography.* A Guggenheim Fellow, Hovannisian serves on several editorial and scholarly boards and represents the State of California on the Western Interstate Commission on Higher Education.

Leo Kuper is Professor Emeritus of Sociology at the University of California, Los Angeles. His main writings include *Passive Resistance in South Africa, An African Bourgeoisie, Race Class and Power, The Pity of It All, Genocide,* and *The Prevention of Genocide.* He received the Herskovits award for *An African Bourgeoisie,* and the Spivak Fellowship from the American Sociological Association for his contributions to the study of group relations.

Robert Melson is Associate Professor of Political Science and for 1985-86 the Chairman of the Jewish Studies program at Purdue University. Among his major publications are *Nigeria: Modernization and the Politics of Communalism* and articles in the *American Political Science Review* and *Comparative Studies in Society and History.* Melson has been a visiting fellow at several research centers, including the Harry S. Truman

Institute of the Hebrew University of Jerusalem. He is working on a comparative study of the Armenian genocide and the Holocaust.

Donald E. Miller is Associate Professor of Religion and Director of the School of Religion at the University of Southern California. He is the author of *The Case for Liberal Christianity* and has published articles in a number of journals, including *Religious Studies Review, Religious Education, The Christian Century, Anglican Theological Review, The Oral History Review,* and *The Futurist.*

Lorna Touryan Miller is Associate Director of the Office for Creative Connections, All Saints Episcopal Church, Pasadena, California.

Vahé Oshagan is a poet and a teacher. With a doctorate in comparative literature from the Sorbonne, he has taught Armenian literature and humanities in several universities, including the American University of Beirut and the University of Pennsylvania. He has published five books of poetry in Armenian and a sixth, *Suburbs,* will appear this year.

Index